P1
Stark R___ ___ ___

"A disorienting, funny, sad book."—*The Boston Globe*

"Henderson pulls off the hat trick: a breezy, highly readable character study, an indelible modern fable set in the kingdom of The Idol Rich, and a titillatingly oblique consideration of The Pelvis himself. . . . There is dark fun to be had in *Stark Raving Elvis*, and Henderson has it. This is a nifty, aptly titled read."—*Philadelphia Inquirer*

"A sharp, well-written work about the hopes and crumbling dreams of a man who struggles to live his dreams of another man's life."—*Houston Chronicle*

"An alternately funny and scary look at one man's American Dream corrupted into nightmare."—*Heavy Metal*

"Fascinating and frightening . . . at the heart of rock there is cold-blooded nihilism, nowhere more aptly captured than in the contest for Elvis impersonators that is the core of Henderson's novel.—*St. Louis Post-Dispatch*

"*Stark Raving Elvis* is no mean feat. It possesses an authentic feel, its language is raw and energetic . . . the real thing."—*Houston Post*

"Henderson has a real feel for the sad, ridiculous squalor in America. . . . What he does best, though, is transform the seedy into musical prose."—*Boston Magazine*

I, Elvis

CONFESSIONS OF A COUNTERFEIT KING

William McCranor Henderson

For Sebastian —
It was great getting to
know you. * Let's start a
band! *

Bill

Boulevard Books, New York

* P.S.
Come see us in Chapel Hill

I, ELVIS: CONFESSIONS OF A COUNTERFEIT KING

A Boulevard Book / published by arrangement with the author.

PRINTING HISTORY
Boulevard trade paperback edition / August 1997

Acknowledgments

First of all, my thanks to John Talbot, who had the inspiration, and Miriam Altshuler, who helped connect the dots, then tossed me the pen. If not for them the world would be short one middle-aged Elvis impersonator.

For their interest, participation, and support along the way, I'd like to thank T.J. Anderson, John Cady, Patty Carroll, Liza Collins, Doc Franklin, Jackie Franklin, Charles Gauthier, Gary Goldstein, Everette "Lumber King" Greene, Peter Guralnick, Ollie Hallowell, Keith Henderson, Todd Jones and Huge Sound, Larry Lee, Bruce Lichtenstein, Sebastian Lockwood, Ray Maas, Fetzer Mills, Rebecca Mills, Dale Volberg Reed, John Shelton Reed, Mike Rosen, Yaniv Rozen, Caroline Saltonstall, Lee Smith, Skip Snyder, Cheryl Trapanier, Rooster Van Dyke, Robert Washington, David Williamson, and John Lincoln Wright.

And many, many thanks to the indispensable Rick Marino, mentor and guide, and all-around great guy.

Chapter

1

When the letter came from my agent, I let it sit on the table for a while—generally, agents telephone when the message is urgent, as in *money*. Besides, I was in summer mode, not doing anything promptly if I didn't have to. My family and I were on vacation in Rhode Island. The days were balmy and golden and we were spending them on the beach or the tennis courts, or (in my case) taking long Dagwood Bumstead naps on one of the couches. When I finally opened the letter, it was at the end of a long day swimming, riding bumper boats, and taking a few swings at a local batting cage with my young daughters. I was feeling every bit of my fifty-plus years. "I've been talking to an editor at Berkley about you," Miriam wrote. "We discussed a possible mass market edition of *Stark Raving Elvis* . . ." (My interest level perked up sharply. This was my first novel, by that time ten years old, and we were trying to get it back into print.) "But he has another idea too."

With great tact she described what was an absurd proposition for a guy in my position: a college teacher, a middle-aged father with a young and demanding family, but (and here was the glint of plausibility) a man who had once, years ago, written a novel about an Elvis impersonator.

1

The editor was looking for a writer with exactly my background—and someone who was enough of an exhibitionist to "take on the life of an Elvis impersonator"—that is, don a wig and jumpsuit and actually perform, travel, enter contests, whatever it took to soak up the reality of that surreal existence—and write a book about it.

"What do you think?" I asked my wife.

She reread the letter and her nose wrinkled. "Kind of a strange idea. Like asking you to run away with the circus. And aren't those Elvis suits awfully expensive?"

Yes, they were. I had heard that a proper Elvis jumpsuit could run you anywhere from $2,000 to $5,000.

By coincidence, just the week before I had been on the phone with an old friend from Boston. Ollie was an industrial show producer who had just staged a sales convention in Hawaii for Simplex, the time-clock and alarm company, in which three top executives appeared on stage at the climax of the show as three different incarnations of Elvis. The big cheese, a corpulent giant, wore the white jumpsuit while his two lieutenants cavorted in black leather and gold lamé.

"These were all corporate tough guys," said Ollie. "All pretty strait-laced, but they went for it, wigs and all."

This wasn't as strange as it may have seemed. I had recently heard about a national gathering of CEOs, where a chorus of ten corporate big bosses appeared decked out as Vegas-era Elvises, complete with jumpsuits, phony coifs, and rubber guitars.

Ollie said, "Something about Elvis really appeals to men in menopausal transition nowadays. And there's a lot of that—I mean, all around me everyone's having some kind of midlife crisis. They're sprouting ponytails, leaving their wives, taking up the saxophone. In any case, if you ever want to hit the road as Elvis, I've got the suits."

We had a good laugh.

The truth is, I've always felt that a midlife crisis, like a Land Rover, was a luxury I couldn't afford. Nevertheless, I caught myself starting to think about this project in eerily practical terms: could Ollie *really* part with one of those suits . . . and how much alteration would it need . . . ?

I called Miriam. "Does this editor know how old I am?"

"Oh, sure. Your age isn't a problem. In fact, it's really an advantage. A thirty-two-year-old doing Elvis—that's not much of a story. But *fifty-two*—" She let it dangle. I finished it in my mind . . . *fifty*-two, that really takes you somewhere: MIDDLED-AGED COLLEGE PROFESSOR BUMPS AND GRINDS . . . now there's a concept with real profile!

After all, didn't this kind of foray into the unknown have an honorable history? Hadn't George Plimpton turned a chance assignment at *Sports Illustrated* into a lifetime of "let me try it" books, culminating in his latest caper—horseshoes with George Bush? Hadn't the very term "gonzo journalism" been coined by Plimpton's darker cousin, Hunter Thompson?

Between the two of them, Plimpton and Thompson had defined the outer limits of participatory journalism. Plimpton's unflappably healthy bonhomie was always in good taste, while Thompson literally kicked the story to life by loading up on booze and drugs, placing himself awkwardly at the epicenter of the event.

I had no idea where I might fit along the spectrum marked off by these two notables. But the more I thought about it, the more I understood it was the "gonzo" part—DOING IT—that attracted me/ I had turned out enough free-lance journalism to know that I had no desire to "cover" stories as an invisible reporter, even in the somewhat more visible tradition of John McPhee or Tom Wolfe.

As much as I admired the work of these men, straight reporting wasn't for me. I was always looking at my watch, yawning, daydreaming, wishing I could wrap it up, write the story, and be done. In fact, I had become a fiction writer precisely *because* "making it up" presented such interesting (and inescapable) challenges. I think it was this, the prospect of being allowed to create a good part of the story through my own choices and behavior, that finally won me over. The central events would be of my own devising, yet I wouldn't have to produce them out of the thin air of imagination: what more could a fiction writer possibly desire?

Taking a train into New York, I dropped by the Berkley Books office on Madison Avenue.

John Talbot, the editor, was clearly a man who saw book projects as totems of his own enthusiasms, seeds springing to life when placed in the hands of the right author. Talbot was a lot younger than I thought he would be, tall and boyish, a cross-bred fan of Plimpton, Thompson, and Elvis Presley. To him, the notion of impersonation contained the essence of something resolutely American. He spoke of Cameron Crowe, who passed himself off as a high school student to write *Fast Times at Ridgemont High*. Talbot himself had hung out at a midtown gym, pretending to be a boxer, sparring on his lunch hour, not to write about it, but to experience the zesty thrill of slipping into another skin. (Wait a minute, I thought, aren't editors supposed to *lunch*? A wine spritzer may have replaced the old three martinis, but . . . workouts on the light bag?)

He and his girlfriend had recently made a pilgrimage to Graceland. They had stayed at the Days Inn next door, where you can watch Elvis movies 24 hours a day. When the time came to tie the knot, they fully intended to be married by an Elvis impersonator. His eyes were bright and full of the future.

"There's an organization for Elvis impersonators," he said, "but I can't find them. You must know something about this . . ."

"I'm afraid I don't. Do they have an 800 number?"

"See what you can find out."

When I wrote *Stark Raving Elvis* none of the events I imagined—a major Elvis impersonator's contest, with national TV coverage, a convention of international "pro" impersonators in Las Vegas—had ever taken place. I had to make them up. By now, life had long since caught up with (and passed) art: these things, and more, had come to exist in the real world. And I didn't have a clue.

I, Elvis

Here's what I did know: Elvis, as Mojo Nixon put it, was everywhere, and Elvis impersonators were now a growing slice of the general population. They were generally thought of as nut cases—sad, fat, sick jokes. Some impersonators were, in fact, over their heads, but the good ones—and I had seen a few—hardly deserved to be held in contempt, or treated with campy derision.

John Talbot agreed. "I want to make sure we see eye to eye on this: I'm not interested in knocking anybody, bashing Elvis, that sort of thing. I'm a genuine fan, my heart's on my sleeve. We're talking about something unique and precious here, and I don't want to have any part of trashing it."

There had certainly been plenty of trashing: almost before the King's body had gone cold, there was a flowering of Elvis-related popular fiction. Impersonator fiction had become a virtual subgenre. In most of the stories I had read, the impersonator was a lost, troubled person or else a tool of some evil political force. Impersonator fans were depicted as fat, tasteless, low-class slobs, the kind of insensate rabble that can easily be manipulated to violence by cunning demagoguery.

Not having reread *Stark Raving Elvis* in ten years, I felt a twinge of guilt: were my own hands clean? Had I done a job on Elvis impersonators in that book? Wasn't its hero, the impersonator, a driven borderline schizophrenic? Yes. Didn't it present an international gathering of Elvis impersonators as having something of a circus atmosphere? I suppose so.

Yet the book took the basic endeavor seriously and was probably the only fiction ever written that said, in effect, doing an Elvis impersonation well was more than just okay: it could be majestic.

I left John Talbot's office without committing myself. As a reality check, I tried the idea out on a few old friends. Even the hippest of these—one a writer, another a musician—seemed to greet the notion with caution and the kind of polite reserve you maintain when a friend tells you, "To hell with it—I'm going to join the Marines" or "I've had it with marketing, I'm going to Hollywood to be an actor!"

One old friend, Phillip, actually tried to save me from myself. Phillip's twin passions were literature and baseball. He took me to the White Horse Tavern for a few beers. As we stood at the weathered old bar, where Dylan Thomas had thrown down untold pints, I felt he was trying to push his point by the very choice of venue. This was literary New York, a haunt that stood for twentieth century poetry, respect for the combined tradition of English literature and the flourish of bohemian intellectualism.

"I'm going to tell you something that you probably won't hear from anybody else, okay? I'm going to be an aggressive busybody."

"Well, okay."

"Don't do this thing, Bill. Fiction is in a tailspin. TV has just about killed it off. TV, movies, rock 'n' roll culture and the kind of nonfiction book this guy wants you to write. Don't do it. Don't betray your craft."

"Let me get this straight: you're saying that I shouldn't write nonfiction, or . . . or what?"

"Well, that's part of it."

"What's the other part? Let me guess: it's the subject matter, isn't it?"

"Well—sure. I mean, Elvis impersonators . . ." He screwed his face into a cross-eyed fright mask.

"But I wrote a *novel* about one and nothing awful happened to me."

"But this time they'll have you running around publicly in an Elvis suit. They'll want you to sing 'Love Me Tender' at book singings. Nobody'll ever take you seriously again."

"It certainly didn't ruin George Plimpton to run around in a football uniform or a baseball suit."

"But, ah—"

"Ah, what? It's so different somehow?"

"Sports . . . sports is different."

"How?"

"It just is."

Different. Okay, I got it: sports were respectable. Mainstream. Sports, like war, came closer to holding up the mirror to real life. Elvis? A marginal entertainment obsession hovering on the edges of social pathology.

Back in Rhode Island I asked my ten-year-old daughter, "What would you think if I put on an Elvis Presley suit and dark glasses and a black wig and got up in front of crowds of people to sing songs with a band?"

Her eyes blinked and widened: "Dad," she said solemnly. "That would be *so* cool!"

I had been a musician of sorts, years back. In my single days around Harvard Square I had played fiddle for a singer-songwriter named John Lincoln Wright, who was (and is) something of a legend on the New England barroom circuit. As a member of John's "wall-of-sound" country rock ensemble, The Sour Mash Boys, one of my duties was to provide occasional harmony vocals.

Aside from humming "ooooh" or "aaaah" into a backup mike, however, my singing was restricted to one solo number, called off by John when he had to leave the stage unexpectedly. This was "Fly Trouble," a chatty talk-novelty, originally recorded by Hank Williams, that you could hardly call singing. Not that I couldn't carry a tune. I had sung in church choirs, Gilbert & Sullivan, that sort of thing. But something about stepping out in front of a band froze me. On stage, I preferred the invisible, mute presence of back-up musician; I was happy to be part of the support troops, nothing more.

And yet . . . and yet . . .

I think I had always had the yen to sing. In the mid-60s, when Bob Dylan defined a new pop paradigm, that of singer-songwriter, I was seized with a compulsion to try out my own songs in one of the small, smoky folk clubs that were springing up like urban mushrooms. I bought a guitar and learned a few chords. In the privacy of my own bedroom I crooned standards like "I Ride an Old Paint" from the Pete Seeger songbook. But the leap to public performance seemed impossible.

I took the chicken's way out and enrolled in a course at the New School. It was called something like How to Sing Folk Songs and everyone in it had some kind of social maladjustment that made each class meeting many times more excruciating than it would have been just to show up at Gerde's Folk City on hoot night.

I know that now. Then, however, the icy experience of stumbling through "In the Early Morning Rain" just seemed to prove that this wasn't my cup of tea. No matter how compelling my fantasies, I was just not made to stand up and sing in public.

But now, it was 30 years later. Now perhaps I was dog-eared enough not to be so damned precious about myself. College teaching had worn away my fear of being the focal point of attention. Parenthood had gotten me used to all kinds of public self-expression ("Put the candy bar back in the rack, dear. Back in the rack. Right now. One . . . two . . . three . . .")

Perhaps fear of "looking bad" in front of strangers had gone the way of my hair. Would I now, finally, be able to pull this off? At 52, you recognize a "last chance" when it stares you in the face. I might make a serious fool of myself—but wouldn't I be a bigger fool to let this last chance pass me by?

Chapter

2

There are two standard places to start the story of Elvis: the beginning (guitar-thumping manchild bursts out of nowhere) or the end (fat celebrity drug addict plods to his death). These are the points of visceral fascination: Elvis making it . . . Elvis losing it. And for many, that's all there is. But *That's the Way It Is,* which I always thought was Elvis's best live concert documentary, reveals a splendid Las Vegas Elvis, slim, sexy, and completely in control of an act designed to showcase his charisma. The image is so indestructible it survives even his own impish impulses to undermine it, mock it, in mid-act.

How could I ever hope to get up and do anything approaching what I was watching?

But as the tape rolled on, something curious happened: the more I watched, the more I began to believe in the possibility that I too could do this thing! Gradually, Elvis's charisma stopped intimidating me and started to inspire me. Perhaps this is what great popular entertainers do: connect with an area of imagination inside everyone that is boundless in its sense of possibility.

The late poet James Dickey once offered a theory of why the homespun poet-celebrity Rod McKuen, who wrote so awfully, was so vastly popular with ordinary people: they felt he wrote no better poetry than *they* would write, if they just got around to it. Elvis gave me that feeling: he seemed to be only doing what I could do anyway, if I wanted to. Even as I marveled at his virtuoso moves, something made me feel them in my own body.

I CAN DO THIS! I CAN! I thought.

I grabbed a yellow pad and began to scribble down code names for various movements and gestures.

> the lasso
> the squat
> the arm fling cutoff
> the fist pump
> the shaky leg
> the body palsey . . .

There was a large mirror in the TV room. I tried a few moves. Yes, yes—they looked halfway decent. My wife, an ex-dancer, drifted into the room and watched me try a few pseudo-karate kicks.

"You're not going to have any trouble with this," she said.

"I've made a decision on John's offer," I said to Miriam on the phone.

"Mm?"

"I'd like to do it."

She seemed surprised. "That's wonderful! I was sure you were going to say no."

"Fabulous!" said my friend Ollie when I phoned him. "Do you want me to send the suits overnight? I could FedEx them."

"No, no. We're driving back to North Carolina in a few days. And anyway, I don't exactly have a lot of pressing gigs lined up. There's no rush. Just when you can."

"Oh, this is too much. I *love* it! Beware the jumpsuit, however. It's going to be awfully roomy."

"That's okay, the price is right."

"And Bill."

"Yes, Ollie?"

"Just don't get carried away. Remember the ponytails, new wives, new lives. Be careful."

That was an interesting notion. That I might, as Carol had suggested, run away with the circus.

I didn't think so.

On the other hand, Elvis impersonation did seem to exert a strong psychic influence on its practitioners. Only two years after Elvis's death, a photo study of Elvis impersonators appeared called *All the King's Men*. For years it remained the only extant nonfiction book on the subject, and as I leafed through it, it seemed to have stood up pretty well. What I found remarkable in 1979 (and even more so now) was how mature a phenomenon Elvis impersonation already was at that time, and how fully this early book captured the varieties of impersonator types.

There was the "surgical" Elvis, Dennis Wise, who underwent a number of operations to "reshape his cheekbones, nose, lips, and mouth to resemble the Elvis Presley of 1972."

Another impersonator, Steve Wayne of Springfield, Illinois, displayed a list of "50 similar characteristics of Steve Wayne and Elvis Presley, as compiled by the Steve Wayne Fan Club."

1. Shy
2. Humble
3. Very reserved
4. Gentle
5. Soft-spoken
6. Generous
7. Honest
8. Sincere

9. Loves children
10. Keen sense of humor
11. Uneasy around strangers
12. Likes Lincoln Continentals
13. Likes motorcycles
14. Likes leather jackets
15. Doesn't drink
16. Doesn't smoke
17. Restless
18. Likes to play pool
19. Religious, but keeps it personal
20. Likes petite women
21. Sings all the time
22. Material things and riches mean very little to him
23. Can't keep track of time
24. Not a letter writer
25. Same height
26. Same voice and speech pattern
27. Same teeth
28. Lips identical
29. Weight problem
30. Eye problems
31. Bluish-hazel eyes
32. Same build and physique
33. Doesn't say thank you but gives expensive gifts instead
34. Drinks only water on stage
35. Song arranger
36. Doesn't wear after-shave or colognes
37. Comes from a poor family
38. Was a truck driver
39. Stationed in Germany
40. Has guys around him all the time
41. Must have bodyguards

42. Stays up all night, sleeps days
43. Room goes quiet when he enters
44. Women go berserk over him
45. Exudes sex appeal
46. Charismatic
47. Plays guitar, but not proficiently
48. A smile that melts your heart
49. Prefers soft ballads but will do the rock tunes
50. No one can stay mad at him very long

Not all impersonators identified so intensely with the original. Ron Furrer of St. Louis was even looking around for some other skin to jump into: "Doing Elvis is starting to really bother me. The whole thing has been turned into a joke."

Even the "humble" Steve Wayne quoted above admitted, "I never really idolized him—to be honest, I think I am a better singer than he was."

So it seemed the world of Elvises was divided into those who did it as an act of worship, and those for whom it was purely and simply an act—with room for variations in between.

Working class seemed to be the preponderant social background, but all sorts of professions were represented:

firefighter
forklift driver
upholstery salesman
pharmacist
advertising copywriter
landscape contractor
anesthesiologist
ambulance supervisor
ophthalmologist
Wal-Mart clerk
computer analyst

One impersonator was even a public official: Bruce Borders, the mayor of Jacksonville, Indiana (predictably, he was known as "The Mayor of Rock 'n' Roll"). Apparently you didn't have to be an antisocial misfit to take up Elvis impersonation.

So where would I fit?

I enjoyed Elvis, respected his achievement, but in truth, I had never been the world's greatest Elvis fan. I was on assignment, after all, too focused on the job to become a true believer. This was a tricky project: in order to write this book, I would have to pull off what amounted to a double pretense while "living" my research: to pretend, as it were, to be a pretender. The Dennis Wises and Steve Waynes actually lived in a country I was only going to visit. I would be a tourist, and a professional tourist at that.

Yet now that I had agreed to this craziness, when I projected what was to come, why did I find myself picturing not the reality—a balding, middle-aged man engaged in an apologetic charade—but a supercharged vision of myself as some kind of rock 'n' roll prince, in command of thousands of latter-day Elvis fans, singing with power and precision, making the right moves, creating pandemonium?

What I needed now was a dose of reality. And that would mean finding a way into the real world of Elvis impersonators.

Chapter

3

We arrived home in North Carolina to a houseful of fleas. Why fleas flourish when the dogs are gone I've never understood. But I didn't have to be a mental giant to understand that, with my wife and daughters in various states of torment, something drastic had to be done. I called a 24-hour exterminator and we vacated the house, dogs and all.

The kids, who love motels, were delighted. As soon as we checked in, they fought over the TV remote and then settled into a rerun of *Gilligan's Island*. My wife and I got a bucketful of ice and poured ourselves a couple of stiff scotches.

"Would this have ever happened to Elvis?" Carol said.

"Probably not. But from what I know, if it had, he wouldn't have checked into the Best Western. He'd have loaded his entourage onto the *Lisa Marie* and flown to Palm Springs."

"I thought Lisa Marie was his daughter."

"She was—is. But he had a huge custom touring jet, a sort of Air Force 2, that he named after her. It's sitting in a parking lot at Graceland. When I take you there we can tour it."

"*If,* not when."

"If, then. I won't force you."

When it came to popular culture, Carol was at best a casual observer. I could see that unless the kids caught the fever, my journey into Elvis was going to be pretty much a solo flight.

"Hey, Dad, look at this!"

I focused my attention on the TV, where an announcer's voice was promoting something called *The Night of 100 Elvises*. Snippet images from Elvis movies alternated with flashes of Elvis impersonators in performance. I practically dropped my scotch and vaulted across the room, placing my face inches from the screen. What luck, an information breakthrough! This program, *The Night of 100 Elvises*, obviously featuring impersonators, was scheduled for TBS the following night. If not for the fleas (since I watch very little TV), the opportunity would have gone right by me.

The Night of 100 Elvises turned out to be mostly packaging for three Elvis movies, *Blue Hawaii; Girls, Girls, Girls;* and *Paradise Hawaiian Style*. What I was really interested in (and recorded on my VCR) was the packaging: the all-too-brief moments that framed commercials and station breaks, moments when the Elvis impersonators appeared. TBS had sent a camera crew to Vegas to cover the convention of the Elvis Presley Impersonator's International Association (EPIIA), and apparently they had spent the whole weekend shooting footage at what I later found out was the Imperial Palace Showroom, with exterior shots in the courtyard of the Stardust Casino.

I went over and over the snippets.

High moments from on-stage performances contrasted with informal cameos, Elvises just standing around, chewing the fat, comparing notes, chatting.

"We have a lot of fun," said one guy, who looked like an Italian-American bank executive. "It's just a bunch of guys getting together and nobody thinks, well, I'm better than this one, I'm better than that one. We just have a good time."

There was Nazar Sayegh, M.D., a paunchy red-suited dervish who described himself as "a family practitioner in Yonkers, New York, and one of the EPIIA Hall of Famers" and stressed the fact that he performed only when it didn't conflict with his medical practice.

There was Gary Sanders, "the Alabama Elvis." There was Joe Tirrito, "the Windy City Elvis."

"Everything's real," said one handsome young Elvis, tugging on his hair. "Women yank on it all the time."

Most of the on-camera pronouncements—like "Welcome back to Las Vegas and our annual Elvis performers international showcase"— were spoken by the same Elvis, who had a "presidential" air about him and talked with professional poise. Although he wasn't identified, I assumed this was the organization's chief. He had a sly side to him when he thought the camera wasn't running: "That thing is awesome, son," he cracked, as a white-suited Elvis flashed a gaudy American flag–lined cape. "That thing is *bad*. I want to take that thing and run you up a flagpole with it."

Another Elvis stood out sharply from the pack. Dressed in slick black leather, he was the color of milk chocolate and had handsome features that made him look like a combination of Polynesian, black, and American Indian. "And now . . ." announced this multicultural prince, with the Stardust's facade twinkling wildly in the background, "back to *Blue Hawaii* . . . on TBS."

This convention, I thought, might well be the key to my entire book. Could I somehow contrive to perform there the following summer? Seeing how polished they were made it a chilling prospect in one sense. Yet the writer in me rose to the idea like an old fire dog jumps to the ready when he hears the clang of the alarm bell.

At any rate, these were my guys. Now: where did they hang out?

I called TBS in Atlanta and got passed along to a producer named William White, the guy who had directed the shoot in Vegas.

"You want Rick Marino," he told me. "He's the president of the EPIIA."

*   *   *

Two storage boxes arrived at the house by FedEx. Ollie had wasted no time. Three Elvis costumes spilled out: a fake gold lamé zoot suit, a plastic "black leather" biker's outfit, and a white Vegas-era jumpsuit. Also included were three black wigs, pinned to Styrofoam head forms; fake sideburns; various kinds of glue, dye, hairspray; and a belt of interlinked mystery-metal wafers with fat fake rubies glued to their midst. No shoes—what kind of shoes did Elvis wear anyway? Blue suede?

I held the jumpsuit up to my body. It was speckled with little brass studs, the collar standing high and stiff, the pant legs flared, 70s style. Empty, it looked like a tubular sack—a wilted parade float waiting for its life-giving blast of helium. It was ridiculously large; Ollie had told me the guy had been fat, but obviously he was taller as well. The other two suits were somewhat too roomy, but they were "young Elvis" suits: I knew I was far beyond ever needing them, except perhaps for a Halloween goof. But the jumpsuit—this would be a formidable reengineering project!

Carol and the kids had taken our dogs out for a walk. I stripped to my underwear and wriggled into the suit. It sagged off me everywhere like folds of skin. Zipping up the thorax pulled things together a bit, but I couldn't help tripping over the flapping bell-bottoms as I made a few moves. I tried one of the wigs—it went on easily, stretching like a watch cap—and looked in the mirror. Yes, an icon of sorts was looking back at me, although something about the total effect was more like Al Pacino's sister than Elvis. But no matter—I heard the family at the kitchen door. This would constitute a rough test: what kind of reaction would I get? I pulled the curtains, slapped "Also Sprach Zarathustra" into the CD deck, struck a pose, and waited.

It had been raining. It took a while for the dogs to be toweled off in the kitchen. My leg began to jitter. I tried another pose. Finally the kitchen door burst open, disgorging wife and kids straight from the woods.

"Eeeeeeeeeeeeeee!"

"Dad!"

"Awesome!"

The dogs bounded in and halted suddenly, breaking into a raucous hubbub of braying, whooping, lunging, sniffing, and more braying. Although their reactions were ambiguous—awe and alarm mixed with laughter (dog lovers familiar with a certain kind of tail-wagging canine "laughter" will know what I mean)—I decided to score the totality of it as some family version of Elvismania.

Charisma?

Only in the sense that any rubber chicken will attract attention and get a cheap guffaw.

I decided I should put in a call to Rick Marino, the EPIIA honcho, and the sooner the better.

This was no casual decision, since Marino's cooperation would be the key to what I saw as the "big event" for my book, an appearance at the next summer's EPIIA Convention in Las Vegas. But I had been reluctant to make the contact until I felt I could "talk Elvis" well enough not to set off any alarms. What if he was a paranoid Elvis nut? What if he thought *I* was the nut? Worst of all, what if he pegged me as just one more exploiter, another mocking opportunist, out to make fun of the Elvis impersonators.

TBS had given me his unlisted number in Jacksonville, Florida, so I girded my loins and dialed it late one Saturday morning—and woke him up. "Gimme about half an hour, son," said the foggy voice on the other end of the line.

I knew Rick Marino was anything but foggy. I had watched him and his bodyguard do a very alert, smooth TV interview in *The Night of 100 Elvises*. Against the flashy backdrop of the Imperial Palace showroom, they were dressed in formal black suits (Marino in a tuxedo).

"This is Joe Butler, my chief of security," Marino had said.

The maestro, Rick Marino.
(Photo courtesy of Patty Carroll.)

"How y'all doing?" Butler was a chunky, tough-looking guy in his 50s.

"His job is just to kind of stand there and look mean." The two men exchanged a chuckle.

The video then cut to a jumpsuited Marino, making his stage entrance, surrounded by several bodyguards in red Elvis-On-Tour wind-breakers. Over music, he swept through the crowd and kissed a female fan. The bodyguards each kept a hand clamped to his shoulder. The effect was reminiscent of a boxer's entry into the arena, surrounded by his ring of protectors.

"When we do the shows, we want to be unapproachable. You don't really wanta make yourself to where people think they can just walk up to you, because it takes away from the show." The voice was assured, like that of a football coach explaining to the TV reporters why you throw a pass on third down and long.

By the time I had called him back, the foggy Marino had been replaced by a chipper, public Marino, ready to talk.

The EPIIA was now five years old, he told me. "It started as a Chicago-area thing. Chicago is probably the single biggest location for Elvis impersonators—there must be about 50 big-time working impersonators right in that area alone. Anyway, basically we're a noncompetitive, fraternal type of organization for the world's best Elvis impersonators. The idea is to create credibility and networking opportunities for all the guys scattered all over the world. And of course there's the convention every summer that brings us all together. I'll tell you this, man. My first convention, seeing 150 Elvises all at once just blew my mind!"

I jumped right in and described my project: "The catch is, I have to do some of this myself . . . that is, stand up in front of audiences and do what you guys do, to get the firsthand experience. And what I'd like to arrange, if possible, is to attend your next convention, get some stories from the guys, and perform a few numbers myself."

"Sounds like a hoot."

"Think it's possible?"

"I think so. We could fit you in—one shot, three songs with the band. We'd have to work it out with Jerome in Chicago, who's chairman of the committee in charge of the show. And clear it with Ron, the founder. But I like your idea. I hear a lot of ideas for books and some of 'em are pretty thin, but I like this one. It reminds me of that book of George Plimpton's where he worked out with the Detroit Lions . . ."

At his mention of Plimpton, I knew I was on solid ground: he got it.

"Do you have a suit?" he asked.

"Yes. Well, not an official suit."

"You really should have a good one. Now I could probably help arrange for you to get one at cost. That would be, say, $800, and that's rock bottom."

"I think mine's okay, really."

"What size or body type are you?"

"Just about average. Of course, I don't have any hair to speak of. That's going to be kind of a challenge."

"That's no problem. We've got a guy from Sweden that's slick as a billiard ball, but I guarantee you'd never know it. Just don't make your sideburns too long, you can easily overdo that. How about scarves? You'll need at least a dozen or so. Five or six to give away on stage, when the women come up to you."

"Oh well, I don't think I need to worry about that."

"Hey, be prepared. I'm telling you. I mean, no offense to you personally, but anybody who does Elvis, it could be Bob Dole up there—if he's doing Elvis, there'll be women coming down to get their scarf, so you better be ready. Something else, too: who've you got to give you your scarves and your water on stage?"

"I haven't thought about it."

"You better. Do you have a bodyguard?"

"I've got a couple of writer friends who are pretty tough."

"Well, you ought to be thinking about it. Bodyguards keep the wrong people away from you, but there's more to it than that: it's part of the show. Sometimes I work without a band. I program a whole show with instrumental tracks—backup tapes. It would be just me and an empty stage out there, so I come on with four bodyguards. I don't truly need that kind of protection. Heck, I used to wrestle, myself—I was in the Olympic trials in 72—I can take care of myself. But it generates excitement when you come in surrounded by guys in dark shades and official-looking jackets. Then you fill up the stage with them. You don't have a band, but you've got four guys up there besides yourself. And one of those guys, his job is to bring you a scarf and put it around your neck every time you need a new one, just like Charlie Hodge done for Elvis. Listen: you go to Wal-Mart, okay? Get you some synthetic silk scarves, big ones, and cut 'em up, six inches wide by 58 to 60 inches long. Have your wife hem them or get one of those plastic hemmers for ten bucks and do it yourself. You'll be glad I told you this."

I hesitated. "The thing is . . . I haven't performed much yet. Not at all, to be honest. I mean, I hope to get some experience before the convention—"

"Oh, you will, you will. Can you sing?"

"I can carry a tune."

"Work on it. Sing every day. Take a few lessons. Get you a few Elvis songs that you can handle and listen to them real hard. Then get used to singing 'em in front of people. Start with karaoke, get out to some karaoke bars—all the DJs have Elvis tracks. The rest of it, the moves and so on, that'll come, but you have to learn to sing first. Don't worry so much about mimicking Elvis. Be yourself doing Elvis, you know what I mean?"

"Not exactly."

"Do it the way Elvis would have done it if he was you—or the way YOU would do it if you was Elvis."

"Hm."

"The thing is, the sooner you realize you ain't Elvis, the better off you'll be."

"I don't have a problem with that. I'm still trying to get a suit that fits."

"Well, you're going to go through every stage along the way, I guarantee you. And trying to be more exactly like Elvis than Elvis himself is one of the stages. And then it leaches out into your life. You start to walk around thinking you're Elvis. I counsel the guys not to go around trying to look like Elvis all the time. 'Everybody gives me such a hard time,' they say. Well—what do you expect, dyeing your hair black every three days and this and that. I tell 'em: guys, there's a switch—you turn it on, you turn it off. Once you learn that, you're okay. Until you learn that, you're not entirely yourself—and in performance terms, that hurts you, it holds you back.

"I tell you what," Rick went on, "I help put on a small fan convention down here every June at Jacksonville Beach. Why don't you come on down. It'd be a good way to break you in. You'll see Elvis impersonators of different types, some of 'em just beginners. You can get up in front of some real Elvis fans and do your thing Saturday afternoon. You'll see me do my show Saturday night. Meet some good people."

June was a long way off. Surely by then I would have picked up enough experience not to make a complete ass of myself. It seemed safe to say yes. My cousin Larry lived in Savannah, about halfway to Jacksonville. Larry was an Assistant U.S. Attorney and occasionally packed a gun: he would be an ideal bodyguard if I could pry him away from his legal briefs for a weekend.

Rick's call-waiting beeped and he excused himself momentarily. "I've got to take this one," he said when he came back. "It's a candidate for the mayoral race down here, and I'm doing a concert for him, a benefit. I'm going to be flat out on that for the next month."

We agreed to talk again in a month or so.

Chapter

4

I was startled to learn from an article in the local paper that there was an Elvis impersonator right in my own hometown, and with my own surname. Keith Henderson was to appear at a popular student dive called He's Not Here, along with his band, The Nomads, who were also local boys. Together, they were billed as The Elvis Resurrection Show.

He's Not Here was a back-alley joint that blossomed into an open courtyard, then became a two-story warren of bars and lounges. It was a balmy September night. A stage had been erected in the leafy courtyard. The Nomads, an excellent "classic rock" band were in mid-set. Most of them were in their early 40s, men with families and full-time jobs—carpenter, public relations man, electrician (Keith Henderson himself was an installer for the local gas company). Music was their second line of work, but their first love. They'd played together since high school, and it showed in their casual professionalism.

As the set progressed, the front man impishly reported Elvis sightings ("The King was just seen at a Dunkin' Donuts about 10 miles west of here . . .") and kept the crowd—a mix of college students and hardcore Elvis fans my age and older—in a playful state of anticipation.

Looking around, I saw a familiar face—a white-bearded Ernest

Hemingway clone under a swaggering wide-brimmed straw hat. Frank Boardman had recently won the Hemingway lookalike contest at a publication party for my novel, *I Killed Hemingway*. Not that he was a fan of Hemingway, whom he had called "a horror—the bastard son of Nietzsche." But the visual juxtaposition was interesting: Papa impersonator turning out to see counterfeit King! I asked him if he was an Elvis fan.

"Absolutely not," he practically bellowed. "Loathe the man, can't stand the music."

"So why are you here?"

"Loyalty and curiosity: the lead guitar player has just done my floors."

Keith's entrance, when it came, was preceded by plenty of carney barking and hoopla, so the crowd was more than ready for Elvis—and here he was, in gleaming gold lamé (the suit clearly built for a leaner, meaner Keith—doing the early Elvis numbers, the universal classics that everyone of a certain age, fan or not, recalls.

"This, I suppose, is what put the youthful version on the postage stamp?" Frank Boardman growled. It occurred to me that, in addition to being an intellectual mandarin, Frank was probably just over the age barrier—too old at the time "Heartbreak Hotel," "Don't Be Cruel," and "Hound Dog" had blown across the charts—too old, that is, to recall the thrill of adolescence that fueled early devotion to Elvis.

I wasn't. I had been thirteen that year, 1956. No man or woman ever forgets the musical backdrop of his or her thirteenth year. Looking at Frank, I realized that for him that music was probably the Four Freshmen, the Kingston Trio, Perry Como . . .

"What kind of music calls up your youth, Frank?"

"Mahler . . . Bruckner."

"No, I mean popular music."

He turned his withering Papa Hemingway glare on me. "Jazz, I suppose. Billie Holiday. How's that?"

*   *   *

Keith put on a spirited, authentic show. He freely admitted to being a few pounds overweight, but it didn't stop him from moving well. Vocally, he was on the money. In terms of showmanship, he had a pleasing stage presence, but there was something tentative, a holding back. He seemed reluctant to surge full-force into the identity of Elvis Presley.

At one point, he left the stage briefly, for a costume change. When he reappeared, it was in the circle of a spotlight, on a balcony that jutted over the rear of the stage. The band broke into Richard Strauss's "Also Sprach Zarathustra," the solemn fanfare introduction used by Elvis in his later performing years (also the theme from the movie *2001: A Space Odyssey*). In the circle of a single spotlight, he posed, cape unfurled in full late-Elvis splendor, his back to the audience—a kind of Batman, revealing himself to all Gotham City.

Posing completed, he descended the stairs and made his entrance, with a ritual guitar hanging from the neck of his high-collared white jumpsuit—and now we were into the "Vegas Years" portion of the show, the real meat of any Elvis impersonator's act.

Still there was a reticence, an "I'm-not-Elvis" diffidence in his stage manner that kept him earthbound. But the crowd thrilled to his moves—women came forward like sassy communicants to receive scarves and kisses; one good-looking college girl stepped on stage and sat, as if for her portrait, while he sang "Love Me Tender" directly to her.

"Look at this response to a guy who could be anyone," I said to Frank. "You can imagine what it was like with Elvis himself."

Frank grunted and folded his arms like a cigar store Indian. Watching his stern, skeptical gaze, I decided not to tell him what I was up to.

Keith Henderson—or Cousin Keith, as my daughters referred to him in the southern manner—certainly did not walk around trying to convince the world he was Elvis. In fact, the next time I saw him, he was growing a mustache. For him, the challenge was *not* being

Elvis: this was the stance of proper humility demanded of a serious fan.

"Normally, I do a tribute," Keith told me on the phone. "I don't talk as if I'm Elvis, we don't have all those Dunkin' Donut jokes and whatnot. The Elvis Resurrection producers wanted me to try more of an impersonation. Usually it's just I'm Keith Henderson, we're going to create the illusion that Elvis is here. I'm really not comfortable with the whole concept of 'Elvis impersonator.' "

Keith had a reputation around town as a nice guy, a family man, and a dead-serious Elvis fan. I told him simply that I was working on an Elvis-related book and invited him to drop by my house for a chat. He showed up one lunch hour in his work clothes, a tall, sturdy fellow in his 30s, and we sat around in my basement, watching the video clips I had taped from *The Night of 100 Elvises*.

For Keith, who had been a teenager when The King died, Elvis was an early passion: "I've studied him, seriously studied him, since I was four years old. My grandmother, she always called him her boyfriend. She would call all her grandchildren and say 'my boyfriend's on TV tonight. Watch him on Channel 11' or whatever. We'd take Grandma to the drive-in movies to see Elvis. The only records she owned were Elvis Presley records. I'd lock myself up with her records, stand in front of a full-length mirror doing all the gyrations. So after years of trying to sing like him, if I sang 'Jingle Bells,' it'd come out Elvis."

Keith's defining career moment had been a three-night high school talent show: the Junior Follies. Keith's girlfriend said he ought to do a tribute to Elvis.

"I was gonna wear a T-shirt with a Harley-Davidson eagle on the front and do a little 50s thing. But my mother and grandma decided they were gonna build me a white Elvis eagle outfit. That was going to be a onetime deal. My father played guitar for me, and a few of my friends played other instruments—that was the band. When I went off through the audience, people were all over me, dragged me to the ground trying to grab me, shake my hands, and pull my rings off.

Keith Henderson sees what Elvis saw.
(Photo courtesy of Fred Stipe)

Next two nights I used a couple of my buddies as bodyguards, trying to keep the people off, but it didn't do any good—same thing, they just grabbed me, wanted to touch me. So I ended up having guys surround me. I saw the same type of reaction to what I did that you see in pictures of live Elvis shows—the hands reaching, that sort of thing."

Going professional was the evolutionary next step.

"My first big show, I did twenty-six songs—way too many. Sixteen's about right for an Elvis show. I carried an eleven-piece band, singers—bodyguards, had a fan club, the whole works. 'Keith Henderson Presents a Tribute to Elvis.' My show was fashioned around the '73 *Aloha from Hawaii* concert. That's the era I was trying to sound like—he was picking harder songs with more operatic kinds of endings. We had the same basic format as Elvis. I paid everybody the same as Elvis's band got, we had roadies, top-notch sound system, everybody had three changes of stage costume, got their meals on the road. Nobody drank alcohol or smoked dope when they were with me. I had to fire the best bass player I ever had over that. It got to where it cost us $8,000 to do a show. That was our cost."

So far, Keith hadn't asked me any questions about my book. Without spilling the beans, I tried to pick up some how-to information I could use.

"What would you say is the secret of doing Elvis well?"

He shrugged. "You have to sing every day. Some impersonators can't even hit a note. A lot of people don't really know the difference. They never saw Elvis in concert, they never saw a concert tape. The big thing that Elvis had was a lot of charisma and a massive amount of stage presence. And he knew how to react to what people were doing in the audience: if he gave 'em a little something and they went crazy, he'd give 'em a little more. He'd always give 'em just enough to make 'em want more."

I came to the obligatory question with caution.

"Do you feel that, when you perform, the spirit of Elvis is somehow coming into you, or through you?"

"Could be. When I psych up for a show, I say a prayer. After that Amen, Elvis kind of jumps into you and you don't have to think about it, you just do it."

This was about as authentic an answer as I could hope for. Okay, his cards were on the table: I decided to 'fess up and tell him exactly what I was really up to: "Here's something I haven't told you yet— mostly because I didn't want you to think I was some kind of nut. I'm going to do this myself."

"Do what?"

"Do Elvis."

He looked at me blankly.

"For my book, that is. I have to actually perform. Get a feel for what it's like."

I opened a closet door and revealed my brass-studded jumpsuit, looking as though it would fit an elephant.

Keith's eyes refocused on me as though I had slipped off a mask and revealed a whole new face. One side of his mouth curled slightly in an Elvis grin.

"Man, you better do your homework."

Chapter

5

n the midst of a total brain bath in all things Elvis, I broke away for something completely different, a Hemingway conference up in Michigan. I am not a Hemingway scholar, but *I Killed Hemingway* had gotten me invited to give a speech at dinner and hang around with the conferees, many of whom would be familiar faces from the previous summer's international Hemingway-Fitzgerald conference in Paris. Some of these were the pros—ambitious young literature professors on their way up, elder scholars anchoring the proceedings with the weight of their reputations—but the ones who most interested me were the pure Hemingway aficionados: not academics, but ordinary people who for one reason or another had discovered Hemingway and gone beyond simply reading him and going about their business.

They were fans.

These folks and others like them planned their vacations to take them to Paris, Michigan, Idaho, Pamplona, Key West, and other locations sacred to Papa, specifically to attend Hemingway get-togethers. They subscribed to the *Hemingway Journal* and the *Hemingway Society Newsletter* (they were members). They owned first editions and collected Hemingway memorabilia (cups, T-shirts, pens).

I learned that Hemingway fans like to get into minute detail about whether some actual piece of geography corresponds to its presumed fictional counterpart in some story or other.

On walking tours I heard remarks like this:

"The general store looks exactly the way he described it in 'Up in Michigan.' "

"You know, in 'Ten Indians' I think he took that two-mile stretch between Petosky and Horton's Bay and shortened it to a half mile."

There was a breakfast the morning after my talk—which had been a rant about how Americans could no longer tell fact from fiction (with boundary-teasing fiction writers like me as prime culprits in this degenerative process). At my breakfast table, there was lively talk of Oliver Stone's *JFK*, the three TV histories of Amy Fisher and how Hemingway's *A Moveable Feast* was so falsified a memoir that it's no wonder Papa wanted to call it a novel. Someone asked me what I was working on now. "A book on Elvis Presley impersonators—mostly from the standpoint of being one." All talk stopped. "I mean, it's going to be an account of my own experiences. As an impersonator. Elvis impersonator. A kind of memoir." (When the hell would I master a crisp one-line description of the damned thing?) The pause continued.

"Goodness, that's quite a leap," said a middle-aged woman, who had told me she taught high school English.

"Oddly enough, it's not such a great leap at all," I challenged her, cartwheeling out on a limb. "You'd be amazed at the similarities between Elvis and Hemingway."

"You're right. I *would* be amazed."

"Well, I don't want to overstate the case—I'm not saying they were separated at birth or something, but look at the similar forces in their lives: both overwhelmed by early fame, both intensely ambitious, hard workers, and early successes. Both needed entourages around them, both had formidable mothers, had to have women as anima figures, both struggled with their celebrity, both were substance abusers, both lost their powers tragically in the end—and on and on."

One young faculty member from a small midwest college drew a bead on me from across the table. He wiped his mouth with a napkin and cleared his throat. "With all respect to Elvis Presley—" he began.

His wife squirmed a bit and, I believe, nudged him under the table. "No, no, I mean that. Elvis Presley is surely deserving of respect. But then . . . what about this mostly Southern, white trash content factor at work there—why do *so many* Americans embrace this in him?"

Sure, it was a question with an edge to it—but a good question. I remember, as a 13-year-old Southerner, asking essentially the same question in my own way as I watched Elvis's early TV appearances—on slick "Yankee" vehicles like the *Milton Berle Show*, Tommy and Jimmy Dorsey's *Stage Show*, the *Ed Sullivan Show*—and heard the New York studio audiences going wild. Something in me had felt pride that another Southerner was causing such a fuss, nationwide, but truthfully, I wondered how a guy like Elvis, who would have been snubbed socially by most of the "nice" kids at my high school, could mainstream his southern hick-greaser act with such immense impact.

That was then and this was now; but almost forty years later, with the hillbilly cat himself long dead, the miracle of his apotheosis was still a nagging mystery to those who saw nothing but alien content there. I thought of a relative of mine and his wife, whose take on Elvis was still, after all these years, "I don't get it. Why Elvis?" But there was a calculated stolidness to their resistance, and beneath that, I believed, a deep resentment of Elvis for inspiring immorality, glorifying defiance, and promoting rudeness. These had been *nice* kids in their day; Elvis to them was the kind of boy who'd spoil a dance by getting into a fight. The young professor was "just curious," but there was a shrill resonance to his question too—as though he took it personally, this white trash content, and was daring me to account for it, acknowledge it, deal with it.

"I'm afraid you've got me there," I said, ducking the issue squarely.

* * *

*   *   *

Why Elvis?

I was to encounter this question in so many guises along the way that I came to anticipate it. It meant many things.

Sometimes it meant simply, *Hey, I think he's terrific, but how did he get so much bigger than anybody else?* At other times there was a social edge to the question. One elegant lady put it to me this way: "What has Elvis *brought* us?" (By which, of course, she meant, what has Elvis brought *them*?) Asked this way, there was unspoken elitism coiled in the question.

The suspense movie *The River Wild* took a crack at depicting the two great white American social divisions: one low-class, white-trash, criminal, threatening; the other intellectual, nonviolent, high-achieving, yuppyish. Although the movie (made by Hollywood yuppies) surely sides with the latter, it is an accurate projection of how the two Americas regard each other. The "nice" classes associate Elvis Presley with fans who are tasteless, vulgar, and probably dangerous. In turn, Elvis people think of the country club set as snooty, out of it, cold, snobby, and effete. Both views are myopic—and in the movie, it's the Meryl Streep character, a class-blind mother, teacher, and hell-raising white-water rafter who strides the two worlds (she's a townie married to a yuppy)—and she's probably the *real* Elvis fan.

So my answer was: For some of us, Elvis had brought . . . nothing. No explanation—his star power, his musicianship, his historical timing—would ever suffice. The question would always contain an implicit social challenge.

Why Elvis? Why all these Elvis impersonators?

But what did we expect in the way of mass-entertainment icons, a legion of Van Cliburn impersonators? Elvis, after all, was quintessentially American, and only doing what quintessential Americans, like Jefferson or the Wright brothers, have always done: redefining himself, then reinventing the world in terms of the new definition; doing it his way; not giving a damn what others might think, socially or otherwise.

I thought of this, watching old tapes of his *Ed Sullivan Show* appearances. Here was certainly the wordless, surly, greaser Elvis. Behind him, in respectable suits, like a row of courtiers, were the Jordanaires, class-president types whose stiff dorkiness contrasted wonderfully with Elvis's cool sexuality. Was Elvis aware of the perfect irony of this social juxtaposition? Was this his subtle revenge on the kids with penny loafers and Ivy League collars who scorned him in high school? To place these nice-boy hirelings, these finger-snapping sycophants *behind* him, reducing them to a mere backdrop?

Often I picked up another shading in the way the question "Why Elvis?" was asked. I could hear an insinuation that there had been a terrible mistake, something had malfunctioned and instead of more Pat Boones, we got . . . Elvis. If we could only dive under the hood with the right tools, maybe the malfunction could even be corrected.

When rock 'n' roll was new, this kind of thinking led to public record burnings, make-it-go-away political speeches, denunciations from the pulpit. At the root of it was a profound misunderstanding of what popular culture is. Societies get the popular culture they deserve, not because they choose it, but because they *are* it. It isn't created; it is one more expression of a society's very identity.

People whose judgments about popular culture lead them to wish they could change or suppress it don't realize what they are dealing with.

You might as well try to change your dreams.

Chapter

6

My first task as an Elvis impersonator was to get my suit looking right. "I can't do anything with it," Carol had told me. "When something is this out of proportion, you can't just take it in. You have to start from scratch."

"But you realize what 'scratch' means, in this case. You said yourself these Elvis suits are hideously expensive."

"I thought the whole idea is that you're just an ordinary guy, doing it for a lark. Does it really matter so much if your suit doesn't fit?"

"But look at me! This is Bozo the Clown."

"All right. Try a professional seamstress."

Halloween was only a few days away, so I figured I wouldn't raise too many eyebrows if I showed up somewhere with an Elvis "costume"; I opened the Yellow Pages and looked for the biggest ad I could find under SEAMSTRESSES—and one that didn't sound too exclusively feminine—or too men's-shop tweedy, for that matter. One image caught my eye: a cartoon figure of a typical American housewife of the 50s, smiling an Ipana smile and waving a pair of scissors the size of garden shears. The ad said:

EVELYN'S HOUSE OF ALTERATIONS. CUSTOM TAILORING AND ALTERATIONS
FOR MEN AND WOMEN. FORMAL WEAR, WEDDING ATTIRE, DRESSMAKING

That seemed global enough. What I didn't want to hear on the other end of the line (punctuated by giggles) was: "An Elvis suit? I'm afraid we don't do Elvis suits."

Evelyn, it turned out, was a small Chinese woman, working her sewing machine like Horowitz on the piano, stopping only to peer at me over her spectacles and smile expectantly. "Help you?"

"Yes, it's an unusual job for you. It's . . . well, let me just show you."

I unzipped the bag and let the jumpsuit billow out like a collapsed parachute. Evelyn's eyes widened. "What is this?"

"An Elvis Presley costume."

"What kind?"

"Elvis? Elvis Presley?"

She wasn't with me. It occurred to me that, world famous as The King was, there still might be people from elsewhere on the planet—whole cultures, even—that would draw a blank on the name "Elvis."

"It's for Halloween," I said, trying to ease things forward. "A costume."

"To fit you? But this is lot of work. Sorry. Not enough time for Halloween."

I swallowed. "Then . . . just take your time."

"You don't need for Halloween?"

"Well, not really. It would be a nice Halloween thing, of course, but . . . Well, actually, I need it for . . . a book I'm writing."

"You professor?"

"Yes."

"Ah," she smiled and nodded firmly, then fixed me with another strange look. "Writing book about . . . what?"

"Elvis Presley. That is, people who imitate Elvis Presley."

"Lot of people who do that?"

"Hundreds of them do it. Thousands. And the thing is, you see, I have to do it myself."

"I see." I realized I had completely lost her. She motioned toward a changing room. "You go try on."

A few moments later I emerged, like a shimmering extraterrestrial from its space ship, rekindling Evelyn's wonder.

"Somebody from the Bible?" she said.

In her fitting room, she stood me on a pedestal and started gathering and pinning. The pedestal was in full view of her front door, and just then, two well-dressed suburban ladies entered. The older of the two, a gray matron, saw me and backed up a step. The younger, a slim Junior Leaguer of about thirty, let out a playful "whooo!" *She* got it.

Evelyn hastened to tell them that all this had something to do with a book the professor was writing. I had to explain, lamely, what I was up to, and, while Evelyn continued to stick pins, and the ladies moved on into the waiting area, I overheard the older one say, in a stage whisper, "Must be a sociologist."

Evelyn and I eventually struck a deal. She would alter the suit for a reasonable price if I myself removed the two or three dozen studs that would have to come out before she could start cutting. This was no problem for me and gave me an opportunity to sit at one of her cutting tables and chat with her (which, because of her limited English, was not an easy matter). Although she had accepted the terms of my obsession, it was with a "why pry any further" insouciance. (I could imagine her shrugging it off to her family later: "You know I get all kinds in there.") I was determined to raise her consciousness.

"You know what rock 'n' roll is, don't you?"

She fixed me with a condescending frown. "My nephew is rock 'n' roll drummer."

"Okay, then. Elvis Presley was the first rock 'n' roll star. Big, very big. All over the world. He's dead now."

Something about "dead" got through. A connection was made, and her face suddenly came alive with revelation. "Oh! Pree—slee! Ah-vis Pree-sleee! Oh, yes, yes! His daughter just marry Michael Jackson!"

"That's right! That's the man!"

"He wear this?"

"I'll bring you pictures next time."

"Of course. Ah-vis Pree-slee. He was very poor. And you know what color car he bought his mama?"

"Pink!"

"That's right! He wear this?"

"Much fancier than this. He had them in all colors. Jewels all over them."

"He was good guy. In Chinese, he called 'King Cat'—I don't know why. He die young, right? After his mama."

"Sort of. But now, like I said, he has hundreds of imitators—thousands—who wear suits like this."

She stared back, skepticism returning: "Ahhhh, I see now," she lied politely.

It didn't take me long to learn that no piece of Elvis symbolism came closer to pure iconographic white heat than did The Suit.

This was grasped early on by satirists: I remember an old *Saturday Night Live* mock concert promo in which a jumpsuit was shown on a headless dummy; a hysterical announcer's voice touted, "Live, onstage, at Madison Square Garden . . . the King's *SUIT*."

There were three archetypal Elvis costumes. The gold lamé suit captured history's imagination as the last word in the early look, although Elvis hated it and hardly ever wore it.

The black leather motorcycle suit was worn only once, in the 1968 television special that launched Elvis's comeback. Among impersonators, black leather came to signify a mythical era: Elvis's transition from youth into full manhood.

The bejeweled jumpsuit was the penultimate Elvis look, and served him from his return to Vegas in 1969 until his death in 1977. According to some accounts, Elvis ordered up something simple, like the *ghi* he felt comfortable doing karate in, but before long, he had traded up to the expensively designed one-piece jumpsuits that gave him a superhero look.

Whatever the case, for Elvis impersonators, The Suit is the benchmark of credibility. If your suit is up to standard, you are in the ballpark. Without one, you ain't nuttin' but a hound dog. B&K Enterprises, one of the current Elvis suitmakers, puts it this way in their catalog: "Remember, your costume is your tool in the entertainment business. The better you look and feel, the better your show will be! The better your show is, the better your bookings will be!"

Eventually, thanks to Evelyn's magic, my suit fit . . . kind of. To be more precise, it no longer surrounded me like a shroud. You wouldn't call it skintight, the kind of custom job that made Elvis look like a god in the early 70s, but at least it wouldn't be an embarrassment. The wig was another matter altogether. All I had were the cheap black costume wigs from Ollie. Here was where I was going to spend serious money, I suspected: on a proper wig, since my own hair was going quickly to white and what was left of it on top only thinly covered my pate.

I looked up wig shops in the Yellow Pages. They all seemed to be geared toward women and cancer patients undergoing chemotherapy. The listings specifically for men seemed concentrated on various hair replacement systems, the kind of heavy-duty fakery that I had always told myself I would avoid. I got the feeling that they weren't looking for the "occasional user" type of customer.

"Do you have a few moments to take a roll of pictures?" I asked Carol, after the kids were off to school. I had spent some time in front of the full-length mirror in our bedroom and felt ready for the logical next step.

"Sure," she said, so I handed her a camera. "But you really should have a better wig."

"I know, I know. Let's just go with this one for now."

Direct from *Planet of the Apes*, my first attempt to dress the part.
(Photo courtesy of Carol Henderson.)

The wig I chose easily covered my whole head. It rose from a pronounced widow's peak into a torrential black swoop, and fell to almost shoulder length. There was a simian quality about it. In fact, it looked like something out of *Planet of the Apes*. But it accomplished the effect I suppose I was after that morning: it completely and unambigu-

Note dirty sneakers: I would be dogged by lack of proper footwear.
(Photo courtesy of Carol Henderson.)

ously erased the 52-year-old "professor." When I looked in the mirror, the first half of my transformation was accomplished with overkill: I was gone.

I posed against a bland beige curtain in the living room. I hadn't thought of shoes (what kind of shoes did Elvis wear with this getup?), but I threw on some dirty, once-white sneakers—they were comfortable and wouldn't restrict movement. Carol could aim the camera so that my feet didn't show.

"Let's put some Elvis on the stereo," said Carol, getting into it. I struck a few classic late-Elvis poses, most of them karate-style, cheerfully macho, "king of the jungle" poses. Keith Henderson had taught me the most basic Elvis move, a kind of pigeon-toed inward thrust of both knees, and I found it was natural. As Carol shot the roll, asking for a little of this or that, something flowed into me, a sensation of physical ease with myself as Elvis; it amounted to an illusion—hallucination, as it turned out—that in terms of my body anyway, I was *there* . . . As Keith Henderson had put it, Elvis just "jumped into me."

I rushed to the 1-hour Photo Quick.

What I saw when the pictures came back sucked the air right out of my sails. The suit (semitailored though it now was) wasn't anywhere near splendid; nor was my body, showing through it. In some shots it looked like I was frolicking in my pajamas. In the facial closeups, my attempt to capture Elvis's sexy half-grin made me look bemused, rattled, as if someone had just waked me up by shining a flashlight in my face. The wig was a comical pile of shag, a bad joke. My poses—the ones that had felt so "right"—were flaccid and unfocused, like someone trying to hypnotize a small animal.

With a sinking sensation, I recalled Keith's reaction when I told him where I was headed: "Whew. You better do your homework!"

I realized how far I had to go before I could stand on a stage in this getup and represent myself as anything other than—let's face it—a clown.

Chapter

7

When I began talking to people about this book, I right away ran into what I called The Clown Archetype. "Oh, what a riot!" people would say, when I told them I was becoming an impersonator myself. The next thing I would hear (I began to anticipate it) was, "Have you seen *Honeymoon in Vegas*?"

I had. It was a popular movie when it came out. It takes place in Las Vegas, and though no single Elvis impersonator figures in the story, the goonish Flying Elvises perform a deus ex machina plot function by coming out of nowhere at the crisis to fly Nicholas Cage from Hawaii to Las Vegas just in time to get the girl. The catch—he must don a jumpsuit himself and make a nocturnal jump with them.

Elvis impersonators are what you remember most about *Honeymoon in Vegas*. And because this movie has caused more misapprehension than any other cultural artifact I've come across, it's worth taking some time here to look in detail at just how it does its job.

Honeymoon in Vegas (1992):

Elvis impersonators, as featured extras, are everywhere in the lobby of the Bally Casino. This draws a smirk from tough-guy gambler Tommy Corman, a psychopathic ball-buster played by James Caan. He watches two bumpkin Elvises alight from a taxi bitching over how expensive the ride was. One of them snorts that the "hound dog" driver couldn't even speak English. The other one gloats that he didn't leave a tip. Message: Elvis impersonators are more than just laughable, they're mean-spirited, miserly, and xenophobic.

Also watching are a young couple, played by Nicholas Cage and Sarah Jessica Parker, who snicker at these louts the way snotty English tourists would titter at the sight of kilted chimpanzees. When four Sufi Elvises in turbans and jumpsuits drift past, Cage cracks a lame, mild joke about how they must have loved Elvis's movie *Blue Calcutta*.

Later, in a poker game, the James Caan character insults a short, pudgy Chinese Elvis, who blandly signals "Hey, no offense," by striking a self-demeaning Elvis pose. Cage remarks he hasn't seen so many side-burns since *West Side Story*, and the poker players, including the hapless Chinese impersonator, yowl with laughter. Caan compliments Cage on the joke and observes proudly that it is an example of "New York wit."

In the midst of a tough hand, the Chinese Elvis inexplicably bursts into a chorus of "Viva Las Vegas" and has to be shut up by Cage. Again, he has no reaction, except to announce grandly that "Babeh, the King must fold." Later, he bothers Cage with another spontaneous vocal outburst: "Wise men say, only fools rush in . . ." Again he's shushed; again the film allows him no reaction. Message: don't think of Elvis impersonators as real characters; they are merely the butt of the joke here.

The film's sucker punch comes in the form of the Flying Elvises, a team of wigged and jumpsuited sky divers whose dopey Elvis routine is an idiot's delight. On the plane, they stare straight ahead at nothing, bouncing and jerking in place to "Burning Love." Their leader is a hoo-boy Chill Wills type whose bad jokes evoke the by-now predictable hyena fits of disconnected laughter. When it comes time to make their jump, they join hands and lurch back and forth in a weird parody of male bonding. Standing, they shuffle toward the hatch like drooling automatons. Later, when Cage and Parker get married in a Las Vegas wedding chapel, these same goofballs witness the ceremony. The lead Elvis has an attack of hysterical wedding-cliché tears (more New York wit), and we all laugh.

Whew.

All this—in an entertainment vehicle with a larger audience than every show by every Elvis impersonator in the history of the world—has been a hard stigmatization to overcome. "Have you seen *Honeymoon in Vegas*" is always code for "Can you believe these morons?"

Some images from fiction are so strong that the public simply believes they *must* be real. *National Geographic* has received thousands of requests for the back-issue containing the photo portfolio of the Madison County bridges. It doesn't exist. Rather, it exists only in the made-up world of *The Bridges of Madison County*. Similarly, Castle Rock, the production company that developed *Honeymoon in Vegas*, began receiving requests for the Flying Elvises. As the calls poured in from bookers for state fairs, mall openings, air shows, parades, sporting events, the callers were simply told the truth: "They don't exist."

Hearing of this, an enterprising Las Vegas producer, Dick Feeney, said, "Well, they do now."

Feeney pulled some of the original *Honeymoon* jumpers together and established the Flying Elvi ("Elvi" so as not to conflict with Castle Rock's established trademark rights). A splinter group calling itself "The Flying Elvises" broke off and managed to get themselves licensed by Elvis Presley Enterprises (aka "Graceland"). Feeney sued, convincing Graceland that prior trademark rights were being violated and (most interesting) that Graceland's very right to license *any* Elvis impersonator *anywhere* was doubtful, on the grounds that such a license would be unenforceable.

Rather than fight a losing battle, Graceland agreed to stop doing business with the renegades and to "license" Feeney's Flying Elvi instead (even though such a license would have no legal force). Feeney would be able to say "Licensed by Elvis Presley Enterprises." In return, a piece of Feeney's action would flow into Graceland's coffers, and since the Flying Elvi were in great demand, performed for big bucks, and would be easy to track, this appealed to the Graceland money machine.

The deal was particularly interesting in that Graceland's general attitude toward Elvis impersonators seemed to have always been that they were regrettable eccentrics, an embarrassment, a nuisance, and wouldn't it be nice if they would all just go away. Yet here was "the Vatican," publicly sanctioning the biggest embarrassment of all—these creepy Flying Elvi, the most ridiculous possible stunt-clown version of the Elvis Presley image in existence!

A curious footnote to *Honeymoon in Vegas* concerns its costar, James Caan. Caan married a woman named Sheila Ryan, who had once been romantically involved with Elvis—the real Elvis. The marriage was on the rocks by the time Caan made *Honeymoon in Vegas*, so you can't help wondering whether Caan the actor read his impersonator put-down lines with a little extra relish—maybe even improvised a few of them—given the wickedly ironic circumstances.

In any case the Clown Factor, as I was coming to know it—Elvis the fat buffoon—was just as far from the truth as the Savior Factor—Elvis the suffering giant who, like Jesus, gave his life for us. But one seemed a function of the other: Elvis the Clown existed as a corrective to Elvis the Savior. On the supermarket tabloid racks (the communications equivalent of a national Elvis bulletin board), the two archetypes sat side by side: *Holy Vision of Elvis Cured Her Cancer . . . Porky Elvis Scarfs Donuts at Weight Clinic*.

All this was on my mind one evening as I taught my graduate fiction writing workshop, a fairly mature group of students ranging in age from 20s to 40s. The subject of reader expectation—built-in cultural spin—came up and I observed that, from my perspective as a (ha-ha)

Elvis impersonator, the Flying Elvises had put a hopeless spin on the subject for all future Elvis impersonators.

"What is it," I asked, "that causes a formidable cultural icon like Elvis Presley to evolve a counter-icon that takes the form of ridicule—a joke?"

Ellsworth, an older student, didn't even buy the premise. "Elvis is formidable? I don't know what you're talking about."

"Well, where do I start? Are you denying that the Elvis phenomenon is significant in size?"

"I'm just saying what's so great about Elvis? Is he really any different from any other entertainer?"

"Well, I think so, to say the least. Let's put it this way," I said. "If you had a phenomenon similar to Elvis in ancient Rome or thirteenth-century France—someone who had been watched at one point by one third of the people alive in the world, someone who twenty years after his death had thousands of people going around impersonating him, someone that 10 percent of the population of the world thought was still alive, nobody would question the propriety of a formal study of it. So let me ask again: how has the Elvis-Is-a-Joke phenomenon evolved out of this?"

"Could it be distance in time?" asked one student.

That didn't convince me. "But why then is Elvis a joke and, say, Jesus is not a joke?"

Ellsworth bristled: "Excuse me, but I just don't see equating Elvis and Jesus."

I could feel the emotion rising in his voice: this wasn't detached academic speculation—Ellsworth was standing up to challenge a blasphemy.

"I'm not equating them."

"Yes, you are."

"Wait a minute—if you look at what I said, I was actually doing the opposite: I was saying that, after two thousand years, Jesus has *not* evolved into an elaborate pop culture joke, whereas in just over fifteen years, Elvis has—at least for some people."

But Ellsworth wasn't through putting Elvis in his place. "Well, you can't compare Elvis to Jesus. Again, what was so great about Elvis anyway?"

Allison, a woman I knew was an Elvis fan, piped up. "He was awesome. He was more than an entertainer. He made people feel good about their lives. It's been all this time and his cult—if you want to call it that—is even stronger than ever."

"I'm just saying *Why Elvis*, that's all," said Ellsworth. "The Grateful Dead have a huge following, but nobody compares them to Jesus."

"*Nobody* was comparing him to Jesus!" I stressed, realizing as I said it that my sin was to have merely talked of Elvis and Jesus in the same breath, the same general frame of reference. Whatever had actually been said, Ellsworth, clearly a pious Christian, had reacted emotionally to the mere proximity of Elvis to Jesus in the discussion.

Once, years ago, John Lennon had been decrying the superficiality of fan worship and ruefully observed, "We're more popular than Jesus." What he meant, of course, was that *this should not be*. But Christians ignored the context, and a flap of major proportions erupted.

"Here's the point, Ellsworth: Check back fifteen years after Jerry Garcia dies—assuming he will someday—and see if there's still a major Grateful Dead cult. See if there are ten to twenty thousand Grateful Dead impersonators around the world. I don't think group-ness can live on in the person of an icon. If all we had were twelve apostles, there would have been no Christianity."

"But as far as Elvis is concerned," said Ellsworth, getting the last word, "I still don't get it."

"And you never will," breathed Allison.

Having read around, I was aware that a well-worked subgenre of Elvis fiction was based on the premise of Elvis worship. The stories were usually set in the near future, when established Elvis cults and churches had come into being. Here's that world as it exists in the novel *Elvissey*, by Jack Womack (which is written in an invented style of English mirroring Womack's idea of how the language may have evolved a hundred years hence).

> Millions wanted the King now, wanted without cease, full-faithed and overt; but which King? The C of E [i.e., Church of Elvis] was one church become many . . . the Prearmyite [i.e., pre-army] denomination was but one: amongst the Elvii were the Hosts of Memphis, the Shaken, Rattled and Rolled, the River Jordanaires; the Gracelandians, the Vegassenes, the Gladyseans; the C of E Now or Never, the Redeemed Believers in Our Master's Voice, the Church of the True Assumption of His Burning Love, and a hundred dozen more. Each chismatrix knew their King true, and saw their road as sole and only; their only given was that, for whatever reason, and—they supposed—at no one's command, the King would return.

In "The Elvis Cults," a rather dark short story by Michael Wilkerson, Elvis worship has grown to massive presence: "Elvism had become the second largest religion in America . . . The cults were centered in the south and midwest; they ranged from the quiet, meditative 'singalikes' of Wisconsin and Minnesota to the more severe, cloistered 'lookalikes' of Elvisville [in Indiana], portions of Illinois, and the Deep South. All Elvists were required to visit Memphis once during their lifetimes. Each day they turned toward that city and sang His lyrics; the songs varied from cult to cult."

Both worlds were based on the unflattering premise that Elvis fans were little more than mental robots who would allow themselves to be organized into doctrinal systems with articulated codes of belief, morality, worship, and so on. This was where the religious parallel fell apart for me.

If anything, the myth of Dionysus came closest to describing the reality of Elvismania. Like Elvis, Dionysus was young and nocturnal and inspired mindless passion from women, who went crazy in his presence. Even in those primitive days, orgiastic passion was seen as hostile to social order. But worship of Dionysus was so widespread that eventually it was tamed (as was Elvis), made public and official, and became the ritual basis for what we know as Greek tragedy.

Greek religious life possessed a free-wheeling quality that suggests today's entertainment "pantheon." The Greeks could choose which of the many gods they followed, much as modern fans choose which star they venerate. For all we know, there might even have been "why Dionysus?" conversations between devotees and nondevotees at Greek cocktail parties!

In Greek terms, anyway, Elvis fills the bill as a possible Dionysian avatar. His mortal origins wouldn't be a problem: heroes could be raised to immortal status—the ultimate meritocracy—so Elvis could have been a minor demigod at the very least. His birth, if not miraculous, was appropriately symbolic (surviving a dead twin brother), and certainly his early achievements were classically heroic. Like any god, he would intercede (sometimes interfere, especially sexually) in the lives of ordinary mortals: making nymphs pregnant or appearing out of nowhere to buy Cadillacs for chance strangers. Elvis didn't grow old— or when it seemed that he would, he disappeared, like Dionysus, in a confusing manner, seemingly swallowed up by chaos and darkness.

But most fascinating to me was the mask, the key functional link between Dionysus worship and its evolution into the secular ritual of tragedy (Greek tragic actors, like the priests of Dionysus, wore larger-than-life masks). The wearer of the mask (and here, of course, I wasn't thinking "mask" so much as Wig, Shades, Jumpsuit) was himself—*and yet not himself*.

In other words, through wearing the mask (persona), the priest of Dionysus took on the power (charisma) of the god. Now here was something I could relate to: it seemed to hold out promise that charisma, so necessary to an Elvis performance, could be put on and taken off. There might be hope even for me!

Ultimately, the question "why do they worship him?" seemed to beg itself. I wasn't coming across any "C of Es" or any organized cults that had anything more in mind than being after-death fan clubs, stretching the fun of "loving" Elvis as long and as far as possible. But this notion of charisma as god-power that could be simulated, in the proper context, by use of a mask—this alone made the religious parallel (though it was usually drawn in scorn) compelling and fascinating to me.

Chapter

8

t was time to start singing.

Rick Marino was right: doing Elvis was first and foremost *singing* Elvis. Where to begin? "You ain't nuttin' but a . . ."? No. By now "Hound Dog" seemed almost too much of a novelty song and beyond that, too emblematic of the young Elvis. Regardless of how the country had voted in the great Elvis stamp election of 1992, the Vegas years had to be my period, by default. So, by this reasoning, I should be learning emblematic jumpsuit favorites like "My Way," or "It's Now or Never." My problem seemed to be that, the older Elvis got, the more technically demanding his repertoire seemed to become.

I had never been to a karaoke bar. I didn't even know there was a karaoke craze, much less that it was a $10 billion industry, when I saw the film *Black Rain*, with its extended karaoke sequence. I was charmed by the idea that for once a piece of Japanese pop culture had swept the United States rather than the other way around. Once I started looking in the local entertainment listings, I discovered that there were karaoke nights in clubs all over the place. Could I simply walk into one of these clubs, throw down a few beers, stand up, and belt out a song anytime the spirit moved me?

"That's the way it works," said a young lady's voice over the phone from Shooters II, a nearby country and western nightclub.

"When I go on stage, can I take the words to the song up with me?"

"Don't have to. Lyrics come up on a monitor screen, right in front of your face."

"A monitor screen?"

"Like a teleprompter thing."

That sounded good. My chief fear, of course, was that I would blow the words, go blank, and stand there like a fool with my tongue lolling out and my brain in reverse.

Come on, you can do this, I told myself. Surely karaoke wasn't rocket science.

But I was damned if I was going to do it alone. I called a friend, David Williamson, whose taste for the offbeat made him the perfect companion for this adventure. Dave was a writer, a husky guy with thick blond hair going to gray. He lived in the country with his family and a ton of animals. He rode a Harley and carried a gun when it suited him (as a reserve cop, he was allowed). He was something of a hangout artist, restless, a hardworking journalist, but ready to go out and play when the sun was down. And he knew the club scene well.

"Shooters," he said. "Yeah, I go there sometimes. Kind of a fancy shitkicker's joint. It can get pretty rough on weekends. Karaoke night's relaxed by contrast. You can actually get on the dance floor. And the music doesn't rip your ears. I have to watch it, I've had hearing loss from too many years of loud music, chainsawing, motorcycles, and gunshots."

"Have you ever sung there?"

"What do you think?"

It was a dumb question. Dave had once been nicknamed Frog and I suspected it had something to do with his voice, which was nasal and atonal, like a battered old boxer's wheeze.

We arranged to meet at Shooter's at around nine.

When I pulled in, the parking lot was full of lavender and neon-green pickup trucks and customized vans. Inside, the ambience was what I would call redneck chic—mostly male twenty-somethings in beards and stubby ponytails, logo baseball caps, T-shirts, and muscles. There were a few ornate Western shirts and some big, high-crowned bull-riding hats. Shooters had formerly been a fish restaurant, and fishnets still adorned the walls in places, along with newer sets of mounted bull horns. A ball-shaped mirror chandelier revolved over the vast, shiny dance floor, spraying darts of light in a pattern of confusion.

There was Dave at a table near the dance floor, in his Duke T-shirt, working on a beer. He waved me over. On stage was a duo act, two skinny men splitting verses on a C&W song. Huge speakers lent a professional gloss to their skulking, hesitant delivery. Dave ordered me a beer and pointed to a loose-leaf ring binder on the table top; BRENDA'S KARAOKE was emblazoned on its cover.

"You look through that, find something you want to sing, fill out the slip, and turn it in to Brenda."

Brenda, the MC, was a spunky little blonde who controlled traffic, found the right back-up CD for each performance, and occasionally belted out a number herself in a sassy, Dolly Parton style.

After a couple of beers, my nerves began to damp down a bit. Nobody I saw was that good. Expectations were low. Energy was low. A plump girl in a huge white hat sang a Reba McIntyre song as though her voice was escaping by accident. An apish guy sang "Pretty Woman" with a voice that seemed to come from the far end of a fifty-foot pipe. Several pairs of lovers huggy-beared around the dance floor, using the slow ballads as an opportunity to rub bodies together. I thought it odd that nobody applauded at the end of a song. It was as if, when you took the mike and joined the highly produced mélange of back-up tracks, your reality temporarily merged into that of an intricately produced electronic artifact. In that light, it made sense: no one applauds a jukebox, after all.

"See anything you'd like to try?" said Dave.

"Maybe a ballad? Here's a whole Elvis page. 'Can't Help Falling in Love'? I don't want to break up the romance out on the floor."

"Don't worry, they'll be doing the electric slide before you know it."

"What's that?"

"A line dance. Kind of like the old hustle."

"Hustle?"

"Disco. Remember disco, Bill?"

"Not very well."

"Pick something up-tempo. She's probably ready for a change of pace."

"Mm. 'Don't Be Cruel,' I guess. It's simple, I know it pretty well. It's kind of emblematic for me, you know. I was thirteen and in love with all the girls when it came out. If that goes well I'll try something more challenging. Here's 'Polk Salad Annie.' "

"I like 'Polk Salad Annie.' "

"Okay, done." I filled out two slips, turned in the first one to Brenda, and waited to be called.

Dave took a long pull on his beer. "I remember being in love with all the girls. I still am, actually."

We watched one of the waitresses pass by, looking as if she were molded into her rough-knit sweater and stone-washed jeans.

"That one, for example, is the kind of woman who could almost make me write bad checks—"

"All right!" blared Brenda's voice into the mike, "*Bill*—get on up here!"

Summoned, I rose and sauntered, or tried to, across the suddenly empty dance floor. As I feared, I was overwhelmed by a wave of self-consciousness. *What's he doing here?* I imagined everyone thinking. Not that I consciously cared so much how I went over—I was just so super-aware of every segment of my body that the simplest movement became a challenge. Attempting to vault the five inches or so to the stage, I tripped.

"Whoa, Bill—get a grip, fella!" said Brenda, her voice filling the room.

"I've never done karaoke before," I chuckled stupidly.

"That's okay, just pick up one of those hand mikes and watch the screen. When the words change color, you sing 'em."

But my mind was still busy revising itself. "Well, I mean I *have*, uh . . . sung into a mike. Twenty years ago, that is—"

"Watch the screen, Bill. Here it comes."

Something wasn't right. It was the music—familiar, but not right. And the words on the screen . . . "Some of y'all never been down South too much . . ."

It was "Polk Salad Annie."

"This is wrong. I must have given you the wrong slip!"

"Huh?"

"I must've—"

"Jump in, Bill!"

Okay, jump in. The opening section was a spoken monologue: "Some of y'all never been down South too much . . ."

"Turn your mike on."

"SOME OF Y'ALL NEVER BEEN DOWN SOUTH TOO MUCH."

But the line was there twice. Why? Oh, yes. I recalled a recording where Elvis said it once, then again weirdly, as if to mock it. But why? Who knew? Whatever the case, I said it twice too. Then I realized I hadn't waited for the words to change color—we were still vamping. So I said it again. Then again. Damn it, when was the verse going to kick in? This song was a loose, rambling improvisation—what an awful choice for karaoke.

"I could do Elvis all night," Brenda said cheerfully. "There goes your cue."

Yes, there it went—red stained the words from left to right. I raced to catch up, rapping like a Gilbert & Sullivan patter singer. My gaze was glued hypnotically to the monitor in front of me. No one was dancing.

I was only vaguely aware of the crowd, but they seemed to be waiting at the edge of my vision, like a ring of quiet vultures.

A new verse appeared, with four dots over the first word. I started singing.

"Wait till the dots go away," Brenda said. -

I broke off. Wait till—what? I hadn't the foggiest idea what she meant. Then, sure enough, the dots started to disappear, in backward sequence: four . . . three . . . two . . . one . . .

"Go."

I could hear my voice, coming back at me like a stranger's, off-key, soft, and rubbery. On screen, the words turned red lazily, not indicating *precisely* when to sing—more like a warning device than a self-pacer. In the pauses, I tried to move around a little, but my feet wouldn't budge. My principal gesture was to clutch the microphone cord and bow my head. I was sweating.

A hundred years later, it seemed, the song was over. I struggled to replace the mike in its holder and get out of there.

"You got some more, Bill."

Sure enough, more words were coming up. "Chang-chang-chinga-chang . . ." The scat ending. This I knew went on and on and on. Stupidly, I read the words (the equivalent of *reading* "dum-de-dum-de-dum") and plowed ahead. Finally, just as I thought I was nailing one of the chinga-changs, I heard the big held chord that signified the end.

I put the mike back to the sound of one hand clapping. Was there a Zen master out there?

No, it was Dave.

Brenda was very sweet. "Not bad for your first time, Bill." Then she added, "Folks practice this stuff, you know."

In the awful vacuum of my retreat to the table, she had already anticipated the need to do something drastic and had a loud, brassy, up-tempo Hank Williams, Jr., song cued and ready to spin. "Get on up here, everybody!" Energy erupted and the floor was suddenly full of line dancers. Thank God for the diversion. I wanted to get out of there now.

But where was Dave?

Up on the floor, of course, doing the electric slide. I drained my beer and sat, dripping sweat inside my shirt, watching him bob and weave expertly in casual unison with the other line dancers.

All right. I had done it. I had drawn first blood—even if it was my own. A journey of a thousand miles begins with a single step, I reminded myself.

Even if that step is a stumble.

Chapter

9

nother phone chat with Rick Marino.

"Okay, there's good news and bad news," Rick said. "I'll give you the good news first: I talked to Jerome and Ron and it's cool for you to do what you want to do at the convention. Now the bad news: we've been knocked out of Vegas. It's politics with the Imperial Palace, where we use the showroom. I don't want to go into the details. But, bottom line, there ain't time to find another showroom. So we're going to a fall-back plan, which is: we're holding the convention in Chicago instead."

"Chicago!"

Yes, it was bad news. As it turned out, it wouldn't even be Chicago proper, but a suburb somewhere northwest of the city.

"Jerome's getting out a letter that'll explain the whole thing. Well, it won't explain the *whole* thing . . . what happened, I mean."

"Can you tell me what happened?"

He paused. "Ah, why not? See, we need a real showroom. That's what you want for a real Elvis show. With a full stage and all. At our level, you just don't do this thing in any old lounge. So we had an arrangement with the Imperial Palace: we shared the showroom with the Legends in Concert Show, which is big in Vegas and other places too. We took Friday and Saturday afternoons and cleared out for Legends at night, then we finished up big on Sunday night, which is a night they don't have a show. So everybody was happy, right? But then their contract with the Imperial Palace came up for renewal and they said, 'We want the EPIIA out of here.' So we're out. Simple as that. We got run over by a bigger truck."

"What was the problem?"

"I guess they didn't like seeing a hundred Elvises competing with their one Elvis."

"Hm. Chicago."

"I know. Nobody's happy about this. But we'll make the most of it."

Within a week an envelope arrived in the mail that included the EPIIA's official performer's application form for the "6th Annual Elvis Performers International Impersonators Association Showcase Convention." Making the most of the Las Vegas setback, the form was headed: "DIRECT FROM VEGAS . . . BACK TO THE WINDY CITY!"

There was a "Dear Performer" letter from Ron Bassette, EPIIA chairman, that even recast the Chicago fallback as a net positive: "In our constant effort to keep the convention fresh and exciting, we have taken on the theme of 'Return to Our Roots' and thought it would be refreshing to bring it back to Chicago again. Chosen as the venue for this year's showcase is the SABRE ROOM, a Las Vegas–style theater and convention hall that features an ornate setting, spacious stage, and quality atmosphere. The SABRE ROOM has been the home of many EPIIA Mini-Conventions in the past, so they are no strangers when it comes to hosting a successful EPIIA event."

For the second year, the convention would boast "the best Elvis tribute showband in the midwest," the "Exspence Account" [*sic*], who could handle any conceivable Elvis back-up chore. A one-page music roster of close to 150 song titles and keys was included.

Ron's letter ended: "We strongly urge all non-members and newcomers to audition by sending in your application, promo-pack, and re-quired videotape. We are looking forward to meeting you."

At the bottom of the application was a query: "WHAT ERA OF ELVIS IS YOUR SPECIALTY?" I entered "Vegas-Aloha," referring to the best of the jumpsuit days, 1969–1973. There was a place to list a dozen songs in order of preference and key. "This list will not guarantee you these songs, but it will be relied on heavily. Future changes can be made."

Scanning the Exspence Account's music roster, I tried to estimate which songs I would end up most comfortable with. It was something of a shot in the dark but I chose—wisely or not—in order of prefer-ence:

1. That's All Right, Mama
2. All Shook Up
3. A Big Hunk o' Love
4. Viva Las Vegas
5. A Fool Such as I
6. Stuck on You
7. Are You Lonesome Tonight?
8. Can't Help Falling in Love
9. Suspicious Minds
10. Burning Love
11. Love Me
12. I Was the One

As I look back on my shot-in-the-dark list of possibles for the con-vention, I'm struck both by how right it is and how wrong: I would learn that "Burning Love," for instance, is so hard to sing that even Elvis dropped it from his live performances; "Viva Las Vegas" is a bracing number, but relentlessly demanding, and again, Elvis hardly ever per-formed it live. Some of the other choices, however, were dead-on ac-curate for me, as it would turn out. With the exception of "A Fool Such as I" (another song Elvis never performed) and "A Big Hunk o' Love" (which I learned, with pleasure, but never sang live), every one of the other songs was destined to enter my repertoire. "That's All Right, Mama" would be the first Elvis song I performed live. "Can't Help Falling in Love," Elvis's show closer, ended my own "shows." "Suspicious Minds" became one of my favorite performance songs—although Elvis ended it on his knees, shimmying his shoulders in a series of moves that I never came close to mastering.

But at the time, I remember staring at the entirety of the EPIIA music roster, intimidated by the sheer bulk of Elvis performance, and realizing that I'd better start closing my knowledge gap. Obviously, even this list was only partial; Elvis Presley had left a huge performance legacy, not just the handful of standard hits that nearly everybody, fan or not, is aware of. One of the compendiums of Elvisiana told me that he had actually recorded close to 750 songs. If you count the songs he performed live but didn't record (some of them well-established items in the impersonator repertoire), the number swells to 800—and he knew a zillion more. Where performers like Tony Bennett, Frank Sinatra, Bob Dylan, Led Zeppelin, have each had a retrospective CD boxed set, it would end up taking not one but three 5-CD boxed sets to encompass Elvis's career. I felt like a fish, raised in a tiny pond, suddenly released into the Pacific Ocean.

One day, scanning my car radio's dial, I locked onto the majestic opening of "Also Sprach Zarathustra" and heard it segue into an announcer's stentorian chatter: "SUNDAY . . . JANUARY 8TH . . . THE 60TH BIRTHDAY OF THE KING OF ROCK 'N' ROLL . . . ELVIS PRESLEY! THIS WEEKEND, OLDIES ONE HUNDRED POINT SEVEN, WTRG, CELEBRATES WITH ELVIS, A TO Z—ALL YOUR FAVORITES IN ALPHABETICAL ORDER—ALL WEEKEND!"

Of course! Elvis was sixty—today.

As a salute to the King, the station had programmed an entire weekend of Elvis material, airing alphabetically, by title, from A to Z. The entire selection would air several times. For me, it was a gold mine of free Elvis songs, a selective overview of the Elvis Presley canon that I could never have put together by myself. After making a dub that cut out commercials and promos, I had three 90-minute all-Elvis cassettes, which I could play and replay, in the car, in my Walkman, on the home stereo.

Within a couple of weeks, the basic Elvis repertoire was wired into my head. The more I listened the more impressed I became with Elvis's sheer verve and virtuosity—his ability to sing his way through almost everything. I had begun with the typical *Rolling Stone* what-a-waste notion of Elvis as a rocker who had once had infinite promise but lost it when he got soft and fat on middle-of-the-road ballads and was never a factor again. Now, confronted with the evidence, I was rapidly revising my opinion.

What struck me as I listened now was how slick a vocal quick-change artist he was. There were many Elvises. It wasn't long before I could name each distinct persona:

The Hillybilly Cat
The White Negro
The Lonely Teenager
The Falsetto Weirdo
The Evangelist
The Secret Stud
The Suffering Lover
The Man's Man
The Opera Star
The Swing Band Finger Snapper
The Hollywood Hipster
The Power Balladeer
The Nashville Countrypolitan

On some songs, he pulled from multiple roots to put together a virtuoso mishmash of styles. Not every one of the A-to-Z performances was top-notch, but a surprising number of them struck me as fully realized—10 on a scale of 10. Some of these were so obscure that casual listeners would never have heard them. Who among us has listened carefully—really carefully—to "It Feels So Right"? Elvis turns in about as accomplished a performance of that song as could ever be imagined—it's airtight, a gem of a recording, a minor masterpiece.

So, where to start? Should I listen for his vocal mannerisms—the bumblebee vibrato, the Italianate sob, the baby-talk yammer, the straining tenor, the booming baritone—and try to drill them until I had developed some capability? Fat chance. That would be like trying to imitate the one-on-one moves of a Michael Jordan: a nice idea on paper, but just try it. I could pick out certain "easy" songs and narrow my focus, ignoring anything that seemed beyond my range. The problem there was that *nothing* actually turned out to be "easy." Wherever I began, I concluded, I would be unmercifully challenged.

So I made an executive decision: I would not be overly demanding about it "at this time." No need for Type A desperation; there was plenty of time to tailor my repertoire. For now, I would keep listening, sing along where I could. Whatever I wrote on the EPIIA application could surely be changed down the line. Now was the time to stay in research mode—just keep sponging it all up—and leave the performing decisions until later.

Chapter

10

The word was out around town that I was "into" Elvis impersonators.

My friend Tawnee, at the copy shop, told me that a touring Elvis named Ray Maas was scheduled to appear not far away, at a large mall where her boyfriend ran a Katy's Pretzel franchise. It would be about an hour's drive on a Saturday. Maas, as it turned out, had been featured 15 years back, as "El-Ray-Vis," in *All the King's Men*. They photographed him inside an airport, striking extreme karate poses as bemused travelers stood in line, grinning or gawking at the antics of this intense, skinny kid in a white Elvis jumpsuit. I wondered how he had evolved in fifteen years on the Elvis trail.

I arrived just as the show, "Ray Maas Ontour in . . . The Elvis Illusion" was starting. A high platform stage had been set up in the mall's atrium, dead center, under a dome of afternoon sunlight. A lithe blond soprano was singing "Part of Your World," from *The Little Mermaid*, which put out the message that this Elvis was going to be G-rated. Then Ray bounded out, an older, heavier, mellower, black-suited version of the youthful El-Ray-Vis. As shoppers wandered by, some stopping, some moving on, he used back-up tapes, run by the blonde (who turned out to be his wife, Dawn Marie) to put on an affable, low-key show that could have been subtitled "Intro to Elvis 101."

The former El-Ray-Vis was now a friendly, chunky-cheeked man who bore a slight resemblance to the ex-Rev. Jim Bakker, but whose charm and rapport were genuine, not slicked up or canned. He was decidedly anti-charismatic, working hard to project an I'm-Not-Elvis brand of humility. As he sang, as he spun out factoids about the real Elvis, as he bantered with the elderly ladies in fold-up chairs, as he made a few simple karate moves, he was as wholesome as a loaf of sweet potato bread. I wondered if the kid, El-Ray-Vis, might have been a little wilder, a little sexier. Perhaps, but for Ray Maas, there was absolutely nothing suggestive below the waist. I later learned his young daughter was also on the road with him, along with his dad. They were a clean, wholesome, religious family (Catholic), and the little girl was being home-schooled as they traveled.

Ray seemed perfectly at home in the decidedly nontheatrical atmosphere of a mall. He left the stage to scatter scarves to the ladies—staying away from the babes and sticking with the blue-haired elders—and mugged willingly and playfully for photographs. He dutifully plugged the mall—even individual stores in the mall, and later, talking to him, I learned that this was his niche: just like Santa Claus or the Easter Bunny, Ray Maas had made a seasonal enterprise out of being . . . a mall Elvis.

"I do this full-time. So when we're not on the road I'm at home, working out of my office, doing the marketing, sales, trying to create ads to play around themes for shopping malls. Like for February and Valentine's Day we try to work around 'Can't Help Falling in Love,' 'Love Me Tender.' May is Mother's Day, so we direct it towards 'That's All Right, Mama.' We try to put little themes in there that the malls can play off of, and I enjoy that. The shopping mall season starts in January, which was Elvis's birthday. And once November is here, as you know, shopping malls start putting out Santa Clauses and reindeers, so our season is January through October and we try to do two weekends a

"Mall" Elvis Ray Maas, working his niche market.
(Photo courtesy of William McCranor Henderson.)

month. Maybe in April, where there's Easter, we won't do any, or only do one. But then in the summer, we make it up—in July and August we may do three weekends a month. But we average about 20 malls a year. Sometimes a little higher."

For years, Ray had traveled with a six-piece show band but now preferred to work with a back-up tape system.

"Malls started changing their budgets as time went on, and I felt that I had to change, because it takes that much more budget to bring in five or six additional players, provide two or three extra hotel rooms.

So we started whittling it down a little bit. Two years ago we went to four pieces. And then from that I thought, well, the tracks are beautiful, they're well done—and actually, in a shopping mall atmosphere, where you don't want to blow people away like in an auditorium, I think this is going to work out very well for us."

Ray's motivation to do Elvis had a particularly poignant beginning.

"My brother got killed in a car accident when I was five, in 1962. And Elvis had just come back from the service; he'd been home two years and he was very hot. Movies, records, he was there. And my brother was my hero; he was the one that was the Elvis fan. So I would play his records and mimic Elvis, and so forth. I suppose that was kind of a link to my brother, playing those records, you know? Coming home from school, even though he wasn't there, *they* were there—to a five-year-old, that's a tie. And of course my parents thought it was wonderful, because it had been such a tragedy for them, that I would continue it. So what I did was, I kept up the record collection: when a new record would come out, I'd have to go get it; when a new movie would come out, I'd have to go buy the soundtrack. And I guess one thing led to another and that was my influence. Elvis became my hero, my Mickey Mantle.

"See, Elvis was dynamic in his looks, in his stage presence. His movements were dynamic, his voice—none of these guys like me really have that, but you know you try. Nobody, I don't care if you're Tom Cruise, John Wayne, Clark Gable, nobody could've pulled off those corny Elvis movies but Elvis. Nobody could've. And guys, no matter how cool—they don't want to tell you at the pool table, the poker table—they *watch* those Elvis movies, because Elvis was cool. Watch 'em—maybe you have. He was cool in the movies, and he made them work.

"So there are people, like these here, that congregate, since Elvis isn't here anymore, to have somebody still give them that feeling of . . . wow! There's no more John Waynes, those were the good old days, there's no more Clark Gables, John F. Kennedys, but there is somebody in that outfit, with that heart-thumpin' music, you know, with the style and the stage presence, recreating and giving them that feeling of the joy and the happiness that Elvis's persona created."

"Hi, Elvis," said a little boy who had inched closer and closer, his face showing the thrill of being adjacent to the living icon.

"How're *you* doing, son?" Ray glanced at me. "Does that say it? What is it that makes that little boy come up to me—he don't know who Elvis was. But yet he *does* through his parents' records or a book, or he's seen Elvis on TV. It's like Mickey Mouse. There's only two people like that, Elvis Presley and Mickey Mouse, and only one of them's human."

On my way back I had planned a stop in Cary, to catch traveling Elvis expert Steve Christopher. Christopher, a radio smoothy, is one of a small cadre of certified Elvis mavens who roam the world lending their encyclopedic trivia knowledge to Elvis gatherings, for a fee. He had joined the promotional activities on Oldies 100.7 and would be meeting the public live at Red, Hot, and Blue, a Memphis-based barbecue chain.

I had been listening to Christopher's radio segments on the drive to the mall. He was affable and slick as he provided colorful detail in answer to listeners' questions. (Q: What's so funny in the infamous live cut of "Are You Lonesome Tonight?" where Elvis starts laughing and can't stop? A: A guy at a front table got Elvis's attention and while he had it, whipped off his friend's toupee.)

"If you've got an Elvis record that I don't have," he promised, "you win $30,000 and a Cadillac from Thompson Cadillac-Olds." (When a collector called in with an obscure record, no longer available, Christopher led him on—"You know, gosh, I don't have that record . . . but guess what—I have it on CD because it's on the brand-new 60s boxed set. Sorry pal.")

The Red, Hot, and Blue was jammed with Elvis fans of all ages, and by the time I parked and walked in, they had been keeping Steve

Christopher busy for at least an hour. He was a handsome guy, in his thirties, with flashing dark eyes and wearing a stylish black leather Elvis athletic jacket. Someone had asked him, on the air, if he was working for Graceland and he gave a cagey, noncommittal answer that implied that something was in the works. Clearly he was an emissary from the establishment wing of Elvis country, and I was curious to get his take on Elvis impersonators as a general phenomenon. I managed to corner him in a momentary lull and put the question to him.

He shrugged disdainfully. "I have to tell you: what I know about impersonators, you could put on the head of a pin. I pretty much adhere to the Graceland policy, which is, you know, hands-off. Most of 'em are weird. They think Elvis has seeped into their skin."

I asked him if he thought that applied to all of them, even the professional Elvis "illusionists."

"Well, I guess not all of 'em think they're literally Elvis—you know, going around and saying 'yes, sir' and 'yes, ma'am' and all that. Actually, some of them are pretty good. I saw one once, in Jackson, Mississippi, who was something else. Man, the fans went just as wild as Elvis's, and in the same way too—grabbing their hair and all. And this guy sounded just like Elvis."

The head of Steve Christopher's pin was getting larger.

I said, "Ronnie MacDowell sounds so much like Elvis it's hard to tell them apart." (MacDowell had supplied Elvis's voice on the soundtrack of the TV docudrama *Elvis, the Movie.*)

"Early Elvis," Christopher specified, raising a finger. "Early Elvis."

Steve Christopher's natural tendency as a know-it-all was overriding his desire to promote the official Graceland party line. Clearly he knew as much about Elvis impersonators as he knew about anything else, and I was getting a demonstration.

"It's actually amazing, what those guys, the good ones, can do to the women and all. Actually, in Memphis there's a contest every year," he went on. "They used to have it at a club called Bad Bob's, but now I think it's at the Best Western—not the one out in Southaven, the one near the airport. Democrat Road. It sounds like fun, too. Who knows . . . ? If I could sing, I might be one of those guys myself."

Smooth as he might be, the trivia master Steve Christopher was a sincere Elvis fan: at some point, like Ray Maas, he had experienced a massive psychological identification with Elvis and, like Ray, had built an entire professional life around this magnificent obsession.

Fans always spoke of a powerful experience that brought them to Elvis (live, or recorded), a single shining moment when the earth shifted and they "knew" that for them, Elvis's music and life would be the coordinates by which they would plot the course of their lives. For the women, that first moment was described as "falling in love," and it was a love that could be fiery and consuming. There were stories of women who moved to Memphis from all over the world, just to be near Elvis's grave.

I was often to hear male fans (especially impersonators) use the word "love," as in "we love you, Elvis" or "my deep love for Elvis." There was nothing sexual or romantic in it. For the men, the *really* operative word for what attracted them to Elvis was "cool." Elvis was cool: his behavior suggested ways you could stay on top of any situation, be admired, get what you wanted in life, and still be good to people—all without compromising yourself.

Elvis fans were not always blue collar. I encountered an intense short story by Julie Hecht, whose work chronicles neurotic suburban obsessions and is often published in the pages of the very white collar *New Yorker*. The heroine of her story "I Want You, I Need You, I Love You," is (unambiguously) genteel, yet harbors a passion for Elvis so hot that it defies her high-class background, her Radcliffe degree, her horn-rimmed glasses, and the contempt of the rest of her family. Tepid devotion to more suitable icons—JFK, for instance, even her own husband, poor guy—is diminished to nothing next to her seismic need for Elvis. *Class has nothing to do with it*, the story cries out between its lines: *I heard "Heartbreak Hotel," I saw* Love Me Tender, *I reeled, I swooned, and now my soul belongs to this "adorable" man for all eternity—and who the hell CARES whether or not he knows his forks!*

Non-fans didn't connect: "What do they see in him? I just don't get it."

Elvis fans, I decided, were people who desired nothing grander than to be, in some way, in the presence of Elvis, and for whom there was no greater pleasure and nothing in life more meaningful to do than to listen to Elvis, watch Elvis, think about Elvis, talk about Elvis, and be around others who did the same.

It all reduced to that.

With my karaoke disaster well behind me, I began once more to try singing along. At first, my efforts were intermittent, timid: while listening to "I'm All Shook Up," I would chime in on the chorus: *Uh-huh-hunh . . . huh-hunh . . . yaaay-yay, I'm all shook up!* I took to humming and mumbling around the house. One evening, in a lull in the dinner conversation, I piped up spontaneously with a piece of "C'mon Everybody." My daughter Olivia, after a moment's assessment, pronounced it "the bomb, Dad."

The next morning, with everyone else out of the house, I went looking for my old vinyl *Elvis Live at the International Hotel*, plopped it on our stereo at just below "blast" level, and lost myself in the sheer volume of the full Vegas show, with all its bells and whistles—the crack TCB Band, back-up groups, orchestral forces (tip: the louder you turn it up, the easier it is to imagine yourself sounding great).

The excitement began to get to me. Wanting full impact with no distractions, I switched to headphones. For the first time, alone in a sea of sound, I started to move, to dance around at the end of the headphones' long coil cord. Heaven knows how it looked, but it felt great. I bopped back and forth to the rhythm. I toed my knees in, as Keith Henderson had taught me. I was loose. I was cool. And I was singing—

belting it out full voice, matching Elvis lick for lick. Or so it seemed. Especially with my eyes closed.

Suddenly, as I boogied past our full-length picture window, I realized I was about six inches away from someone on the other side of the glass. I ripped off the headphones and looked. There, frozen with amazement, was the FedEx deliveryman, mouth agog, a parcel dangling irrelevently from his hand.

"Caught me doing my aerobics," I heh-hehed as I signed his register.

He was polite, as FedEx people usually are, and pretended to have witnessed me up to nothing more than practicing putts on the living room rug.

So where to rehearse, let it all hang out?

I soon found the ideal space for singing as loud as I wanted to: the car. People do all sorts of things in cars—they sleep, eat, have sex, die of heart attacks, go crazy, all in that confined, absolutely defined space. The car, open as it is to visual scrutiny, is still one of the most private areas in American life. It certainly was for me, as I skimmed along I-40, my Elvis tapes turned up full. I was learning more lyrics now and could sing along with raucous confidence. But I had to watch it on the road: the combination of adrenaline and distraction caused by double tracking Elvis on "Burning Love" could quickly push my speed so high that cars were blinking their headlights at me. Even stuck in traffic, at a sedate 25 mph, I would catch people glancing oddly at me when I vocalized inside the moving isolation booth. I didn't care. "Yes, I'm crazy! How ya doin'? Just a hunka hunka burning love . . . whoooooo . . . a hunka hunka burning love."

V ocally, I was getting there, and that was crucial. But what about the other skills? And what were they? Obviously there was a basic skills set. I had already isolated some of Elvis's standard moves. Now I drilled them, in sets, in front of the mirror. Boogying around the living room was one thing; replicating actual stage movement was another. I found it physically exhausting and discouraging. For one thing, it made me acutely aware of how little I resembled Elvis physically. This came back to me in people's blank stares whenever I told them I was going to be "doing Elvis." I could almost hear their thoughts: "Oh, please, give me a break. *You*—as Elvis?"

The fact was that, as long as I wasn't trying to cast myself as a whip-thin, athletic "young" Elvis, I had extreme latitude to build my own Elvis. At the elder end of the Elvis spectrum, the platform was wide and accommodating.

"A lot of impersonators don't realize this, but you know Elvis didn't move half as much as you'd think," Rick Marino observed. "He'd suggest a move, he'd tease. Especially toward the end. Some of the guys are bumping and grinding every second because they think that's the way you put it across."

Elvis impersonators came in all shapes and sizes. That was comforting. Looking exactly like Elvis would be nice, but it wouldn't be necessary. Back during the Elvis stamp brouhaha, the postmaster general had put it this way: "[The portrait on the stamp] doesn't have to look too much like Elvis. It has to look like *the image of him in people's minds*" (my italics). That was an interesting thought: what he was saying was that Elvis had floated beyond identity into the realm of pure image. Plato understood this state and called it "ideal." So, it was the Platonic Ideal of Elvis that now counted, not whoever or whatever the real Elvis actually was, or had been. The King had passed into the realm of the archetypal, and impersonators were so many living versions of the ideal. This opened the door wider than ever for pretenders like me, who didn't have a prayer in hell of being mistaken for Elvis Presley. But just like the stamp, I wouldn't have to look all that much like Elvis, but only to suggest "the image of him in people's minds."

As I'd predicted, my teaching schedule kept me too busy to work up a performance. But there would be plenty of time to prepare before Rick Marino's convention in June, my first gig. Although there was already a hint of spring in the air, I felt ready. I was belting out my singalong versions with great and greater confidence. And I could observe the beginnings of a phenomenon that would grow more and more intense as time went on, something I can only call "going native."

I had read *Salvation on Sand Mountain* by Dennis Covington, an Alabama writer who covered snake-handling churches for the *New York Times*, and ended up joining one. It's a phenomenon that occasionally befalls the journalist who becomes so identified with the story that going native is the sometimes funny, sometimes dire result. At the start of this story, my attitude had been, "whatever happens, no matter how much of a fool I make of myself, it will simply be *the story of this book*." But now I was seeing things in a different way: now, as I worked away at this stuff, I found myself *wanting to be good*. I wasn't beguiled anymore (if I ever had been) by the idea that I would get up on a stage somewhere, flop around a little, and go off to write about it. I wanted to take on the task in earnest, master what I could, learn this art form, get the body movement into my muscle memory, and build a vocal apparatus supple and expressive enough to make someone think, even if for just a split second, that I just could be Elvis.

Moreover, I was beginning to believe such a miracle was possible.

I was like a 50-year-old distance runner dreaming of a sub-four-minute mile.

I was no longer laughing.

It was in this context that a phone message from Jerome Marion arrived. Great, I thought. He got my application, he thinks it's a fabulous idea, he's calling to welcome me personally to the EPIIA. I returned his call right away.

"Hollywood Lookalikes," he answered.

"Jerome? This is Bill Henderson."

The voice was matter-of-fact, a little glum. "Oh yeah, hi." (Not, 'He-e-ey, how you doing'!) I tensed. Was he going to bump me?

"Got your application and the check. Thanks for responding, but here's the thing: we're canceling the convention for this year, it's just too overwhelming a challenge, the logistics of having to move it back to Chicago and all. Just too much."

Abruptly I stopped anticipating mere rejection and felt a pang of utter desolation.

"We just haven't had enough response. People are spoiled after Vegas. Bringing your family to Chicago in August just doesn't compare. It's a different kind of area—affordable lodging's hard to secure, there isn't enough to do, either for families or for the guys, after hours. Compared to Vegas, well—we'll work on getting back there in 96. We've talked to one hotel owner already who's interested. Also a dude who calls himself 'the Colonel'—probably a logo name—says he wants to do it now and take it around the country. Probably just talk. But stay tuned, I guess. And thanks again for your interest."

I hung up and settled into a chair, feeling old and blue. There went my Big Event. Perhaps there went my book!

Oh, come on, I told myself, it wouldn't be that bad. There was Rick Marino's fan convention in Jacksonville; perhaps the impersonator contest I had heard about in Memphis was still a going thing (with my luck it would have gone out of existence just this year). I shoved my *Night of 100 Elvises* video into the VCR and let myself mourn not just the loss of this gathering of so many—so many—Elvises, but also the glittering venue of Las Vegas, this perfect backdrop for the most American of pop-fantasy events.

"You can't really blame 'em," Rick Marino said. "I don't think there was much interest from the international Elvises—I mean you come all the way from Sweden or Japan, you want something like Las Vegas on the other end. Vegas is a draw, there's no doubt about it. That's where we ought to be, and we'll be back. But for you—as far as your timing is concerned, it's too bad, but you know what I'd do if I was you?"

"What?"

"Throw yourself into the big contest in Memphis. I mean, it *is* a competition, guys aren't as friendly, maybe, or as fraternal, you might say. But next to our weekend, it's the biggest thing happening. I'll give you the name of the guy who runs it. His name's Doc—he used to be Elvis's veterinarian, took care of all the Graceland animals. But Doc and I don't get along so well, so don't mention my name, you hear? And I wouldn't even say you're writing a book; that might complicate things. Just enter, like anybody else. You'll probably have to submit a tape and a picture. Heck, when you come down here, I'll dress you in one of my suits and we'll take some pictures, and you can send in a tape of anybody; they won't know the difference. Doc won't even care. As long as you got a picture he can put in his brochure and your entry fee is in the envelope, you'll be in."

I called the number Rick Marino had given me and ended up speaking to the contest impresario, Doc Franklin, at his animal clinic a few miles down the road from Graceland. Doc was pleasant and chipper, and because his voice sounded somewhat like Ross Perot's I envisioned a small man, trim and efficient, bustling around his clinic in a white coat, like a pint-sized research chemist. I decided not to lead with the I'm-Writing-A-Book gambit; I would be simply another Elvis impersonator calling for information.

Busy as he was ("Excuse me a second, I've got to send an X ray out—"), he seemed concerned to show an interest in me and make me feel welcome.

"Here's what you do," he said solicitously. "I'll send you an entry form. You got a tape?"

"Uh . . . sure."

"Well, you send back the entry form with your tape, and a picture—make it black and white if possible because we want to be able to pull it for a composite brochure—and we'll see."

We'll see? What did that mean?

Was it possible that I might be turned down? Not according to Rick, but Rick's viewpoint might be skewed by competitive bad feeling. It sounded conceivable to be *denied* entry here—"Dear applicant. We were overwhelmed by the high quality of the turnout for the Contest this year. We are sorry to inform you that we were unable to act favorably on your application." And then where would I be? After awkwardly answering a few questions about my "career" as an impersonator, my occupation ("teacher"), my age ("I'm in my 40s")—I've never been a good liar—I felt more comfortable spilling the beans. I decided to abandon the anonymous pose and tell him about my book project.

Doc didn't miss a beat. "Oh, kind of a Plimpton thing, that's interesting. Well, we've got plenty of people doing books. Got a girl who came down last summer, a professional photographer, Patty Carroll, set up and took everybody's picture. She puts out the King Kards, have you seen those? A deck of cards where every card is a different Elvis impersonator. She'll be back this year. Got a girl doing some damned kind of a book, I'm not sure what. I get calls all the time from researchers, TV people, documentary film people, *Entertainment Tonight*, ABC. We're really the dead center of this whole thing. The boys who go through here come back year after year. My son maintains a database on his computer which is probably the most comprehensive source of information anywhere about Elvis impersonators worldwide. We've got black impersonators—Robert Washington's one of our finalists for this summer—got Korean impersonators, Japanese impersonators, women impersonators. You'll have an experience here, I'll tell you; there's other contests but there's nothing like what happens here. I mean, you tell me where you could sit in one place and watch sixty or seventy Elvis impersonators, one right after another, and six or eight of those would be the best Elvis impersonators in the world."

I thought of the EPIIA Convention and almost brought it up, but remembering Rick's warning, I decided it would be better not to challenge Doc with the EPIIA. After all, I still had to get myself accepted into this thing. And besides, the EPIIA Convention had just gone up in a wisp of smoke—at least as far as this summer, *my* Elvis summer, was concerned.

"Well, how do I enter?" I asked.

"Just like everybody else. I don't make the decisions because I don't know a damned thing about music. I'm just a veterinarian. But I've got a selection board who knows more about it than I ever will and I leave them alone. So you'll have to get selected like any of the others. Just do like I said, and we'll see."

Chapter

12

A few days later, an envelope arrived from "Dr. E. O. Franklin." Inside was an informational flyer and the entry form. Across the bottom, Doc had scrawled, "Nice to talk to you 'Professor.' Send info, and good luck."

I loaded my camera, this time with professional black and white film, and Carol shot another roll of stills. The *Planet of the Apes* wig was out of the question. I discovered that one of Ollie's alternate mops was close enough to acceptable that I could hold off the wig maker for now.

More important was the required tape. I felt I had to have a good one—and it really should be mine, not a forgery.

I called a few karaoke services and got quotes on Elvis backup tracks—usually it came to something like $5 per track. Everyone was offering the same twelve numbers, and (suspiciously) in what seemed like the same order. There must be a professional source, a supplier I could tap into. I subscribed to a glossy fan magazine called *Elvis International Forum*, and had just received my first issue: sure enough, in the classifieds I spotted an ad—"Elvis Tracks . . . huge supply, etc." I called an 800 number and within minutes, two karaoke CDs—Pocket

Songs' *You Sing the Hits of Elvis Presley, Vol. 1 and 2*—were on their way to me by UPS Next Day Delivery.

Now I needed a recording studio.

I called a musician friend, Todd Jones, a singer-songwriter somewhat in the "alternative" mode, whom I knew had a seat-of-the-pants basement studio in his house. Todd's stationery was emblazoned: "*HUGE Sound Generating Facility ... the sound of sounds being sounded*." He was not particularly into Elvis.

"What was that tacky song that came out back when I was in high school? Something about . . . caught in a trap?"

"Suspicious Minds."

"Yeah, yeah. And he did that sort of hey-I-care song about 'the ghetto'."

"Yeah, well. 'Suspicious Minds' is actually a good song."

"If you say so."

We agreed on a night the following week and Todd told me to come prepared to lay down five tracks, "in case we get hot." In the more likely case that we didn't get hot, we'd mix down three out of five as keepers.

I felt a tightening in my gut. Turning fantasy into reality, for me, was as simple as that: here's a date—put up or shut up. As soon as I hung up the phone I was reaching for my Pocket Songs CDs.

The Elvis "hits" CD (a total of 20 songs), showed a reptilian impersonator on its cover, modeling Elvis in two distinct looks, gold lamé (Volume 1, all early stuff) and black leather (Volume 2, post-comeback). Inside was a booklet with the song lyrics and photo images of ordinary folks, obviously models, with mikes in their hands, having a high old time imitating Elvis. Presumably, this was Pocket Songs' target audience: party show-offs, all in stylishly flamboyant go-go poses. Something about them inspired me to fantasize about their lives: a young woman in jeans and boots—probably a bank teller married to a paint store manager (they like to go out line dancing). A middle-aged dude with elbow patches and tan buck shoes—most likely an assistant high school principal, between wives (a pipe smoker). A professional-looking black guy in after-hours flannel plaid and baggy corduroy—an actuary (loves old movies). A trim young tuxedoed kid with garish crimson cummerbund and tie combo—a wedding guest (plays weekend rugby).

All these people were having a hilarious good time.

I, on the other hand, had a recording session to prepare for. I was dead serious.

"Please don't disturb me for a while," I called out to my family and commandeered the stereo.

I slid Volume 1 into the CD player and began to listen, over and over. The singer on the guide vocal didn't sound much like Elvis, but he took care to replicate Elvis's most obvious mannerisms, and the arrangements were mostly faithful to the originals (with the odd exception of "Return to Sender"—which was given a hard-rock edge).

Finally I had listened enough. I put the headphones on. It was time to sing. Shyly, I attempted "All Shook Up." Each time I paused, the house seemed unnaturally silent. Was I being spied on? I fiddled with the volume, searching for a level that would allow me to hear myself, but not too starkly. The more I turned the tracks down, the more exposed I seemed—and the better I could hear what the kids called my "Daddy" voice.

I spent some time on the lugubrious spoken verse of "Are You Lonesome Tonight?", trying to suggest Elvis's diction without aping it. The trick is to talk over the music so that it sounds impromptu but ends up in the right place at the right time. After a while, I was getting it: ". . . and if you won't come back to me, then they can bring the curtain down." Yeah!

I moved on to Volume 2 and found a few more congenial cuts— "(Let Me Be Your) Teddy Bear," "Stuck on You," "Can't Help Falling in Love"—although some of the later songs—"Kentucky Rain," "If I Can Dream"—were way beyond me, technically. Perhaps my voice was simply giving out, but it seemed to be taking on a nice rough edge. I couldn't sing the ballads anymore, but the rockers had moments of growly bravado.

My confidence was picking up when my daughters suddenly appeared, wearing black Elvis wigs, and shoved me aside to listen to their new *Lion King* tape. This was fine. I had made some progress: I'd picked the songs I was going to record, I'd tried them out. I was ready to make my move. Now, I let myself relax and watch the girls perform a kooky Disney version of karaoke—brandishing flashlights for mikes, as they improvised Elvis moves and lip-sinched to "I Just Can't Wait to Be King."

Long after Olivia, my 10-year-old, had moved on to something else, Colette, 7, kept at it. Doing Elvis came naturally to her—the sneer was almost innate and her little limbs fell gracefully into Elvis poses. She was bizarre, with her blond hair peeking out the sides of the *Planet of the Apes* wig—bizarre but focused. As I would observe many times along the way, children grasp the basic Elvis attitude without even having to learn it. Later, friends would say, aghast, "You mean there are actually kid Elvis impersonators?" The answer was: yes, absolutely, and some of them are damned good at it, better than a lot of adults.

But that knowledge was yet to come. Now, I was just enjoying one of my own, watching her do a mean Elvis as she had once done a wicked flamboyant Julie Andrews, flopping through a meadow with her guitar case in *The Sound of Music*. Preparing to mime "The Circle of Life," Colette faced an imaginary crowd of "ladies and gentlemen" and addressed them in a gruff, halting stutter: "Thank you, ah, th-thank you vurry much. Here's a song that I would have done if I was still alive. And I'm pretty sure I would've loved it if I would have been . . ."

Would have been . . .

The more I learned about Elvis, the more I ran into what I began to call the "would-have-been" factor. Jane and Michael Stern, in their book *Elvis World* (not to be confused with Bill E. Burk's excellent fan magazine of that name), referred to it as the "if only" factor, and observed that *Mystery Train*, Greil Marcus's lament for the lost pure rock 'n' roll icon, is shot through with it: "If only the Colonel hadn't enslaved him; if only RCA hadn't cheapened him; if only Hollywood hadn't beckoned . . ."

Certainly people wonder what "would have been" if Elvis had been more aggressive about, say, defying Col. Parker and taking the role of the over-the-hill rocker in Barbra Streisand's remake of *A Star Is Born*.

What "would have been" if death hadn't claimed him at age 42? Some say he was about to become evangelist Rex Humbard's musical eminence. Some say it would have been political office—a senator? President of the United States? Apocalyptic world leader? Elvis Presley, emissary to the far reaches of the universe?

The ultimate document in this line was a seven-part comic book series I stumbled upon, *The Elvis Presley Experience*, in which Elvis dies and enters the afterlife, where (like all new dead folk) he has to undergo "therapy" to help him better understand his days on earth. To speed the process, his IQ is jacked up to genius level and he's assigned a curvy therapist named Jennifer, who takes him through the well-known eras of his life, in rueful flashback.

Comic book techniques exploit famous moments—there's a pagewide frame, based on a famous photographic grief image of Elvis and his dad mourning Gladys Presley. They are sitting on a curb, arm in arm, grieving. A garish banner, meant to visualize their shrieks, spills across the panel: "EEEOOWAAUGH!!"

Jennifer the therapist arranges a "comeback" concert: Elvis is backed by Jimi Hendrix, Roy Orbison, and Albert Einstein (on violin).

The plot thickens as Elvis forces a meeting with the guy who runs Eternity, "Mr. Merrin," an L. Ron Hubbard type in silk cravat and smoking jacket ("The icy stares I get from disappointed feminists when they find out that God really is a white male Republican are priceless!"). A special viewing device makes it possible to scan and evaluate Elvis's possible alternate futures—the lives he "would have" lived, *if only* . . .

- He disengages from Col. Parker, makes *A Star Is Born*, *Star Wars*, wins an Oscar, stars in the stage play *Equus*, dies of AIDS.
- He's a dashing Yale college professor, bearded, an ecoactivist, attacks and destroys a Japanese whaler for Greenpeace.
- He's an ordinary radio repairman, drives a pickup truck, lives a simple, anonymous life with his wife and little girl (it's Pat Boone, not Elvis, who sticks "Hound Dog" in the nation's face!). He gets into fights defending blacks against KKK bullies and ends up lynched.
- He doesn't die in the 70s but manages to repackage himself in the 80s as a Springsteen-style working man's rocker.
- He becomes a professional wrestler, The Tupelo Tornado.

Mr. Merrin decides to bypass these possibilities and send Elvis straight to the Omego Field, a kind of Valhalla. But Elvis bucks: "Is it true that what I am will vanish into some 'cosmic whole?' If I learned anything from looking at my life it's that I was always free! My learning here is wasted unless I can apply it to life as I knew it. You gave me freedom. I'M EXERCISING IT!"

He stalks off, followed by Jenny ("Nice speech . . . wait up!").

In an act of cosmic favoritism, Mr. Merrin lets Elvis return to earth—as the newly inaugurated president of the United States.

"Go take care of business, m'boy," he says, and sends Jennifer with him, in human form, to help Elvis run "the greatest nation on earth."

Pretty grand stuff.

But the "would-have-been" factor operates just as provocatively at more trivial levels: Col. Parker, when he was asked why there was an Always Elvis Wine even though Elvis himself never touched the stuff, replied: "This is the wine Elvis would have drank if he had drank wine." Some Elvis impersonators wear clothes "that Elvis would have worn if he were alive today." Some perform post–Elvis-era songs (or other songs Elvis never touched) "as Elvis would have performed them." Here's impersonator Mike Albert's would-have-been rationalization: "If Elvis were alive today, he would be performing current hits and gospel songs, mingled with a few old medleys and new originals." True enough—Elvis was nothing if not eclectic in his repertoire—but I began to wonder how far you could stretch it: How about Elton John's "Rocket Man"? Or Aerosmith's "Crazy"? Or "I Just Can't Wait to Be King"? Was it legitimate to use the would-have-been factor to cover these anomalous possibilities?

For me, the beauty of the would-have-been factor was the way it threw open the door to Elvis impersonators in the first place. Anyone, or almost anyone, could use the power of the phrase to legitimize what was absurd on the face of it: anyone could say, without appearing to be insane: "What you're about to see now is, in some small way, the Elvis you would have seen, the Elvis that would have been—young, transitional, or mature—if he were still alive today."

Enter . . . me?

Chapter

13

"**T**he King!"

Todd's 12-year-old son Max was greeting me at the door. I couldn't tell if he was in awe, in a state of sympathetic dread, or just putting me on. Whatever the case, he led me downstairs to Huge Sound's "Studio A" (the basement), where Todd had set up a mixing board and some recorders amid the clutter of the half-finished cellar.

Todd had a day gig, something to do with computers, but by night he was Todd Jones and Thing. His girlfriend Bridget wrote about rock for a local alternative weekly and had a family story about her mother, who, as a high school journalist, had interviewed Elvis in Florida. During the interview, Elvis held her hand with one hand and ate a hamburger with the other.

"Ah, Big E!" Todd called out as I entered. He was tinkering with a huge black box that hung from the wall. "You're in luck, dude, these are my new studio monitors that just arrived today. Although there seems to be an unwelcome noise in one of them . . ."

While he ripped off a front panel to peer into the guts of the thing, I was trying to pace my nerves off, running through my five selections silently, at double speed.

For five days I had practiced obsessively, nearly flaying my vocal chords in the process. I was beyond self-consciousness. "Dad, you can hear it all the way down the street," Olivia said one day, coming in from the schoolbus. Good, I thought. At least I'm able to project.

Miraculously, after a day's rest I was now in possession of considerably more sheer voice power than I could have mustered just a week ago. Yes: I could now sing LOUD.

But something about the intimacy of Todd's basement was thrusting a challenge at me: you didn't have to be loud here, you had to be *good*. Todd, in fact, would be using his prize possession, an antique Neuman U-89 studio microphone, an instrument designed to serve the likes of Pavarotti. Never mind that the vocal booth was a tiny half-bathroom (causing Todd to observe that, since Elvis died on the toilet, there was something mystically appropriate in this setup). After all, hadn't Elvis recorded his early Sun classics in a ratty old studio the size of a two-car garage?

"We could pretend this is a bootleg," Todd suggested, as he babied the Neuman into position, "Call it 'Bilvis—the Huge Sessions,' or 'the King's Final Dump.'"

He dubbed the CD tracks onto tape, which didn't take long, and we were ready to lay down vocals. "Will you step into the throne room, your majesty?" said Todd, clearing some unidentified electronic parts out of the path to the bathroom door. My mouth was dry as cotton.

"Can I have some water?"

"Cold or tepid? All the *real* singers ask for tepid."

"Tepid, then."

Inside the WC, I was suddenly face to face with the intimidating gray eminence of the Neuman; only a small circular wind screen separated us. "Don't wave your arms around," Todd warned me. "If you hit the Neuman I'm out of business." He put headphones on me and left me alone with the Neuman (a fact that, in itself, astounded Max, who had never been alone with the Neuman). Then he went back to his control board and set the level for my headphones. Through these, I would hear both myself and the background tracks, mixed, with re-verb—a live approximation of what would end up on tape. As I tried a little "Stuck on You," for levels, it sounded warm, lush. Reverb, I discovered, is good for confidence: nothing can freeze you up faster than hearing your utterly unadorned voice in all its nakedness.

But I was beyond freezing up now. I was loose. From now on it would be like method acting: if I felt like Elvis, I would sound like Elvis. It was as though Elvis were there, a power potential. The trick was to remove all barriers. To let Elvis jump in. The metaphor reminded me of the way Christian evangelicals spoke of "just letting Christ into your heart. He's waiting. It's up to you." Or sometimes it was the Holy Spirit, which was supposed to be this sacred neon-like *thing* that zapped into you, and when it did, you burst into spiritual color, hopped around possessed, and jibbered in tongues. In terms of doing Elvis, I felt like one of those sputtering neon signs that can't decide whether it's on or off.

When we began to record in earnest, I'm sure Elvis came and went a bit. Song for song, sometimes I thought I had nailed one. Then there were the ones that seemed to never get off the ground; on those, Elvis had temporarily left the building. But even the losers ("Teddy Bear" was one) had a not unpleasant quality; it's just that they contained some violation of pitch or diction that put them firmly in the reject column.

Todd nodded kindly as we listened.

"We can comp there," he would say when a boo-boo went by, meaning we could switch transparently back and forth between Take 1 and Take 2. But before long, just as he had predicted in our first con-versation, three keepers emerged out of the five.

Once that decision was made, we could ease up a bit. Todd left the room and returned with two bottles of what you might call "alterna-tive" beer—something with a name like Xyoxacle. "Here's my most im-portant piece of studio equipment," he said, reaching up to a metal ceiling plate and retrieving a magnetic beer opener.

We drank and listened.

It was not bad.

Todd finished his beer and said, "I know it's late, but I gotta play you something." It was a song called "17 Girls" he had written and recorded with his band. It came blistering off a tiny DAT cassette, out of his new monitor speakers, with a clarity and force I could hardly stand. Todd's voice was supple and full of "punk" wit and sassy assurance. I realized I had been locked into the muted scale of my own voice for the last three hours; now I was hearing a real singer. How could my sorry version of Elvis compete? Closer to the point, how could it—how could I—be so bold, be so out of it, as to *represent* Elvis? Would friends of mine judge Elvis according to my poor version? Was this the ultimate fallacy of Elvis impersonation—that it would slowly but surely deconstruct Elvis? I had a compulsion to run out to my car and bring in a tape of the *real* Elvis, to show Todd—who would surely appreciate it, being a singer himself—what Elvis could do with a song. But I was digging "17 Girls" too much to move. It was a good song. In fact, I found myself wishing Elvis were there to dig it too.

We had a party not long afterward at which everyone was dying to hear my tape, or so they said. But the only guest who really pursued it was a composer, T. J. Anderson, who literally followed me around until I sat him down with headphones at the stereo. As the party went on around him, he gave each track a careful, judicious listen. T. J. Anderson is a virtuoso composer, if such a term exists. He is an African-American, with roots in every form of music from jazz and other "black" forms to the contemporary Western classical tradition (he studied composition with Darius Milhaud). The point is not so much to blow T.J.'s horn (though he certainly deserves it) as to establish just *who*, in the professional sense, was listening to this tape. It was a man with a lifetime of relating to music at the highest levels, whose particular experience as an artist was so inclusive, so eclectic, that his reaction would be informed to the maximum, and free of prejudice. As he listened, without betraying any reaction, I pretended not to take much notice, but I was watching him out of the corner of my eye.

"Not bad," he said generously, laying the headphones aside. Then his smile turned into a frown of concentration. Here came the message: "You've got to pay closer attention to Elvis's diction. His diction was very precise and sometimes stylized in a very deliberate way. And the other thing is—more energy. Moment for moment, he produced energy. You've got to infuse it with that same level of energy."

He was right. I could hear it, too. There was a lassitude in my singing, a lack not only of energy but of focus. Elvis had the vibrant intensity of a butterfly on speed built into every note. What it amounted to was vocal charisma, pure and simple—and here we were, back at the charisma issue again. Did I have it? If not, could I come by it somehow? Was it, in fact, something you could acquire? Of course, as Rick Marino had said, the best Elvis impersonators filter Elvis through their own personalities. Given that no one can *be* Elvis, was the "me" of my filter interesting enough? Was my challenge going to be to find or fashion a *character*, part me, part Elvis? To find my way to a charismatic presence, using what I possessed, *plus* what I could create or acquire to craft a cunningly arresting persona?

Or was I just getting carried away with the whole project—and the wrong part of it at that?

In any case, I now had a complete entry package for the contest in Memphis, which I FedExed to Doc Franklin. A week or so later, a letter arrived, on Images of Elvis, Inc. stationery. "Dear Bill," it read, "We received your package and are delighted that you want to participate in this August's contest. To confirm, you will be in the Wednesday night preliminaries, August 16. As of now, sound check is scheduled for 4:00 P.M. on that day . . ."

I was in. The die was cast.

*author—narrator
(speaker)*

character

Chapter

14

One question kept nagging at me: What did it *mean* to be a "good" Elvis impersonator? To be doing it at the level of a Rick Marino, a Keith Henderson? Did impersonating Elvis Presley, even at the highest level, have any intrinsic worth? Or was it too far downstream to be anywhere close to mainstream?

Was my friend Phillip right to worry how I could have so little artistic self-esteem as to back burner a half-finished novel and do this thing, this bizarre thing that possessed none of the *Field of Dreams* cachet of baseball, nor even the macho legitimacy of football? This, of course, was George Plimpton's subtext: he took his reader (and himself) on a fantasy walk into worlds his mostly male readership found significant. Every male has fantasized about pitching to the great hitters, taking the snap in a real NFL game. Has every male fantasized about going on stage as Elvis?

What was my subtext, anyway? FICTION WRITER GOES BANANAS, INFECTED BY THE LURE OF HIS MATERIAL, CROSSES THE LINE, IS TRANSMOGRIFIED HORRIBLY, TURNS SELF INTO TERMINAL LITERARY JOKE?

I thought of the great Japanese fiction writer Yukio Mishima, who wrote obsessively about hara-kiri, portraying it again and again in his work. Even as an actor in cheap movies, he disemboweled himself before the camera any number of times. Then, finally, he did it for real. Was his greatest accomplishment his superb writing? Or was it (as I think he ultimately came to believe) his carefully designed, semibotched, real-life suicide?

Where was the line between action and art? Was there such a line?

It was time to break free of questions like these. I had no answers anyway. Perhaps if I got a look at a Big League professional Elvis, my doubts might go away. Spring break was coming up. Olivia, my 10-year-old, had been pestering me to take her to the mountains. Rick Marino had told me that Pete Willcox, a solid pro, was performing nightly in a tourist destination called Pigeon Forge, in the mountains of Tennessee. I called the phone number Rick gave me. It was the box office at Memories Theater, and yes, Willcox was there, doing a full-dress Vegas-style Elvis show. Not only that, I was told, but Charlie Hodge, Elvis's own back-up singer, majordomo, pal, and scarf-and-water man was in residence there too, and part of the show. Pigeon Forge was only a few hours away by car. I decided we'd go.

I had barely heard of Pigeon Forge at that point, although I was well aware of its main attraction, Dollywood ("Entertainment Capital of the Smokies: 40 Live Shows Daily, 29 Rides and Attractions, 50 Craft Showcases"). A trend had arisen for even marginal Vegas and C&W stars, when they began to fade, to build roadside theaters in towns like Branson, Myrtle Beach, or Pigeon Forge, where they could do two shows a day, presumably until the end of time, for endless busloads of tourists. Dolly Parton, however, was still such a formidable entertainment force that she could pull off an entire theme park. What we hadn't realized was that the weekend of our trip coincided with Dollywood's seasonal grand opening, a guaranteed mob scene.

"You won't be able to book anything in Pigeon Forge," said the accommodations woman at the Tennessee Welcome Center. "There's Dollywood and the Antique Car Parade. But Gatlinburg's only eight miles down the road. I can put you into Gatlinburg."

"Whatever," I said. Let the experts handle it.

Gatlinburg seemed to be all motels and marriage chapels, with a musty 50s flavor, laid out claustrophobically in the winding gap between two chains of mountains.

We checked into our motel and asked the desk clerk for directions to Pigeon Forge.

He shook his head. "I'd stay out of there if I was you," he said ruefully. "Unless you want to end up in the Car Parade"—he checked his watch—"which starts in about an hour and a half."

But we had no choice: tickets had to be picked up in person by six or we could lose our front row seats.

"Let's hit it," I said to Olivia, and we took off without even unloading our bags.

Sure enough, traffic slowed to a crawl entering Pigeon Forge. What we saw was a break in the mountains that broadened into a flat plateau down which ran a six-lane boulevard called the Parkway, Pigeon Forge's main drag. On either side of the Parkway were some of the most bizarre roadside attractions I had ever seen. Star Wars thinking had built an entire city of water parks, go-cart tracks, and simulated cyberwar battlefields.

"Dad, I think we *are* in the parade," said Olivia from the passenger seat.

Sure enough, in front of us was a burnished green Model A Ford with a rumble seat. In the rearview mirror I glimpsed something that looked like an ancient wood-paneled fire engine. Crowds of onlookers, some in lawn chairs, lined our side of the Parkway and gawked at us, clearly wondering why a 1991 Subaru was in the parade. We were going about three miles per hour.

"Just keep looking for Memories Theater," I said through my teeth.

As we crawled down the Parkway, Olivia described what was going by: elaborate water slide installations (she wanted to stop!); slick go-cart tracks; golf biomes as elaborate as ancient jungle temple complexes, including one "featuring waterfalls, fountains, old mill, western scene, castle, mansion and miniature houses on a waterfront." Then there was Ultrazone, a place where you could fight laser wars and have "fierce family fun" and "destroy enemy base stations."

"What's that thing that looks like the Pompidou Centre?"

"It says indoor sky diving."

"What?!"

"Simulated, it says. I guess you jump into artificial gravity or something. Dad, can we go back to the water slide?"

"Absolutely not. If we lose our place in this caravan, we'll never make it to the Memories Theater on time."

On we went, miles it seemed, past wedding chapels, scenic-view helicopter landings, Hillbilly Golf, Bunny Land Golf, Fantasy Golf, Smokey Bear Golf ("golf with bears and other wild animals"). Finally, after we passed the clogged entryway to Dollywood, traffic began to lighten a bit. Just a few blocks before the Parkway strip seemed about to end, several "live show" theaters sprouted out of the asphalt, one of them Memories Theater. I pulled into the nearly empty parking lot. Looking toward the mountains behind the theater I saw . . . motels! At least half a dozen of them! Brand-new. With similarly empty parking lots.

"I could kick myself," I muttered.

"How come, Daddy?"

"Well, here we are, tired, ready for a meal and a rest, we could *walk* to that Bugetel Inn over there, and just because some functionary at the border gave me bad information, we'll have to pick up our tickets, spend an hour driving *back* through Pigeon Forge, and by the time we change clothes in the motel in Gatlinburg, we'll have to turn right around again or we'll miss the show."

"You won't even make it to Gatlinburg and back in time," said the woman in the ticket office. "There's no way, with this car parade and all. There's plenty of rooms right around here. Why don't you call your motel and cancel?"

"I've checked in already."

"Well, you can try. Sometimes people are nice. You can use our phone."

She was right. Sometimes people are nice. Reluctantly, the motel clerk in Gatlinburg decided to be nice (after first putting up a gruff show of reluctance) and released us, on my scout's honor to drop off the key in the morning.

Now we were home free.

As I hung up the phone, who should roll up in the parking lot, lounging in the back seat of a black Cadillac convertible, but an Elvis impersonator in a white jumpsuit who resembled the young Abe Lincoln.

"Is that Pete?" I asked the ticket lady.

"Yeah, he was in the car parade. I guess he was on this end of it."

Must have been about 10 cars behind us.

He was out of the Cadillac now, a lanky, ectomorphic Elvis, idly watching his driver fiddle with some speakers that had been mounted on the limo's fenders.

I approached and introduced myself.

He looked back at me, without saying anything, and I had the sensation that someone had just walked across my grave. The silence broadened. I realized he wasn't going to say anything to break it.

"We drove up from Chapel Hill to see your show," I gushed into the vacuum of his nonresponse. "I've heard you do an excellent show."

Again, he stared back, mute.

So what do I have to do, I thought, stand on my head?

"Pretty hot out," I ventured.

He shrugged and looked away.

I stumbled on, "Anyway, I'm writing a book that has to do with Elvis performers and the Elvis legacy and I'd like to chat with you, if possible. If you have some time."

The chill around him thickened. Had I offended him with the mention of a book? Maybe I should really blow his mind by telling him I'm an Elvis performer too (I had even been careful to avoid the term "impersonator" just in case he had that particular sensitivity).

Okay, I thought, let's try a name: "I've been working with Rick Marino. Rick suggested I come see you."

Nothing. Was I being iced or what?

"Do you know who I mean? Rick Marino?"

"I was at his convention."

"Ah . . . okay then. Can I arrange to talk to you?"

"I sign autographs in the lobby after the show." It came out with velvet softness, like the dying words of a mourning dove.

I began to sense something crafted in this limp unresponsiveness, a ploy: *I'll be so unlikable you'll go away.* It was an interesting contrast, I thought, to Elvis Presley's own dogged respect for his fans, even when they constituted a hideous nuisance.

Rick Marino had told me a story that said reams about the "good" Elvis, and why his fans loved him then and continued to love him now:

"Elvis treated the fans like gold, never turned away from 'em. One night in Vegas there was a fat lady in the audience, and Elvis's guys were making fun of her, y'know, fat slob and all that. Elvis ordered one of them to bring her and her friend up to a front table and made two of the guys be their dates, sit with 'em all night, get 'em whatever they wanted. Elvis took care of the whole thing. Afterwards he told the guys: don't you ever let me see you do that again."

Charlie Hodge was a living link to Elvis's Honor-Thy-Fans tradition. Hodge was known principally as the sunny little pop-up guy in Elvis's show band, but his principal task had been that of valet—on stage and off. His on-stage duties included catching Elvis's guitar when he tossed it over his head, bringing Elvis his water, following Elvis around with new scarves as Elvis gave them out during the Scarves and Kisses portion of his 70s show. Charlie had been like a mascot, a friendly little tyke among the growling hound dogs in Elvis's entourage. I had read that nowadays he was venerated at fan conventions all over the world, one of the latter-day Elvis saints. It would be interesting to see how

Charlie Hodge's well-known warmth would fit into Peter Willcox's chilly universe.

We dressed up a bit and, just before show time, strolled through the spring night to the theater. By now the lobby was bustling with tourists, most of them ages 30 to 40, but buttressed by a stiff shot of elderly bus trippers—the same folks you might find on a similar outing to the Lawrence Welk Theater in Branson.

Inside, we took our front row seats and watched video projection screens on either side of the gold-curtained stage, showing an episode of the *Andy Griffith Show*. What was the connection there? Nostalgia, I suppose. My mind went into analytical gear: People wanted a world that already *was*: that way, they could dwell on what was nice, and there would be no surprises. Elvis *was*. Thus Elvis shows, like Andy Griffith reruns, had to be seen as part of that general embrace of the sweet, safe past—

"Dad!" said Olivia, bursting my thought balloon. "The lights are going down."

Show time. As I watched the excitement in Olivia's face, I saw one factor that made Elvis impersonation a going thing: the irreplaceable thrill of a live performance. No amount of Elvis LPs or Elvis on video could recreate the experience of going out to see a living performer.

The curtain lifted to reveal a full show band—your basic guitar band plus not one but two keyboard players, brass, and pedal steel. A trio of young, permed, white women in spangled dresses bounded on stage, representing the equivalent of Elvis's black trio, The Sweet Inspirations. They got the crowd tapping toes to a set of classic oldies, then yielded to Bubba and Redneck Ranger, a Gomer Pyle–type rustic comedian (in function, if not in style, equivalent to Elvis's Jewish comic, Jackie Kahane).

Bubba would have been a hard act for anyone to follow, but he closed the first half of the show—again, following the template of the typical Elvis show of the 70s: by the time Elvis finally emerged, the crowd was always more than ready for him.

After intermission, there came Charlie Hodge himself, looking like a fragile gray-haired talk-show host, in a tuxedo, to do his own version of a stand-up routine. It started slow, with "The question I'm always asked: is Elvis still alive?" The answer being no, this led to a series of Elvis-in-heaven jokes, one of which had to do with the return of Elvis on the occasion of Lisa Marie's marriage—the proof being one blue suede shoe imbedded in a certain part of Michael Jackson's anatomy. Not very tasteful material, but there was an innate charm about Charlie that overcame the bad taste, and he left the stage to a round of genuinely appreciative applause.

Finally the moment was at hand. "This is the closest you'll ever get to what a real Elvis show was like," Charlie had said before leaving the stage. Now we would see. The band went into "Also Sprach Zarathustra," the lights cued wildly, and at last—enter The King—or a gangling, red-suited version of him, guitar-slung, fully caped and sun-shaded, singing Elvis's traditional opener, "See See Rider."

"How do you like me *now*?" were Pete Willcox's first spoken words, as he whipped off the shades and shot a Healthcliffean glare at the crowd.

There was something aloof—almost lordly—in the way he went about it. I wondered what kind of act he might do in his own right, since he could clearly (as Elvis, anyway) dominate a stage and drive a show. Yet there he was, this lean, towering pseudo-Elvis. Rick had told me Willcox had done some acting. Was this just another part? Or was it devotion? What was it that made one kind of performer wrap himself in Elvis, when another performer—perhaps not even as good a performer—wouldn't consider anything but an original act? I wanted to ask this of Pete Willcox. Although after our brief encounter in the afternoon, I rather expected I wouldn't come away with much of an answer.

But I had to hand it to him: Pete Willcox was the most impressive living Elvis replica I had seen yet. Aside from his coldness—a saturnine disdain that lay just beneath the surface, coloring even his occasional flashes of humor an ironic gray—he seemed to have it all: catlike physical grace, a voice that, though it lacked Elvis's southern diction, delivered all the power and nuance of the original. His direct interaction with the audience seemed stilted, mannered, not the sort of thing that came naturally, but he was an experienced showman, knew when to talk and how to move things along.

Charlie Hodge had slipped into his spot in the band by the time Willcox was ready to give out scarves and kisses. The scarves and kisses business had been ritualized by Elvis in the 70s: by now, any Elvis impersonator's audience would be full of women who knew exactly what to do: approach the front, as a communicant would for Holy Communion, and wait. Scarves were bestowed one at a time, direct from the impersonator's neck. Kisses were usually chaste, occasionally hot. A scarf, given away, was immediately replaced by the on-stage scarf-and-water man.

Charlie Hodge had created this function for Elvis himself. Watching, I found it odd—bizarre, even—that here was the same Charlie Hodge, performing an exactly similar function for Pete Willcox and doing it with the same snappy crispness with which you could see him servicing Elvis in many a concert video.

Why bizarre? It was the mixture of real (Charlie) and facsimile (Willcox), neither acknowledging the slightest strangeness about it. It was as if a man's second wife was consciously impersonating his first wife, while the man, in turn, consciously impersonated himself in the role of husband to the first wife.

Whew. Lost in an Elvis hall of mirrors.

Willcox moved the show toward its climax, "American Trilogy," complete with a massive American flag backdrop. Fluttering Old Glories sprouted on the video projection screens, triggering a patriotic reflex that brought the audience to its feet. But although he inspired a kind of intense regard from the audience, no one seemed to love Pete

Willcox like they loved Elvis. The question that had brought me here was getting at least a partial answer. What did it *mean* to be a good impersonator? One thing it meant was that technical mastery only got you in the door. You had to have something else that brought out the juice in your audience, that made them love you, at least a little. In his favor, Willcox's show gave good value for an evening in the theater, but random pulse checks would have shown that the general emotional response level was in the reptilian range.

By this time, Olivia's long day had caught up with her and her head was on my shoulder.

An announcer's voice assured us that "Pete has *not* left the building," and would be autographing copies of his tape and video.

Charlie Hodge, the voice went on, would be signing copies of his book and "home movies" video compilation *Me and Elvis*. I could see he was already standing at the rear center aisle, like a minister, ready to meet the congregation and shake each departing hand.

"Come on," I said to the semicomatose Olivia, "let's meet Charlie."

Coming close to a celebrity can bring you into a strange force field of high-intensity magnetism that both pushes and pulls. Body magnetism is palpable, an almost visible force-field pattern: the vibes are simultaneously saying "love me" and "go away." Nothing as complicated as this surrounded Charlie Hodge. He greeted each patron with simple, genuine warmth, as if he or she were, momentarily anyway, the only creature in the universe.

"How are you, sir?" he asked me, and from ten inches away, it felt like he actually meant it.

Bubba the Redneck Ranger had taken up his station around the souvenir counter and flirted oafishly with the older women as they lined up to buy scarves and mugs with Pete Willcox's image on them.

Willcox himself finally made an appearance, in casual black leather, and slumped behind a table piled with souvenirs. Slowly he affixed his signature to the product offered up by a long line of waiting fans that had formed almost instantly. Most likely it would involve at least a twenty-minute wait to have my word with him. Unless I cut in, flacklike: "Excuse me a second, folks. Pete, great show. Say, about that chat? Is it all right if I wait around till you're through here?" or some such obsequious wording designed to pierce his icy remoteness.

"Dad, can we leave now?" said Olivia. "I'm exhausted."

"I'm all set, honey. Let's go."

Chapter

15

A s spring ripened I realized that one important piece of experience was missing from my résumé: I had never been to Graceland.

I knew I would be in Memphis in August, but then I would be entirely focused on the contest at the Best Western, leaving little time for sight-seeing. The trip to Graceland was a rite of passage that I felt I needed now, not later, so I had been testing various weekends on the calendar, when one night I received a phone call from the holy city itself.

"Bill," said a deep southern basso profundo (it came out "Bee-uhl."). "This is Fetzer Mills." The voice suddenly disappeared in a crackle of static.

"Fetzer?"

"I'm back. It's my cell phone messin' up. I'm at work at this storage depot, nothing but me and the trucks out here."

The last time I had talked to Fetzer Mills, he was a political consultant in Alabama, teaching liberal candidates how to appeal to redneck voters. As a swarthy, half-redneck himself (the other half was old-family southern) he knew instinctively how to be persuasive in these matters. But now, as he drawled on, it seemed this part of his life was all over: his marriage had collapsed, he was living alone in Memphis, working as a security guard—and here things got a little hard to follow. He was (a) about to publish a book on how to run your own low-cost political campaign; (b) about to cut a rockabilly record at Sam Phillips's Recording Service (hiring ancient surviving Elvis-era sidemen), about which he would write a magazine article; and, of particular relevance, (c) was about to start a new security guard job—on the force at (of all places) *Graceland.*

"What happened to politics?" I asked.

"It's a long story. I could tell you, but I'd have to kill you."

"That's okay."

"Well, it's really not so heavy as all that: what happened was I started drinking one day and didn't stop for about three weeks, ended up in Memphis, in detox, separated from Becky, life blown to pieces, all that. But it was due, it was coming. We had a lot of stuff to work out in the marriage. Things are better now. We're even seeing each other again. Doing okay now."

"When do you start at Graceland?"

"Next week. I've had my employee indoctrination and orientation and all. I'm ready. It's actually kind of ironic, because when me and Becky took a tour there some time back, I intentionally started a ruckus in the Meditation Garden, just for fun."

"A ruckus?"

"Aw, somebody asked a guide if Elvis's body was under the slab and I piped up and said hell no, in fact, Elvis was still very much alive and I had even seen him in a Wal-Mart in Wadesboro, NC, buying a shotgun. You can imagine how that played out. I was rolling my eyes around and talking real loud—Becky kept trying to shut me up. The guide started whispering in her walkie-talkie, calling up security. Now they've got self-guided tours and *I'm* gonna be security. What a world. But I don't know, the people at Graceland are a little too far on the happy scale for me, too chirpy. They're like the staff at Disney World."

"But I guess you'll get some interesting material to write about."

"Yeah, I'm thinking of a TV series, kind of a cop show, based on Graceland security, called EPD."

"Elvis Police Department?"

"Yeah, that's right! Each episode, Graceland security thwarts an attempt to steal the body, or break into the upstairs bathroom, or murder an important Elvis impersonator."

"Elvis could be a running character, a ghost."

"Yeah! Like only certain people can see him. He comes and goes, like *I Dream of Jeannie*."

"Or George and Marian, in *Topper*."

"*Topper*. Oh, yeah! Great."

Fetzer had heard about my impersonator project and wondered when I'd be showing up in Memphis, hence the phone call. With this development it was going to be pretty darn quick. I began to fantasize that with Fetzer as my inside source, I would see Graceland in a way ordinary tourists could never imagine. Maybe he could even get me into Elvis's strictly off-limits bedroom and the forbidden death-bathroom! As soon as I hung up I threw a dart at my wall calendar to finalize a weekend, set up a stay with some old friends in the Memphis suburb of Germantown (Fetzer's downtown apartment would be too small), and speed-dialed my travel agent.

I had always thought Memphis was an interesting music city. Geographically, it had served as a magnet for ambitious or desperate country people in the upper Mississippi Delta who needed a city to move to. This made it the unofficial urban capital of an area composed of parts of four different states.

Elvis and his family moved to Memphis. So did W. C. Handy, Muddy Waters, B. B. King, Jerry Lee Lewis, Johnny Cash, and a ton of other musicians with country blues and jazz roots. Nashville might serve as the capital of the more mountain-rooted "country" music, but Memphis, with its gloriously heterodox tradition, had probably fed more life into more forms of American popular music than any other city on earth.

Fetzer Mills, who liked things loose, loved this combination of easygoing mobility and funky cross-fertility. He had been an international studies major, spoke three languages (four, if you count redneck as a language), had military police experience and, because of his combination of good-old-boy affability and brick wall toughness, he could qualify as an ideal security operative if it came to that—which it had, apparently (he described security work as the 90s equivalent of pumping gas).

But his real love was rockabilly music. Insecurities about his singing talent had kept him from ever performing. But now the priorities of his life had shifted and he was ready to *just do it*, take action, pay whatever it would cost—which meant working security, pawning his pawnables, even cutting off his phone and utilities—to finance a recording session with his heroes.

"And where else but Memphis, man? I can call up Malcolm Yelvington or Roland James! Just call 'em up! They're right there in the book! Punch the buttons and talk to history. Do you think I could do that in Nashville? Everybody's unlisted there."

And then there was Graceland.

"First day you get to Memphis, you ought to really devote most of the day to Graceland," Fetzer advised. "There's a lot to do out there. I'll be assigned to the Plaza, so we can kind of hang out a little. There's food and a post office right on the premises, and some kinda weird souvenir shops off the reservation, and places to just sit and write in your journal. And there's a video show, it's free, every half hour—you can just go in the theater and watch it all day long if you want to; some fans do."

I flew into Memphis late Friday night and after securing my rental car (which took hours, it seemed) drove out to Germantown, where my friends, Mike and Cheryl, had waited up for me. Mike and Cheryl weren't into Elvis at all. Even so, Mike had found a memoir, by a Memphis kid who had grown up to become a journalist. The author, James Conoway, described himself in high school as a nice middle-class Memphis boy, contemptuous of—and afraid of—the greasers from the projects. Yet all of a sudden, "Heartbreak Hotel" had launched Elvis as the world's hunkiest teen avatar—this greaser from right across town! It was hard to handle. Mike and Cheryl, I think, were on the writer's side of the fence, a little bemused by my foray into Elvis World, but quite content to enjoy the trip vicariously, through me.

I was up bright and early. Fetzer had told me to try and make it down to Graceland by 7:00 A.M., when free access to the Meditation Garden was allowed for about half an hour prior to the first paid tour of the day. This was to accommodate certain pilgrims who came to the grave every day—chief among them was Kiki Apostolakos, one of the extreme female fans, who had left her family in Greece to move to Memphis, supporting herself as a waitress to be near Elvis. (Richard Thompson's song "Galway to Graceland" describes an Irish version of the same syndrome.) But by the time I arrived, that magic hour had come and gone. The first few cars were arriving in the Graceland parking lot, in the cool of the spring morning, and only a handful of visitors were at the ticket booth.

Across a wide expanse of traffic, the mansion sat, removed and protected, at the top of a rolling, green rise, recalling Hank Williams's "Mansion on the Hill." But the business end of Graceland was now a slick theme park, referred to as the Plaza, which included restaurants, shops, museums, offices, and a parking place for the *Lisa Marie*, Elvis's gigantic Convair 880 touring jet. An adjacent strip mall, Graceland Crossing, was devoted entirely to even more Elvis merchandise.

At the time Elvis bought it, as a haven for his parents, Graceland was an isolated country estate. The mansion still sat in the midst of several acres of green, but urban sprawl now surrounded it. Ticky-tacky housing had grown up just across the property lines, and Elvis Presley Boulevard had matured into an ugly four-lane urban drag, its dreariness broken only by the sudden appearance of the mansion, and across from it, the Elvis memory factory, Graceland Plaza.

"Bee-uhl."

Fetzer Mills, on the beat at Graceland.
(Photo courtesy of William McCranor Henderson.)

I heard the growl as I entered the plaza, after crossing a cute oriental bridge from the parking lot. Fetzer was waiting for me, seated on a bench, in his Graceland security uniform, looking like a police officer in summer whites. He stood up, tall and bulky, puffing on a cigarette, and flashed the all-inclusive "platinum" ticket he had managed to arrange for me.

"I'll be working the parking lot all morning, it turns out, but there's a place I want to show you later. It's the First Church of the Elvis Impersonator. We can shoot over there after my shift."

"It's a church?"

"Sort of. You can get married there. It's the kind of thing they ought to have here at Graceland, but they don't."

We made plans to meet for lunch, and I hooked a place in line for the next Mansion tour.

To comprehend greater Graceland in its present-day totality, you first have to realize that it is "open" around the clock. Although the exhibits themselves close, the Plaza is accessible and populated throughout the night. Fans from everywhere can be seen at three or four in the morning, gazing in the direction of the Mansion across the street, smoking, contemplating their lives, weeping, or in the case of the maladjusted, walking in geometric patterns or assuming ritual postures.

Fetzer told me about encountering some of these night people—the German Elvis wanna-be (he doubted the man was a working impersonator), who loomed up out of the night and fog, in a fully caped jumpsuit, like a rhinestoned Dracula, singing Elvis in guttural phonetic English . . . or the four-foot Philippino, dressed all in black, who stood on the wall and told the world, "Hi, ahm Johnny Cash!"

The Mansion, Elvis's home, was situated by itself across the Boulevard from everything else. Little European buses shuttled tour groups over and back every 20 minutes. I picked up my self-guided tour (a large black cassette player with headphones) and boarded my bus feeling a thrill of anticipation—at last to stand in the very space I had read so much about!

It's a baronial home, the kind that might house a monied CEO in Princeton or Greenwich or Kenilworth or Whitefish Bay or any old-money suburb. The muted stone facade promises third- or fourth-generation-wealth artifacts inside—oil portraits of prominent forebears, and so on—but this impression ended once I was inside. Graceland is not, as you often hear, "oh, so tacky" or "unbelievably garish." It is simply what you would expect to find in any midcentury American mansion furnished and decorated with sudden new wealth—mostly a combination of 50s modern and sentimental glitz. The fans' most common complaint is that Priscilla Presley or Elvis's later girlfriend, Linda Thompson, altered color schemes and redecorated areas that were once products of Elvis's pure momentary inspiration.

For me, the most memorable part of the house was the stairway to Elvis's second-floor suite, hidden behind funereal green velvet curtains. My hope that Fetzer could get me in was pie-in-the-sky. The bedroom has hardly been touched since his death. No one goes there, Fetzer told me, not even most staff—only a handpicked high-security cleaning crew occasionally pierces that upstairs miasma of gloom and time, which includes the infamous bathroom, where Elvis was seized by an arrhythmia, while reading on the toilet, and pitched to the floor, dead at 42.

Oddly, the house seemed smaller inside, less expansive than the exterior lead me to expect (after all, hadn't Elvis lain in state there?). There were stables off to the back, as well as outbuildings that now housed exhibits of records and memorabilia. Some interesting items were on display. Early merchandise: Elvis Presley's TEDDY BEAR eau de parfum; an "*Oy Gevaldt Elvis*" button; Elvis Presley lipstick ("Excitingly Alive"); and a very 50s Elvis Presley "Party Game for the Young at Heart." A piece of documentation tells you that if all the records Elvis sold were laid end-to-end, they would circle the world and then some. Elvis's private racquetball court has been turned into a museum that holds his gold records, framed and hanging on flat-black walls. A TV monitor runs with the image of Jack Soden, Graceland's CEO, giving a speech at the dedication of the space.

Soden is generic CEO material, smart, blank, unprepossessing, yet with an air of quiet competence. He was turned out at birth to head a corporation, any corporation. He might or might not be an Elvis fan (my guess is he isn't), but that's not really what's important for the leader of today's Graceland: what's important is that he can manage for growth and profit. I used to write speeches for men like this. They can change jobs as easily as they might change country clubs: after all, golf is golf, wherever you go; and corporate business is corporate business; widgets are widgets, whether you are marketing soft drinks, automobiles, soap, banking services (Soden's former widget), or the legacy of Elvis Presley.

The soul of Graceland is the Meditation Garden. This is where the true Elvis pilgrims linger—and lingering is allowed (if you miss the shuttle bus back to the Plaza, there's always another one). Here, amid the Italianate marble and iron-filigreed kitsch, was finally something of the numinous drawing power of the dead Elvis: yes, this *could* be the burial place of a saint. The grave was covered with small tributes. One stood out: a simple wooden cross made of garden stakes, the kind that are driven into the hearts of vampires, with I LOVE YOU . . . SHIRLEY hand-burned into it.

By lunchtime I had seen the rest of the exhibits. There was the Automobile Museum (I wasn't interested in cars, but Elvis owned a lot of nifty ones). The video theater presentation was clever. The *Lisa Marie*, little more than a touring bus blown up to jet liner proportions, was worth about three of four minutes.

A modest museum, the Sincerely Elvis exhibit, was essentially a procession of window displays, one of which I found fascinating: it contained a selection from Elvis's wildly eclectic private record collection. I jotted down the titles in no particular order . . .

Mormon Tabernacle Choir: *Best Loved American Folk Songs*

Leinsdorf, Boston Symphony: *Mahler Symphony #1*

Bernstein: *Dvorak, New World Symphony*

Gilels, Reiner: *Brahms, Concerto #2*

Patti Page Sings C&W Golden Hits

Dean Martin: *French Style*

Mahalia Jackson: *Everytime I Feel This Spirit*

B.J. Thomas: *Everybody's Out of Town*

Ray Conniff: *'s Awful Nice*

Sam Cooke: *Shake*

Ray Charles: *A Man and His Soul*

Tom Jones: *Live in Las Vegas*

The Clovers: *Dance Party*

Ray Price: *Like Old Times Again*

Jake Hess & the Imperials!

Peter Paul & Mary: *Moving*

Allman Brothers Band: *Beginnings*

Don Ho: *Live in Hawaii*

Kim Carnes: *Rest on Me*

Fetzer's rapport with everyone at Graceland gave me a chance to see the place in ways I never could have managed, either as a casual visitor or an official guest to be shown around by a media representative (I preferred anonymity). For example: while we ate lunch outside, so Fetzer could smoke, I watched a short, round, black woman, uniformed, sweating in the heat, sweeping up cigarette butts. Had I not been with Fetzer, she would have remained, for me, an anonymous African-American Minimum Wage Worker. Fetzer's presence brought her to life.

He hailed her: "Peggy!" She took a break and joined us, and before my eyes, as they chatted, transformed into "Simply Peggy," a rising gospel singing star in Memphis, with a record out ("Ready" on the A-side, a Christian rap on the other), and a manager, lining up her appearances on radio and TV shows. As she talked, confident and full of spunky good humor, she displayed a front tooth lined with gold and inlaid with a star. That star, I could tell, was the symbol of her personal goal. Graceland was just her day job. As soon as God lay the big break on her, she was out of here.

She asked Fetzer about his own recording project. He puffed hard on his cigarette.

"Well, I've got it set up to go into Sam Phillips's studio and do two sides."

"What you gonna do?"

"An old Warren Smith number, 'Red Cadillac and a Black Mustache' and 'The Fool,' by Sanford Clark."

"Elvis done 'The Fool.'"

"Elvis? You're kidding me."

"Yep. Yep. Elvis done 'The Fool.'"

"How about that!" Fetzer turned to me. "I guess that makes me an honorary Elvis impersonator, doesn't it!"

When Fetzer introduced me, with my gray, balding head, as an Elvis impersonator, Peggy didn't bat an eye. It occurred to me that role playing was such a necessary and natural factor in black life that it didn't seem the slightest bit unusual for me to be not as I seemed—even emphatically so.

"Well, I got to get back to it," she said and went off with her broom and her pan, a squat figure in the unattractive Graceland uniform and cap. Now, however, my mind's eye could see her in a flowing blue gospel robe, her hair creamy black, her tooth flashing its star, commanding a church, an auditorium, a Grammy audience . . .

For an early-rock purist like Fetzer, working at Graceland, where they pipe 20 years of Elvis through speakers 24 hours a day, was an eye-opener. Although he had some connoisseurish Elvis favorites, like "The Girl of My Best Friend," ("The best song about adolescent guilt I ever heard!"), he had been largely ignorant of Elvis's massive post-Sun oeuvre. He found the eclecticism of middle and late Elvis interesting but remained a staunch rockabilly purist.

His recording project was benefiting from the fact that in Memphis, the surviving figures from the rockabilly era, now in their sixties and seventies, were approachable and had time on their hands. Right behind Graceland Plaza, for instance, was an old security guard who had once played rhythm guitar for Carl Perkins. Complete amateur that he was, Fetzer had managed to assemble a group for his session that included the legendary Malcolm Yelvington, who with his Star Rhythm Boys was an early Sun artist, and Roland James, house guitarist at Sun, who toured as a member of Jerry Lee Lewis's band.

In fact, as soon as Fetzer's shift ended, we were to head over to Sun Studios so that Fetzer could talk to someone there about his date. But first, since he knew I was interested in picking up some Elvis souvenirs for the kids (and for me), he wanted to steer me to "the good stuff."

"It's all Wonder Bread at the Graceland shops. They've weeded out anything cool, like bottles of Elvis sweat or little china Elvis toilets, and charge top dollar for standard stuff you can get cheaper off the reservation."

Fetzer had tried to promote a potter friend who was turning out very artistic Elvis Buddhas. Graceland turned him down. "The woman I showed one to got real indignant and said, 'That isn't supposed to be Someone We Know, is it?' I just said, 'No ma'am, it's Roy Orbison.'"

Graceland had erected a huge spite fence to hide its neighbors, the competing unofficial Elvis shops. We walked around it and entered a store called Souvenirs of Elvis that looked like a more idiosyncratic environment. Fetzer, looking large in his Graceland "EPD" whites, received the same attention any policeman gets when he makes a casual visit.

"You gonna bust us, Mr. Man?" said one of the gruff, middle-aged white ladies who clerk at these places. Normally you can't get a shadow of a grin out of them, but they, like everybody else around Graceland, knew Fetzer.

"Ain't gonna bust you today. What do you think of that Elvis Buddha I showed you?"

"Mm, don't know. Fifty dollar's a lot of money for a fat little brown Elvis. It ain't very tough either."

"But it's very special, very delicate."

"Well, we ain't said no yet."

"You keep thinkin' about it."

Here, I found even the standard souvenir items to be more interesting than Graceland's "official" caps, T-shirts, and key rings: I bought a cap with an authentic touring patch on it—the one Elvis had designed especially for his road staff. You won't find it at Graceland. Why? Who knows? You find a lot of caps that read "Graceland" or "I ♥ Graceland" or "I've Been to Graceland." In fact, the main priority at Graceland is evident in one key aspect of the layout of the place: every exhibit, bar none, exits into a souvenir shop. In order just to get "out," you must pass through one. Although Elvis's image is everywhere, the Graceland logo is just as much in evidence on the T-shirts, caps, key chains, and so on. This is not lost on Elvis fans: Rick Marino pointed it out to me. "You'll notice when you get there that the Estate is selling Graceland more than they're selling Elvis."

On his way back to work, Fetzer steered me to one official shop, where Elvis's uncle, Vester Presley, was sitting behind a table signing books. Vester, for my money, has the perkiest title of all the "Elvis-and-Me" books: *A Presley Speaks*. More recently, he had weighed in with one of the many Elvis culinary titles, *The Presley Family Cookbook*. My favorite of these, by the way, was a food-oriented biography called *The Life and Cuisine of Elvis Presley*. Sample chapters: "Love Me Slender: The Elvis Diets" . . . "The Tragic Dinners" . . . "The Last Supper" (which, according to all accounts, was four scoops of ice cream and two dozen cookies).

Back in the pre-Estate days, when Graceland was just Elvis's house, Vester had headed a seat-of-the-pants security operation that indulged the fans with spontaneous jeep tours of the grounds, and hours of chitchat at the front gate. He would show heart to the young pilgrims who came with sleeping bags, hoping for a glimpse of Elvis (who was usually away, in Vegas, LA, or on tour). "I let 'em curl up in their bags and get some rest, poor things. But you boys, you run it like the Army."

A strapping man when younger, Vester was frail and palsied now. His wife had died recently, and he seemed depressed. Later I would spot him around the Plaza, in a baseball cap and shorts, wandering among the crowds, invisible, like a ghost, this man who had witnessed it all, from the dirt-scratching poverty of Depression Tupelo to the pristine glitz of this funhouse memorial to his nephew, where no one recognized Uncle Vester anymore.

"I'm the last Presley," he repeated in a mournful litany, as he signed a copy of *A Presley Speaks* for me. I had asked him to personalize it— "To Bill Henderson"—and realized, with a shock, as he hemmed and hawed, that he was semi-literate. Laboriously, he managed "To Bill" and I still treasure it, a first grader's unconnected wavy capitals, sketched slowly, one at a time, as if they were elaborate pictographs.

Vester's sudden moroseness caused Fetzer and me to fall awkwardly silent. "My wife's gone now, everybody's gone, I'm the last one, the last one."

"What about Lisa Marie?"

Vester simply rolled his eyes. Lisa Marie was clearly Priscilla's get, beyond the pale, certainly not his idea of a Presley.

"How about your daughter, Patsy?"

He shook his head. "She ain't been the same since Elvis died." He eyed Fetzer. "You know, I sure would like to go downtown. I ain't been downtown in twenty years." A crocodile tear welled up in the old man's eyes.

Fetzer shifted from one foot to another and made a point of looking at his wristwatch. "Oh boy, I'm late getting back."

Just then a fan engaged Vester and we slipped out.

"See, he wants me to take him downtown to ride the trolley, take the monorail to Mud Island, all that. It's sentimental. He knows I live downtown and he hasn't been there in all these years. He's workin' on me."

I could tell Fetzer was upset by the encounter. I walked him back toward the lower security hut; his arms were waving as he ambled along.

"I guess I've got a big brother problem—I want to take care of everybody. I'd like to take him around, but I just haven't had the time. I never have the time. Or the focus or something. Maybe I'm focus disabled."

Chapter

16

After Fetzer's shift ended, we left his car at Graceland and piled into my spiffy turquoise rental for a ride to Sun Studio, in the industrial no-man's-land of downtown Union Avenue.

Sun, of course, was also hallowed ground. Elvis cut his first record there, a $3.99 vanity acetate. His first commercial records (as well as those of Carl Perkins, Jerry Lee Lewis, and Johnny Cash) had been made there. In later years, Sam Phillips had moved his studio to a new location and sold the name "Sun" to a Nashville operation. The original studio fell on hard times.

When the present owner, a young musician, found it in the 70s, it was being used as a radiator shop. Realizing he had a chance to own a bona fide historical site, he bought the building, restored it, and began using it both as a proper recording studio and a landmark tourist stop. Since the studio is only a single room, "tours" are really set-pieces. The tour guide runs through the history of early rock 'n' roll (which is almost synonymous with the history of Sun) punctuating the rap with brief examples from an old Ampex tape deck. If you'd like to merge with history by making a tape of yourself at Sun Studio—just like the teenaged Elvis once did—you can, on the half-hour, for fifty dollars (back-up tracks provided).

The former Taylor's Restaurant next door has become the Sun Studio Cafe, a bustling diner with a line of Sun Studio merchandise and food specialties like peanut butter and mashed banana sandwiches (Elvis's passion) and (my passion) fried banana pie, served with a scoop of vanilla ice cream. I was told Vice President Al Gore, a Tennessean, orders 30 or so of the pies whenever Air Force 2 touches down in Memphis. Fetzer, of course, knew everyone there, from the waitress to the manager, a friendly long-haired guy named Mark (unlike Graceland, Sun has a funky, "alternative" quality, and the people who run it now are young, hip, and long-haired).

Business was slack in the cafe and the Sun crew, in their black Sun Studio T-shirts joined Fetzer at a table. Mark's assistant, another young longhair, was describing an independent feature film being made by a friend of his. *DamsElvis, Daughter of Helvis* would be a send-up of horror films, Elvis lore, and just about anything else you could think of, with characters named RebElvis, PsychedElvis, Elviscious—

"Elviscious," said Fetzer, shifting his heavy uniform belt with cop-on-the-beat insouciance. "That reminds me of that version of 'My Way' Sid Vicious does. Did you ever hear that? 'Oi did it MOY WOY'—he's totally wasted, kind of spits it out?"

"Yeah, yeah," said Mark. "*The Great Rock 'n' Roll Swindle*, check it out."

"You gonna sing 'Moy Woy,' Bill?" Fetzer asked me, causing everyone to go temporarily blank as they wondered why the question was in any way pertinent to me. Fetzer turned back to them: "Bill's going to enter the Elvis Impersonator contest in August."

"No way! That's cool, that is really COOL!" Mark, wiry, speedy, blowing smoke, shook my hand. "I like that, I like that. I mean, we get impersonators here all the time, but they don't look like you. Hey, I got to show you something, man, look at this." He walked me over to the wall and pointed to one of the many framed photos, this one an attractive young woman blowing a baritone sax along with—yes, it was Bobby Keyes, the horn man who gained fame by touring with the

Rolling Stones. "That's Suzi Hendrix, used to be a waitress here, damn good horn player, and guess what?—an Elvis impersonator!"

What would be the term for a female Elvis impersonator? Impersonatrix? I had seen pictures of a few of them. Generally they were bulky and mannish; they wrapped their chests with Ace bandages to do away with their breasts; they combed their hair in greasy swoops and accentuated Elvis's tough masculine side—a quality that has sometimes been characterized by rock writers as "butch." I wondered what this decidedly unbutch woman did to transform herself into The King. It would be a stretch. Yet if I could do it, I supposed she could do it.

Fetzer was into a story told him by the comedian/musician/wild man Rev. Billy C. Wirtz, who was, of course, yet another friend of Fetzer's.

"Billy was on a talk show one night in Memphis, and he made an offer to buy any original Elvis memorabilia. This teenage girl called in, said she had an authentic Elvis toe tag from the morgue, where her daddy worked, with documentation and all, so Billy bought it for $50. Turned out it was her daddy's prize possession, and she had been real, real mad at him when she heard the radio and just called up on an impulse."

"Showed him."

"Yeah, and later on the guy got him a lawyer, sued, et cetera, but Billy stood firm and kept it. It was a done deal." Fetzer was laughing and cigarette coughing at the same time. "Broke the guy's heart."

"Well," said Mark, "better'n if she took his shotgun and blew his fool head off."

As the repartee went on, my mind began to wander: here I was, sitting at the Edenic center of all American rock 'n' roll—listening to talk about Elvis's toe tag. How did we get from "That's All Right, Mama" to toe tags?

In the Taylor Restaurant days, a pimply Elvis himself might have sat exactly where I was sitting, along with Scottie Moore, Bill Black, Carl Perkins—small-town boys, big-time dreamers. Sun Records couldn't have seemed more than moderately promising to them. I had seen other small recording studios of roughly that era, and they all looked the same: you would walk through a tiny office into a cavernous, dingy room encased in discolored old acoustical tile; a rectangle of heavy glass in the far wall would connect to the dusty control booth. Out-doors, there would be alleys, warehouses, junkyards, auto parts stores, vacant lots. This was the humble reality of Sun Studio in 1954, even as now. Yet from such a bleak nowhere, the unlikely revolution had sprung.

Unlikely? That hardly says it. What a complete long shot it had been for Elvis (or anybody really) to come blazing out of that little hole-in-the-wall, in that blank, run-down area of a music city second- or third-rate in its commercial importance—to become *the world's fore-most pop music phenomenon of all time!*

It was one of those stranger-than-fiction true stories that would be received with utter skepticism in a novel. But it had happened—and with such force and consequence that no one has ever been able to "fictionalize" the Elvis Presley story successfully. Fiction imitates life, feeds off it—then suddenly one day, life turns, like a monster, and eats fiction whole.

"Carter-Young" had been the bohemian district of Memphis, and even though it was now gentrifying, the streets were still peopled by long-haired artists and student types. We had come up here to see the First Church of the Elvis Impersonator and grab a bite of supper. Still bright-white in his uniform, with its Graceland patches and official-looking gold badge, Fetzer stepped out of the car and yawned loudly as several street people gave him a wide berth.

"After we do this, you might want to take a little trip down to the other Graceland," he said, with a sly half-grin. "It's about halfway down to Tupelo, in Holly Springs. It's actually called Graceland *Too*—you know, t-o-o? I've been wanting to check it out. A guy and his son turned their whole house into an Elvis museum; he calls himself the world's foremost Elvis fan or something to that effect. It's well worth a visit, or so I hear."

We turned a corner and there, in a cluster of storefronts, was the "Church," a curious old shop space with its entire display window a shrine to Elvis impersonators. Next to a coin slot was a sign: "Bedazzle, Bemuse, Behold, Believe! 25¢, quarters only, per blessed vista. . . . Wedding Chapel Inside."

The shrine was an impressive example of an art form that seems to be growing: Elvis kitsch, a sculptural, decorative, devotional Elvis-based aesthetic that rides the line between spoof and high seriousness. This nest of iconography was dominated by a painting of an Elvis impersonator with his eyes closed and his hands folded in prayer and a cross about where his penis would be. There was a tombstone in greenish patterned bathroom wallpaper with orange fuzz around it. Written in glitter paint: "Viva Memphis" and "24-Hour Shotgun Weddings—It's Legal." There was a pink toy motorcycle on a 45 rpm turntable with a tiny wedding-cake Elvis impersonator in cape and rhinestones. On either side of the Elvis figurine were two ancient plastic record players turned on their sides. Photo fragments of various Elvis impersonators were stuck to them. There were side items: a backdrop festooned with tiny details—dominoes, a purple guitar, a pink ukelele, a Sun Records button, a picture of two-and-a-half-month-old "Phil, the world's youngest Elvis impersonator"—a doll's head with paste-on sideburns, plastic funeral flowers, a red "hot line" telephone ("Line to Big E"), Hawaiian leis, Chinese lanterns, mirror fragments, a tiny animal skull. Below the praying hands was a small frieze of the Last Supper, about six inches across and two inches high. Up above was a cluster of names of Elvis impersonators against waving American flags: "Joe Elvis, Rob Elvis Dye, Jerry El, El Vez, Eric Elvis Domino. . . ."

"You got a quarter?"

As I dropped one into the coin box, the shrine came robotically to life, for 30 seconds, like a Rube Goldberg 5th Avenue Christmas display. Spooky music—an ethereal choir of some sort—poured from a pair of speakers in the ceiling. The turntables began to revolve, the Elvis figurine along with them, lights twittered on and off in a minimally kinetic pattern.

Some unusual-looking people entered by the main door. "They're not getting married, are they?" I asked. We followed them into what looked like a Disney re-creation of a 50s Greenwich Village coffeehouse. Long-haired, mustachioed beatniks and hippies smoked, sipped espresso, and played chess. These were mostly artists, Fetzer explained, impervious to the stares at his Graceland uniform. "This, to Carter-Young, is like the Dome was to Paris in the 20s." Well, maybe. We peeked into the Wedding Chapel, a grotto off the back; it was empty—no weddings today. There was a coffee bar up front, and I ordered an espresso and struck up a chat with an attractive girl who was waiting for a cappuccino. She worked here, she said, sometimes waiting tables, sometimes performing marriages.

"You're an Elvis impersonator?" I said, with an incredulous rise in tone.

Fetzer, who had joined us, chimed in. "Well, *you're* one, ain't you? You don't look any more likely than she does."

"Good point."

"I'm kind of semi-inactive at this point," said the girl. "I used to do the contest, when it was at Bad Bob's, but it's gotten so competitive."

"Wait a minute," I said. "You're not Suzi Hendrix, are you? The saxophone player?"

She seemed mildly shocked to be recognized. "Yes. Except when I perform I go by another name . . . Elvisira Parsely."

We fell into shop talk—costumes, scarves, all that. She told me her favorite impersonator was El Vez, the famous Mexican trickster who used Elvis performance as a jumping-off point for his campy stage act. Real Elvis fans grind their teeth at the mention of the name El Vez, but ironically, I found El Vez to be the most widely known Elvis impersonator of them all (proving the prevalence of camp over purity) and the only one that "sophisticated" folk would admit to liking.

I could tell that Suzi Hendrix, as Elvisira Parsely, was similarly adapting Elvis to her own decidedly feminine particularities, certainly an "alternative" view of Elvis. She talked of sitting through the contest in its Bad Bob days, basking in a kind of collective spirit that was lost when the contest upscaled. I asked her what look she went for when she performed, expecting to hear how she butched herself up with Ace bandages and Lucky Tiger. But she was going for something that wouldn't erase her womanliness. She wore an unorthodox adaptation of the traditional white jumpsuit that incorporated an Indian belly-dancing halter top.

It was later, after Fetzer and I had finished our coffee and were back in the car, headed for Mississippi, that it occurred to me I had never asked her about the photo at Sun Studio.

"Good excuse to talk to her again," Fetzer said. "Maybe we can come back when she's doing a wedding."

Chapter

17

We grabbed some hamburgers and headed out Lamar Avenue, past the Eagle's Nest (now called the Americana), one of Elvis's first professional gigs, and down the straight dark Highway 78, toward Tupelo. At the Holly Springs/Oxford exit, we went west, into the little courthouse town of Holly Springs. It was getting late. I realized that we didn't have the address of this place, and even if we did, what if it was closed?

"It never closes," said Fetzer.

"Never?"

"Open 24 hours a day. That's what I heard. And I'd venture a bet that anybody in town knows where it is."

Sure enough, the first person we asked (an elderly lady moonlighting in a Zip Mart) directed us around the corner and three blocks down a dark street and there it was: a dingy white antebellum minimansion. At first, nothing about it suggested Graceland. Then I realized it was roughly the same period style—a broad facade, with a Doric portico. But the scale was smaller: single pillars, rather than double, four front windows rather than eight, moldy clapboard rather than stone. Twin chimneys at either end seemed to support the rickety structure, like frail bookends. A pair of stone lions, replicas of the real Graceland's, sat regally on either side of the front steps.

We banged on the front door and, after a minute or two, it was opened by a stocky middle-aged man, dressed in black, with jet black hair and eyebrows.

"Come in, come in the house, welcome." Paul Macleod, The World's Number One Elvis Fan, was up and running. "How much time do you have? I ask you that because I could go for a half-hour, hour, two hours, depending on you, because there's so much here, so much to talk about, we're open 24 hours a day, seven days a week, 365 days a year, and there still ain't enough time."

As we entered, Paul Macleod instantly recognized Fetzer's Graceland uniform. That and my university connection made us significant visitors from the moment we crossed the threshold and signed the guest register. Macleod's son, Elvis Aron Presley Macleod, a hulking gentle giant in his early 20s, about six feet eight, was handling a tour of German pilgrims just in front of us, so Macleod gave us his entire attention.

Yes, this was Graceland Too, built in 1854, and indeed open 24 hours a day—except for the room housing Graceland Too's wall display of first-edition records; this doubled as his 86-year-old mother's sleeping quarters, so Mrs. Macleod had it to herself from eight to eight. Paul and Elvis Macleod slept in shifts, on the floor, fully clothed and ready to jump up and lead a tour at any hour of the day or night, seven days a week, 24 hours a day, 365 days a year.

Graceland Too was Paul Macleod's great dream. After following the living Elvis on tour (he attended 154 live shows) and collecting Elvis memorabilia for 39 years, he returned to his hometown and bought Graceland Too as an archive site for his collection. Now the house was stuffed and overflowing with all things Elvis—anything remotely connected with The King: any magazine that ever published the name Elvis Presley was fair game—example: a full set of *TV Guides* from the 50s with highlighted listings of Elvis's appearances and general references to his name. VCRs and audiotapes were running around the clock to catch on-air mentions of Elvis. Movie and concert posters lined the walls. Stacked footlockers spilled over with newspapers, fan magazines, computer printouts, souvenir plastic bags, fragments of old carpet from Graceland, books and pamphlets written about Elvis. Walls, tables, and display cases were crowded with Elvisiana: posters, ashtrays, movie stills, concert stills, Elvis games, dolls, promotional records, items Elvis may have once owned, perhaps only just touched. As Paul Macleod put it, "You could make my day with a toothpick!"

A large-framed photograph of the young Paul as a stogy-chewing, sideburned dude in a limousine, car phone in hand, hung on the wall. Beside him in the limo was a pretty young woman, in a state of smoldering irritation, by the look of it. "That's me and my wife, outside the International Hotel in Vegas when Elvis was there. My wife, of course, is gone with the wind. She come to me in 1991 and says, 'Paul, either this Elvis collection's got to go or I'm history.'" He paused for effect. "I didn't miss a beat, just told her bye-bye and that was all she wrote—haven't seen her since."

As our tour progressed, from room to red-carpeted room (walls and ceiling included), I began to realize that the real exhibit here was not so much the objects on display, but the mind of Paul Macleod. Just as any object with the remotest connection to Elvis could find a home in Graceland Too, the mind of Paul Macleod, with its mass (some might say mess) of Elvisian connections was, for me, the prize exhibit.

"I got about a hundred and fifty different kinds of dinner plates. You see the *Jailhouse Rock* plate in the center up there? All right, now listen to this: somebody asked me, now what can you tell us about *Jailhouse Rock*? Well, I said, Elvis did thirty-one movies and two documentaries, it's his daughter Lisa Marie's favorite movie, and Elvis wouldn't watch *Jailhouse Rock* because his leading lady, Judy Tyler, was killed in a head-on collision after they did that movie. So okay—I even got her death certificate—and I said, did you know that Elvis wore three wigs in this movie, did you know that? He wore three wigs because his prisoner's hair was about your length and they had to make up the wigs for it to look like his hair was growing out. And to top that off, they was looking for John Wayne's wigs and they found the *Jailhouse Rock* wigs, to the best of my knowledge, stumbled on 'em. And the Beatles' wigs are worth $100,000 last price I got on 'em, but these wigs are worth a fortune, and anyway it took Elvis two takes to do the song 'Jailhouse Rock' because he got short-winded—bet you didn't know that. They got the wrong serial number on that plate also. Not only that, the dance scenes, he choreographed 'em, that's another reason why he liked it. Okay, I've got 10 copies of *Jailhouse Rock*, black-and-white, color, closed caption, everything else. So next time you see the movie in black and white or color, look at Elvis's feet when he's doing *Jailhouse Rock* because he's wearing black and white Japanese tennis shoes, and they've got prisoners shoes on, and as far as I'm concerned that's wrong. The dancer dancing beside Elvis, he used to hire here every night in town for a dollar fifty cents a night, him Lash Larue, with a bullwhip, could take a toothpick outa your mouth at 40 feet, and Charley Feathers, for a dollar fifty cents a night. Then to top that off, Elvis used to rent the theaters here—and the guy's talking about giving me the projector and all the stuff for it—but here's the deal: the Elvis Presley freeway's named for him for a hundred and ten miles, you two probably passed it on the way coming up here, it's a little town called Bihalia, Mississippi. Okay: well, a lady was sitting in the theater when they premiered *Love Me Tender, Loving You*, and *Jailhouse Rock*—so to top it off, the seats are all filled and the aisles are all filled, the lady from Bihalia was sitting in her seat and she kept kneeing the lady in front of her, in her back. That lady got mad and she called this friend of mine that owned the theater, Leon Rountree, and she said, 'Mr. Rountree, would you ask this lady to stop kneeing me in the back, I'm trying to watch Elvis sing.' Elvis did a song in the movie called 'Treat Me Nice.' Strangely enough, he recorded it on my birthday of October 17, so my friend told the lady, 'You're gonna have to calm down.' So he told her once, and he told her twice: 'Lady, you're gonna have to calm down, you're gettin' too excited.' Come over and shook her the third time, she had a heart attack and dropped dead in the theater—and I got her death certificate—age 42, same as Elvis, they had to drag her body out the theater. D'you believe that? If I'm wrong, you can bury me in that gold suit right back there, I swear to God.

"Now here: I don't know how true some of these stories is, okay, but Dewey Phillips, you know, the first man to play Elvis's record, okay, WHBQ? He died at 42, Elvis died at 42, some of his classmates died at 42, I heard the paramedics who got him to the hospital died at 42, Alan Freed died at 42. A lady come here from Pennsylvania, and she was here to see these antebellum homes, see? Because there's some beautiful houses in this town, don't think there ain't. So here, the lady was stayin' there as a guest, see, and she was here to tour the homes. She's passin' by Graceland Too here with a friend, she looks over and she sees this sign 'Elvis,' see? So she tells that friend, 'Is that something about Elvis Presley back there?' Says, 'Yeah, one of his largest fans in the world lives back there, but I ain't never been in there, I heard he even named his son after Elvis, got a pretty nice collection, too.' So anyway she says, 'Well, have a nice day, I'm an Elvis fan first, I'm going in to find out what he's got.' Well, her mind got carried away after she met me and my son and my mother here, and she couldn't get over the sheer dedication, all Elvis, 24 hours a day, 7 days a week. So she says, 'I want a pencil and paper and I don't care if you give me toilet paper, give me something to write on. I got something in my mind I want to write down for this guy.' She writes me a poem, then she rhymes it with Clint Eastwood and 'make my day.' I put it on a T-shirt, right there it is. Now read that. Anyway the lady gets done with the poem, she dies, August 16, 1977, 42 years old. Finishes the poem, she dies. Same day as Elvis. Same age. What do you think of that, now? Ain't that something? Ain't that something? Here's the song the other lady dropped dead to—not this lady, the lady from Bihalia—these here are aluminum dubs—here's the one the lady dropped dead to, from *Jailhouse Rock*."

The dub, which looks like an aluminum 78 rpm, was worn and

scratchy, but it was Elvis—or was it? As we listened, Paul dropped the bomb: no, the voice wasn't Elvis, but Paul himself, recorded on a whim one day at a walk-in studio just outside Las Vegas. In fact, as we all gathered around a big PA speaker across the room, Paul not only sang along with The King's own "Treat Me Nice" right on the spot—and credibly enough—he even threw in some practiced bumps and grinds and a little knee action, too.

It was time to have our Polaroids taken, the climax of every Graceland Too tour. Fetzer stood up tall in his uniform, his face bright with admiration, emotion even, at the prospect of Paul Macleod's pure-hearted dedication.

"I'll put your picture with all the others, by state or country, we've had 20,000 folks from every state, every country on earth, CNN, Entertainment Tonight, Geraldo, articles, newspaper stories, people clip 'em and send 'em to us in the mail, and we don't do nothing to get this kind of coverage, it's just what people are saying about us when they leave here. Read this guy's statement he wrote in the guest book, give you an idea of what 20,000 people are saying, just came out of his head when he was walking out the door—" He thrust a statement into Fetzer's hand. "Read that out loud."

Fetzer recited sonorously:

"THIS HOUSE IS TRULY A MONUMENT, NOT ONLY TO THE LEGACY OF ELVIS PRESLEY, BUT TO THE SHEER UNABATED DEVOTION HE INSPIRED IN HIS LISTENERS. NOTHING ELSE COULD COME CLOSE TO THE JUSTICE DONE BY THIS TRIBUTE TO ELVIS'S INFLUENCE. THIS IS THE DEFINITIVE MONUMENT TO AMERICA'S MOST RECOGNIZABLE GLOBAL FIGURE."

"Ain't that nice? Ain't that nice? There's 20,000 people who wrote stuff like that, just come out of their head real quick."

We were back now where our tour had started, in the foyer. Eccentricities aside, Graceland Too was an awe-inspiring primitive archive. The Macleods were like monks, willing to endure poverty, stress, even ridicule, in their devotion to Elvis Presley. Although they could easily retire for life by liquidating the rarest collectibles on display at Graceland Too, they would have scoffed at the suggestion. Theirs was a higher mission. And an expensive one, too. Proceeds from the $5 admission to Graceland Too ("Lifetime membership and free admission after three visits!") hardly covered daily overhead.

With Elvis studies coming into prominence as academia cast a wider and wider net, I wondered if some smart university might become a silent partner and help with operating expenses, preservation, security. Fetzer, whose big-brother complex was fully activated, had a few ideas—grant applications, letters to southern studies scholars, fee minimums for media sharks like Geraldo.

Macleod listened to Fetzer's dissertation eagerly, but without much notion of what to do about it. Beyond the strict boundaries of Elvis country, Paul Macleod was a naif.

Fetzer seemed to be reaching for some way to express his esteem and awe at what this simple man had accomplished. Words weren't doing it for Fetzer; he needed a gesture. Impulsively he began to strip off his uniform. "Look here, Paul, I want to give you this. I want you to have it. I can't give you the badge, but I can give you everything else."

Macleod was bug-eyed. "Oh my, that's something, all right! Are you sure?"

"Just don't tell Graceland where you got it."

"Lord, I've died and gone to heaven. Thank you so much. Are you sure?"

"I'm sure. You deserve it more than me. I wish I could give you the badge too, but I can't do that yet. That would really land me in deep doo-doo."

Young Elvis ambled in, a 32-ounce Coke in his hand.

"Look at this. He's donating it," said Paul and held the shirt up.

Cooler emotionally than his dad, Elvis still radiated the thrill of a major acquisition. "I've got the perfect display case for it."

"There you go; next time you're down here it'll be pheasant under glass. But now, I sure as heck don't want you to get in any trouble—"

"Don't you worry about it. The laundry lost it, okay?"

First light was a muted purple when we pulled into Graceland. Fetzer had me drop him in the employee's lot, as close as possible to the security gate, where he could sprint to his car.

"I don't want anybody to see me running around half-naked the same night the laundry lost my uniform."

He waved good-bye and ran from car to car, like a lumbering commando, in his sleeveless underwear.

Turning left into Elvis Presley Boulevard, I pulled over in front of the mansion. The floodlit facade, with its eerie familiarity, looked like a movie set. The nocturnal Elvis would have just been turning in for the night now, as everywhere else in Memphis, ordinary folks were beginning to jerk awake to the buzzing or clanging of their alarm clocks, sounds The King probably never heard in his life, certainly not after 1955.

Back in Holly Springs, Paul and Elvis Macleod might well be grabbing a few winks on the floor until the first morning visitors banged at their door. This very second, all around the planet, Elvis fans would be getting up or going to bed, eating, sleeping, making love, all the while inserting Elvis CDs, tapes, and records into the collective consciousness of the world. Writers were writing about Elvis dreamers dreaming about Elvis. The dying were saying good-bye to his still strong earthly presence. Comedians were devising new Elvis jokes. Young girls were falling in love with his image on their screens, his voice in their hearts. Collectors were dusting, polishing, rearranging their private or public shrines. Elvis picnics, dinners, parties, dances were in full swing. Future Elvis events were being planned. Impersonators were concocting ways to add some extra sizzle to their acts. Elvis *was* everywhere.

Idling my rental car at the still, silent center of Elvis's universe, I tried to imagine the alternate reality he lived in, barely conceivable to someone who lived a relatively ordinary life in a more or less normal world.

I wished at that moment I could share his consciousness for only thirty seconds. Maybe fifteen would do.

But Elvis had left the building, though the rest of us were still here, still, in our various ways (as I certainly was), dancing to his tune.

Chapter

18

Once my spring semester grades were in, I had to face the fact that I hadn't yet logged a single performance as Elvis— even though in just over three months, I would be standing on a stage in Memphis, a contestant in the big one. Making my tape had been challenging enough, but the only other human being present that night had been Col. Todd—who thought the whole thing was a goof anyway. And the recording process itself had built-in safety nets: you mess up, you stop and start over. As I had learned from karaoke, live performance is a high-wire act: once you step on the tightrope, you can only go forward—or fall off. Singing around the house or in the car wouldn't do it. I had to go to the next step.

"And now here he is, give it up for William . . . McCranor . . . HENDERSON*!"*

I had a rough plan: I would debut with Rick Marino's Elvis weekend in Jacksonville. Then, once we headed north to Rhode Island for the summer, I would arrange a few other live appearances in New England. By the time August rolled around, I would be seasoned, confident, practiced, and ready for Memphis. Whistling in the dark? Perhaps. But I had a silly faith in all sorts of X factors that would com-

pensate for my lack of raw Elvis-ness. I had always been a quick study:
I could pull it off.

I started to plan my trip to Jacksonville. I needed a bodyguard—
not so much to protect my body as to provide emotional support. My
cousin Larry was up for the adventure, as I had hoped he would be. Savannah was a convenient stop along the way to Jacksonville Beach,
where the fan fair was to be held at the Days Inn.

"What do I have to do?" Larry asked when I phoned him.

"Plan my entry and exit routes. Check out the stage. Be ready for
trouble."

"I see."

"And better bring your gun."

"Excuse me? I think we're about to be cut off—"

"Just kidding. Forget the gun. Mostly I need somebody in my corner. I know it may sound like a complete lark on my part, but there's a
real fear component here. I sometimes wake up in sweats over this."

"You're saying you need someone to wrestle you on stage if you
chicken out or go catatonic."

"Or off stage, if that's what it takes."

"I'm your man."

Larry's problem was that, as a federal prosecutor, he was at the
beck and call of judges and court schedules. A major case was looming
and, as he told me, if the judge set the Monday following our weekend
as Day One, he was out of the picture—a prospect that filled me with
unease.

Meanwhile, I was struggling with the lyrics and coming to grips
with one of the prime unpleasant truths of middle age: the old memory machine isn't what it used to be. Unexpected gaps appear in pre-
viously memorized material. You no longer trust yourself to memorize
an address, a phone number. You struggle all semester to place names
with faces in the classroom, only to blank them all out as the new semester starts. Perfectly obvious names—George Gershwin, say, or

Benedict Arnold—become temporarily inaccessible. And as for memorizing new material, like song lyrics, well—as a 45ish singer-songwriter of my acquaintance told me, "The only songs I really trust myself on are the ones I learned before I was 30."

What made it particularly insidious in my case was the *illusion* that I knew certain songs because I had heard them all my adult life. Elvis standards like "Don't Be Cruel" or "Heartbreak Hotel" had been part of my programming since adolescence. I seemed to be able to sing along with the recordings flawlessly. New material also had a comforting familiarity to it, since I had so recently listened to it all over and over again. This too set up a kind of false confidence.

"You should really perform all this stuff for us," Carol suggested, "Make sure you can get through it."

"Oh, I know I could get through it for you guys. It's stage fright I'm worried about. Going on and blanking totally. No amount of practice runs can guard against that."

"I'm not sure I agree." Carol had been a modern dancer in Boston and New York and had extensive performing experience. I should have listened to her. In my characteristic way, I had it all reasoned out, like the French, based not on reality but on an intellectual notion, some linguistic formulation that I had concocted. Looking back, I can see it as a clear rationalization of performance anxiety. Squatting in my unconscious like a toad was the fear that if I couldn't get through it for my own family, I risked an onset of general panic—fear of failure might rise up like a dark tsunami and drown my confidence altogether, swamp the entire project. I would have to give my advance back. I would lose face with my kids, my agent, my friends, with whom I had been flip about the possibility of failure. ("If I flop? No problem—that's the beautiful part about this project: anything goes, it's all grist for the mill. If I make an ass of myself, so be it—that's what the book will be about.")

But no: that's *not* what I wanted the book to be about. Deep down, I desperately wanted to be good. I wanted to stride on stage, in front of a band, as I had watched Elvis do a hundred times on video, take control of an audience, win their confidence, put on a show—*deliver*.

But wouldn't failure make a better story, a funnier, more entertaining story? George Plimpton's four snaps with the Lions had been ignominious disasters (he was lucky to come out of it alive). If he had thrown a 30-yard touchdown pass, would *Paper Lion* have been a better book? Wouldn't such a freak surprise have blurred his basic working premise (that of Everyman, going naked into the Land of Giants)?

Whatever the case, the big weekend approached without my having gotten around to a full practice run. "I'll be okay," I assured Carol, in full denial. "I know the basic five or six, and I'll practice on the drive down, or I'll go through it for Larry in the hotel room. Don't worry. I'll be fine."

The call I was waiting for came from Larry: "I'm all set. I told the judge I had to guard an Elvis impersonator, and he rearranged the court calendar for the entire federal district."

"Don't forget your lyric sheets," called Carol, as I pulled the car out.

"I really won't need them."

"Take them along anyway, okay?" She ran to the car with the two little booklets that had come with the karaoke CDs.

My lip went up, Elvis style: "Bye-bye, baby. Kiss the kids for me."

"And don't spend a lot of money on Elvis junk at this thing!"

Larry and I arrived at Jacksonville beach on a hot bright June day. As we entered the lobby of the Days Inn, a large poster assured us that "Elvis Is In the Building."

There was a stack of fliers at the check-in desk:

JACKSONVILLE'S SIXTH ANNUAL

ELVIS PRESLEY CONVENTION AND RECORD SHOW

PRESENTED BY "ELVIS ALWAYS FAN CLUB, INC."

SPECIAL GUEST NANCY WALTERS—SHE STARRED AS MISS PRENTISS,
THE SCHOOLTEACHER WITH ELVIS IN *BLUE HAWAII*

ENTERTAINMENT: HERO'S OCEANFRONT LOUNGE

• "MR. SHOWMAN HIMSELF . . . RICK MARINO

• PRIZES

• CONTEST

• ELVIS MOVIES

. . . PLUS MANY OTHER SURPRISES!

PROCEEDS TO NORTHEAST FLORIDA LUPUS FOUNDATIONS, INC.

I supposed I was one of the "surprises."

I could see that the event was based on a microcosm of the standard Elvis impersonator ecosystem: an Elvis Presley fan club (in this case the Elvis Always Fan Club, Inc., of Folkston, Georgia, just across the state line) has a "convention" in a motor hotel; vendors of Elvis souvenirs, memorabilia, and records set up booths in the ballroom; a famous friend or associate of Elvis attends as an honored guest; the club's favorite Elvis impersonator puts on a show (often the club doubles as the impersonator's official fan club); a portion of the proceeds goes to an officially designated charity. This basic paradigm is repeated everywhere, from the humblest small-town fan get-togethers right up to the major Tribute Week extravaganzas in Memphis, involving top vendors, massive foot traffic, big-name friends of Elvis (Charlie Hodge, D. J. Fontana, the Jordanaires, J. D. Sumner and the Stamps), and civvy-clad "Elvis entertainers" (often vocal impersonator Ronnie MacDowell or ex-impersonator Terry Mike Jeffrey, who provide Elvis music purged of the Elvis-made-flesh illusion).

Rick Marino, who makes no bones about being "an Elvis impersonator, period," had told me emphatically, in one of our phone calls: "*I—am—an—Elvis—impersonator*, okay? And I'm PROUD of it. I'm not ashamed of it. I don't say I'm an 'invoker' or I'm an Elvis this or that—I'm an Elvis impersonator, period. Ain't no getting around that. A lot of the guys have a problem with that word: we're Elvis performers, we're

Elvis entertainers, illusionists, invokers, whatever— Well, you know what? You're an Elvis *impersonator*. There's nothing wrong with that word. And the bottom line is that, if you do it properly, you won't get laughed at, you won't get ridiculed, people will respect you. Because the only way they're ever going to experience what it was like to actually see Elvis is through an Elvis impersonator . . . through what you do. That's something to think about, ain't it?"

Larry and I checked in and went for a swim in the ocean, then ordered hamburgers and beer at the poolside grill. We fell into conversation with a young guy whom I pegged as one of the Elvis people (perfect black hair, sideburns). He had spotted my TCB cap from Memphis and gave me a nod. It turned out he was a vendor himself. He remarked on the authenticity of the touring patch.

"I'm surprised you found that in Memphis," he said, in a New York accent. "You can't get stuff like that at the official Graceland shops anymore. They want just the appearance of authenticity, nothing more. Real fans have to go somewhere else for the good stuff."

We went looking for Rick, who was rumored to be somewhere on the premises. I realized I wasn't sure what he looked like. Every picture I had of him gave him a different image—tall, skinny, plump, older, younger—and in the brief clip from TBS's *Night of 100 Elvises*, he had been shot from the shoulder up, a talking head, hidden behind dark glasses.

At the desk, they thought he might be back in the vendor area. One of the vendors said he had just headed for the restaurant. In the restaurant, a huge bullet-headed short-order cook told us to try the bar: "He's arguing with my boss, Kermit the Frog."

Sure enough, at the far end of the bar, two men sat on barstools, in the midst of an intense exchange. One of them bore a distinct resemblance to the famous Muppet. By process of elimination, the other had to be my man. Rick was wearing shorts and a tank top over his powerful wrestler's shoulders. He looked younger than he had on TBS, a 30-ish beachcomber. Nothing about him said Elvis.

Whatever the argument was about, it seemed to reach an impasse. "Well, to hell with you, then—!" Rick spun around on his barstool.

Larry and I, waiting like anxious courtiers, seemed to present a welcome diversion.

"Got to go, man," he said to Kermit, who squatted on his stool and glowered into a half-finished beer. "Got to talk to these good folks."

I introduced us. "We're not intruding, I hope?" I said.

"Heck no, this jerk is just one of the minus-side items we have to deal with, that's all. The world's full of every type and he's kind of playing out his miserable role, you know what I mean? The Lord just didn't give him too much to start with. But we can work around that. How about you, man? Got your suit all ready?"

An anvil fell on my head: though I was sure I had my wig and sunglasses, I had no specific memory of placing the suit in the car. Gadzooks! What a magnificent act of super-denial that would be, to leave the jumpsuit at home!

"Sure, sure," I said.

"Well, here's what we're going to do: a show tonight with a band, just an informal kind of preconvention set mostly for my friends, family, all that. Tomorrow afternoon you can work the other room, with the other impersonators. Then tomorrow night's my big show, with my tapes and bodyguards and all. Meanwhile I've got to persuade the manager here to pay my damn band and loosen up on room charges for my fan club people, which includes you. I tell you, man, if I had known I was gonna have so much trouble with this guy, this Kermit the Frog, I never would've picked this venue. We're paying good money and bringing people in his damn club, and he acts like he's doing us a favor. Well, you know what? I ain't going to make any more fuss. Just when it comes up next year, this guy's out. No way we'd come back here, man!"

His mood brightened as he swept us into the convention hall, introducing us around to the various vendors, to the president of the

Elvis Always Fan Club, and to Nancy Walters, of *Blue Hawaii*. Ms. Walters was now a statuesque middle-aged lady, who in the years since Hollywood had become an evangelical minister. She was selling her own devotional tapes and had a stack of them on her table. I thought about another of Elvis's costars, Delores Hart, the achingly beautiful young actress who had become a nun after two Elvis movies (and was now mother superior of a cloistered convent in Connecticut). I remarked aloud how ironic it seemed that two of Elvis's on-screen opposites "took the veil." One of the fan club ladies chimed in with a perfect anti-ironic rejoinder: "Maybe Elvis just led them to goodness."

A quick search of our room and the car confirmed to my horror that I had, like an idiot, left my jumpsuit home. Whatever self-destruct sce-

Calling home for my lost jumpsuit.
(Photo courtesy of Larry Lee.)

nario was going on inside my twisted psyche, I had to override it and get back on track. I phoned Carol immediately and arranged to have her FedEx it down—priority, Saturday Delivery. I picked five songs and had Larry listen, correcting me, prompting me, as I sang through them.

"How do I sound?"

"Fine. Fine. Elvis sounds maybe . . . oh, lower."

"Lower?" I remembered Olivia's judgment: *You don't sound like Elvis, you sound like Daddy.*

"Deeper, I guess . . . guttier. You might call it . . . Elvis Lite."

I felt suddenly defensive. "Well, I'm not performing, after all; I'm just sitting here in the motel room. I mean, Elvis himself probably sounded a little 'Lite' when he was practicing lyrics in the motel room."

"Of course. Of course."

Lite? What was he saying? Lightweight? No charisma . . . ?

I began to blank on the simplest lyrics.

"Come on," I said, after stumbling one time too many. "Let's go have a few drinks and enjoy the damned show."

Dinner at Hero's (done to order by the bullet-headed cook, whose nickname was Top Job) was awful—pink chicken à la king, sodden broccoli, leather potatoes.

"Should we complain?"

"Complain to that guy? He might come out and finish us off with a wok chopper."

But things brightened up after a few scotches (Larry, the law enforcement professional, stuck to seltzer and lime) and by the time the band came on for their warm-up set, I was feeling super.

Our early arrival had gotten us ringside seats. The rest of the room filled up with Rick Marino fans, friends, family, and convention characters. I hailed the vendor I had been chatting with earlier, but since I was now capless, he had trouble recognizing me, because of the prominence of my near-bald head. This, I found, would be a constantly recurring event (often a blessed convenience) in my tricksterish transformations into and out of the Elvis persona: bewigged, I was, for all practical purposes, Elvis; without wig (or in this case, *sans* cap) I was invisible enough to walk through walls.

The band, a quartet of C&W pros, finished their opening set and on strode Rick, to an improvised "Also Sprach Zarathustra" intro. This was his "informal" show. He wore a nonstandard brownish Edwardian jacket and joked easily with the crowd, most of whom he knew. On "Teddy Bear" he lofted handfuls of tiny stuffed bears into the audience. On the talking part of "Are You Lonesome Tonight" he clowned it up, changing the words and aiming them at his grandmother, at a front table: "Then my little body changed, I acted strange, and why? . . . Hey, you couldn't figure it out, could you, Grandma?" (I would later discover that monkeying around with the talk section of this song is a standard impersonator ploy.) He didn't like the way he ended "Hurt"—so he backed the band up, circled the runway, and ended it again.

"He's loose!" Larry commented.

And he was. Loose, warm, spontaneous—a charmer. The ease with which he moved through his show humbled me and cut sharply into my grandiose fantasy of the full-set show I would someday wow a crowd with. Rick made a nice speech, plugging the convention, mentioning especially the vendors—"These people are the real heroes." ("How Great We Art," I heard one of them quip.) Then it was into the standard live-show closer, "Can't Help Falling in Love," and he was off.

It was an abbreviated show, but—as Rick emphasized out in the lobby afterward—only an hors d'oeuvre, a taste of what was to come tomorrow night. "Man, I screwed up bigtime on 'Hurt.' Trouble is, I'm not singing enough. I usually do 75 shows a year, but sometimes too much time goes by. If I sang more than twice a week, I could really whizz it."

As Rick schmoozed with his fans, I thought I spotted a familiar figure: a short, tough-looking guy in a red tour jacket. He was hanging back slightly from the action, his eyes scanning the lobby like an automatic camera.

"Excuse me. Didn't I see you on the 100 Elvises thing from Vegas?"

His eyes refocused on me. "Yep. Joe Butler. How you doin'?"

"You're Rick's chief of security, right?"

"That's right, you got it," said Joe Butler, pleased to be recognized. His strong-silent demeanor gave way immediately to a chatty intensity, although his eyes never stopped their periodic scans of the room. "I been with Rick five years. I used to have my own martial arts school, then I was selling carpeting for a while. Now it's satellites. Direct TV satellite systems. But this is what I really love. You can say I'm a Red West impersonator, I like that. We just keep it cool, sometimes you need a strong arm. Once a guy attacked me with a hunting knife, cut me right here. I rearranged him a little bit. I carry a gun, but I never had to use it yet. You never know where it's coming from. A preacher's wife pulled a 10-inch blade on me one time—I could've beat her down with my gun but I just talked her out of it: you know, come on, let's grow up. My role is just, come on, guys, life's too short for this, let's be grown-ups, we're just not going to have any trouble, okay?"

Bodyguards had been a way of life for Elvis. Cronies like Red West, a high school friend, were like disciples; they devoted their lives to serving and protecting Elvis (for very little pay, but unbelievable benefits), but sometimes overdid it—in Vegas, Red beat a man so viciously that the result was a multimillion-dollar lawsuit. Red, the most prominent bodyguard, was let go by Elvis's father. In retaliation, he wrote the first of the scandalous tell-all books, and fans believe to this day that its publication, two weeks before Elvis died, hastened The King's demise. All of which goes to reinforce the notion that, with fans, groupies, followers, and devotees, a fine line separates love from resentment and betrayal. Even Judas started as a devotee. Charlie Hodge was not a bodyguard but the original scarf-and-water man. The ideal impersonator "bodyguard," in my opinion, would be a combination of the best of Red West and Charlie Hodge.

My suit arrived in the late morning (we had slept in and were awakened by a call from the front desk). Now I had suit, wig, and shades—no excuses. But one sartorial detail I had never taken care of was the shoes. Elvis wore a certain kind of shiny white ankle boot, with a zipper up the inside. I was sure any shoe department would have a cheap knock-off version, but I had put off the search.

"Wal-Mart," Larry suggested, after three shoe stores had yielded no results.

Wal-Mart indeed had a vast array of knockoffs, but no white ankle boots.

It was already noon. Back on the convention floor, a DJ was setting up his sound system for the walk-on Elvises. My nervousness was mounting.

"We could head into Jacksonville," said Larry.

"No, it's almost show time. I'd better settle for the closest approximation."

"White sneaks?"

"White sneaks."

The DJ was a tall, laid-back young singer-guitarist in a broad felt western hat. Full mutton chops gave him that "urban-cowboy" look that you used to see a lot back in the 70s. He had set up a sound system at the stage end of the ballroom and was tinkering with his microphones.

Everywhere else in the room, the fan fair, like an Elvis flea market, was in full swing. Customers browsed and crowded around the booths, and the vendors seemed to be doing brisk business.

Larry merged into the flow of foot traffic, and I lost him. I saw a couple of other Elvises lurking near the stage area, both younger than I and fully costumed—they could probably Elvis me right out of the building. But so what? I kept reminding myself that I was just a virgin Elvis, just a walk-on: expectations should be set at zero. *Come on,* my mind yapped at itself, *just have fun with it.*

The DJ (I had been told his name was Jeff) had a smooth unflappable demeanor and was completely unfazed when approached by this self-declared Elvis impersonator who looked more like Steve Martin's balding brother-in-law.

"You got your tape?"

"My tape?" I said. "You mean, back-up tapes?"

"Yeah. Your tape."

"Well, I mean—I've got these CDs . . ."

"Pocket Songs?"

"Yes. You Sing the Hits—"

"I've got those too. But you don't have your own tape?"

It hit me what he was talking about: I should have dubbed off the three or four numbers I planned to sing. Made my own custom tape. Another lapse. Another act of unconscious self-obstruction. I was a walking case history for subversion of purpose. Well, too late now.

"Guess I don't."

"No problem. Just tell me what you want to sing, and I'll wing it with the CDs."

"Well . . . let's see. 'Teddy Bear,' 'Don't Be Cruel,' 'Can't Help Falling in Love' . . ."

"That's all?"

"I think that'll be enough."

Larry had linked up with a man who seemed to have about twenty cameras hanging from his shoulders. "This is Jack Luedke from the *Times-Union*. He's covering the convention."

"Yes, I understand you're a professor?—and an Elvis impersonator?"

"Ah—yes."

"If you don't mind, I'd like to come with you guys when you change into your suit. Take a series of pictures. You know, cover the transfiguration?"

Larry had stepped back and was enjoying the moment—his handiwork, his mischief. I hesitated. I was Rick's guest here. Publicity might seem a little brazen, after all.

"Sure," Larry beamed at the photographer, "glad to have you, glad to have you."

Up in the room, it felt like "*Life* Goes to an Elvis Impersonation" as Jack Luedke snapped away at his photo essay. I stepped into the suit, like a toddler into his Doctor Dentons, and zipped it up. The wig went on (Larry had to black out a couple of spots where gray peeked through). The shades completed the "transfiguration"—functionally, too, as they kept the sideburns from skewing out at a silly angle.

We emerged into the long open breezeway that led to the elevators, me and my entourage—bodyguard and photographer leading me. Luedke, waddling backward, crabwise, fired off his camera again and

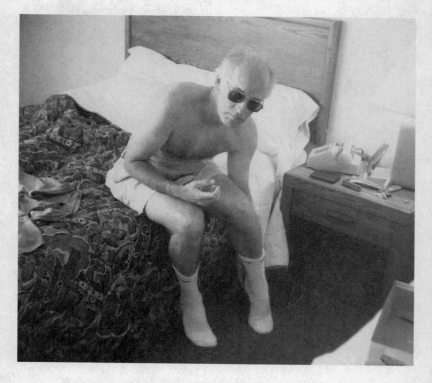

Pre-show jitters: could this whole fiasco be . . .
(Photo courtesy of Larry Lee.)

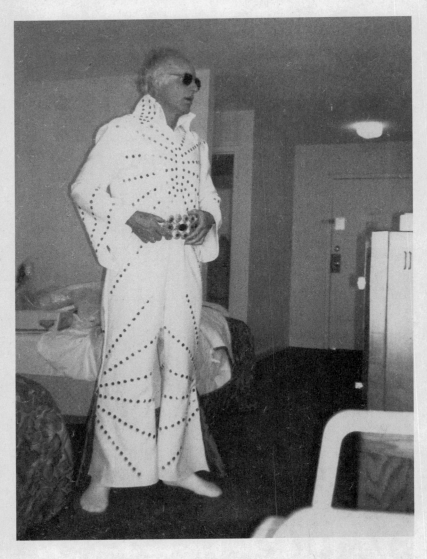

. . . a ghastly mistake?
(Photo courtesy of Larry Lee.)

again. I felt myself stand tall, walk with an indefinable air of gravity—nobility? Yes, nobility! It was almost like the progress of a royal figure. Could this be the beginning of charisma, the source of it: a *feeling* that one is, in all ways, more formidable a presence?

We passed two black housekeepers who kept a straight face. However, the maintenance man chatting with them, an Eddie Murphy lookalike, lost it entirely, and dissolved into fits of muffled giggles.

A mother and child waited for the elevator along with us. The kid looked up at me with panic. "It's just Elvis, honey," said the mommy. When the doors opened on the lobby floor, we drew an array of reactions—all the way from studied nonchalance to back-slapping cordiality. I was getting anxious to enter the fan fair, where, among the Elvis people anyway, I would be a standard, well-accepted icon, not a freak.

One of the Elvises was just wrapping up his set. He was Rusty Dickerson, a portly hospital security officer in a black jumpsuit. He knew what he was doing, and he was serious: I had seen him arriving at the motel with his wardrobe—several different jumpsuits hanging from a rolling chrome clothes rack. He finished strong.

In the lull following, I made a decision: "Give me the damned lyric books," I said to Larry. It represented a defeat, of course, but I wasn't going to go through the nightmare of blanking miserably in front of an audience. Jeff introduced me. As I took the mike, I knew I had made the right decision: suddenly I couldn't remember a single line, a single word. I wasn't even sure which song I had decided to sing first.

" 'Teddy Bear,' " Jeff whispered from the control panel. Some curious onlookers dragged up chairs. Two wheelchair-bound Elvis fans rolled up, ready to rock. I could see Rick, in his beachcomber casuals, at the rear of the ballroom.

"Well, folks," I croaked into the mike. "Here's the deal: to get up here, I sent Rick Marino a tape of me singing three songs, and he told me the first cut was not bad, the second was worse, and the third a disaster. So that's what we've got to work with here. I hope you don't mind if I have to read off the lyrics—at least it's a step up from lip sync-ing."

"Sing!" somebody yelled.

Jeff punched a button and pointed his cue finger at me. The rest is mostly a blur.

I remember the wheelchair people (bless them) whooping with enthusiasm as I announced each song.

I remember the strange sound of my own voice, warmed up with reverb, coming back at me disembodied from the floor-level monitor speakers.

I remember trying (and failing miserably) to flip the pages of the lyric sheet with my microphone hand.

There was plenty I would prefer to forget. But most of all, I re-member the few odd moments when things were going okay, when the voice coming back from the monitors was . . . well, *reasonable*. Discounting the fumbling, the flop sweat, the ignominy of having to read the lyrics (and *still* managing to screw them up), I ended up en-couraged, sensing a potential in my attitude, if nothing else: I COULD DO THIS THING, I felt, in the occasional moments when everything clicked. Sure I had a long way to go, much to learn, but I could do it; I could be my own personal-best Elvis.

Suddenly I was aware of Larry standing next to a TV news cam-eraman who had taped the whole thing. As I finished "Can't Help Falling in Love," (to first-ever applause!) Larry whispered in my ear, "Come on, you've got to work the house." With the TV camera follow-ing, I went from booth to booth, shaking hands, saying Elvis-type things ("How you doin' today, sir?") and receiving not contempt, but warm vibes from the Elvis people—who apparently gave me points for just standing up there, no matter what the outcome.

"I thought you sounded great," said one woman. "You go tell Rick Marino to shut his face."

I stopped to say hi to my vendor buddy, who once again didn't rec-ognize me (surely Elvis would be the ideal Witness Protection Program

Getting through it at Jacksonville Beach-song lyrics clutched in hand.
(Photo courtesy of Larry Lee.)

disguise!), and finally ended my progress at a booth where Rick and his wife, Susie, a tall, pretty blonde, were hanging out.

"You're going to have to do something about that white chest hair," said Susie, staring at my zipped-up thorax. "That zipper ought to be open at least down to your solar plexus."

"Down to your belly button," said Rick.

Nothing was said about my ignominious performance, thank goodness. Rick took up the slack by telling stories: "One night I played a show same night as Elvis, in the same town, and we sold out, too! Now go figure that one!" He plunked a video into a nearby VCR: it was his benefit performance for the mayoral candidate, "with my big band"— a 13-piece show band with a full complement of back-up singers. At one point in the tape he called his dad up on stage, a rugged, white-haired gent in a black bodyguard jacket. "This man was my hero," said Rick to the audience. "I used to watch him sing with bands when I was five!" The old guy did a vigorous rendition of "My Way," with stiff but professional gestures, switching the mike from hand to hand, reliving the old moves.

Suddenly I was drained, enervated. I wanted desperately to sit down somewhere, but my only immediate option was the floor. "Can you tell me what you're doing here?" asked the TV cameraman, pointing his mike at me. I gave what I thought was a pretty good condensed 30-second description of my project, emphasizing my complete virgin status as a performer, the irony of my academic connection and so on. When the cameraman had had enough, I motioned to Larry and we were out of there, avoiding the lobby, up a little-used rear breezeway and into the protective womb of the room. Without changing, I fell back on my bed and slept.

Later, at six, Larry shook me awake. Channel 5 was leading off its news hour with footage (silent) of me singing, working the house, shaking hands with Rick.

"I wonder why they didn't use my statement? I thought it wasn't bad."

Larry, who once worked in radio and is media savvy, pointed out that I went on too long. "Thirty seconds makes work for them—they have to edit it. Give them a solid, self-contained eight-second byte and they'll fall on it like a fumble."

Oh well, for a few seconds, at least, my silent image gave me a flicker of evanescence throughout greater Jacksonville, Florida. As drownings, train wrecks, and convenience store murders took over the newscast, I lay back against the skimpy motel pillows and was almost instantly asleep again.

Rick's Saturday night began with a Shake Like Elvis contest (which I did *not* enter). A swarthy gigolo type got up on stage and swung and swayed to the music, but he was beaten out by a wiry fellow in a business suit, who whipped off his jacket and amazed the crowd by skittering around the stage in a kind of supercharged jitterbug that resembled Elvis in the wildest of his rock-out teen frenzies, those old black-and-white TV showcases that had turned a generation of Bing Crosby–bred parents against him forever.

At last, after a melodramatic buildup ("Ladies and gentlemen, we've received word that The King is in the building!") Rick made a gladiatorial entrance, flanked by Joe Butler and three other burly bodyguards.

This time Rick was resplendent in white—perhaps a little porky (he admitted to me later that he needed to go on a weight-loss plan), but who cared about that when it was assumed that the Vegas Elvis had always been fat? The remarkable fact was that he took over and drove the show with an assurance that, to me—after my timid showing of the afternoon—was almost incomprehensible.

Most important, he was able to reach out and pull in everything around him, making it a part of his show. For instance, to deal with the anomaly of a solitary Elvis, alone on stage (Elvis always made certain his band and back-up singers—cronies as well as collaborators—were only a few feet away), he stationed his bodyguards around him, in a four-corners formation, and interacted with them as he had with his band the night before.

During one ballad, Joe Butler's wife, Judy, ran on stage with a bouquet of roses for Rick. When the two settled into a sexy slow dance, Joe stormed over, mugging and miming the jealous husband.

Later, after tossing about 30 mini–teddy bears into the audience, Rick got sentimental and dedicated "Always On My Mind" to Susie, who was still out in the lobby collecting fees. Someone ran to get her and she joined him onstage, a bit flustered, as he cuddled her gently, placed his hand on her abdomen and announced, "We got one in the oven, folks. Tonight, right here, is the first time I ever sung to my *baby*!"

Throughout the show, he never let his bond with the audience cool down. He was there for them; they were clamoring to get at him. Rick closed with "Unchained Melody," allegedly the last song Elvis ever sang, a soaring, operatic rendition with big moments that the audience

Rick Marino "whizzing" a high note while bodyguard Joe Butler scans the crowd.
(Photo courtesy of William McCranor Henderson.)

received like a bullfight crowd reacting to flourishes of the matador's cape. Tonight, I had to say, he "really whizzed it." And in doing so, he had defined the chasm that lay between my own silly attempt and his solid triumph.

Ironically, we had made the Sunday papers: a nice color shot of Larry fussing with my coiffure. I looked relaxed and confident, although the telltale lyric sheet clutched in my hand betrayed the reality.

TEACHER IS KING FOR A DAY, read the caption. "First-time Elvis impersonator Bill Henderson of Chapel Hill, N.C., reviews some lyrics in his hotel room before his debut performance at the Days Inn Oceanfront Resort at Jacksonville Beach. His cousin, Larry Lee of Savannah, Ga., helps with the wig and hair coloring."

Over breakfast, Larry had a few observations to venture: "You were on key, that's something. You weren't all that bad, really. But you might work on sounding a little more like Elvis and a little less like Bill Henderson." (There it was, the "daddy-voice" syndrome again.)

"Well, how the hell do I go about that?"

"You got me there: you're the Elvis impersonator, I'm just the bodyguard."

It was too deep for me. I was licking my wounds and casting a baleful eye toward the rest of the summer. Larry was trying to be kind and helpful, but he realized as well as anyone how royally I had screwed up.

But I could do better. I *would* do better. I didn't want to write a book wherein I executed one pratfall after another. Yes, admit it: I wanted to be as heroic as I had the stuff to be. I wanted to stand up, without apologies, in the holy city of Memphis, in possession of my own little piece of Elvis-ness, tiny though it may be, and really whizz it.

I had a little over three months to pull it off.

Chapter

19

ow the scene shifted.

Summer had returned and we were due back in Rhode Island, where Miriam, my agent, had originally contacted me with the first breath of this Elvis project; it would be there that I would base my final preparations for the foray into Memphis.

Carol and I had a history in New England. We had met in Boston, twenty years back, when she was an itinerant dancer and I played electric fiddle for John Lincoln Wright. John was still an active presence on the New England music scene. As a matter of fact, I had just recently written him a letter, explaining what I was up to, and—without any idea whether he would shoot the notion down or recommend psychiatric treatment—I asked if he might consider letting me sit in with his present group of musicians (he always had good bands) and, er . . . do my Elvis. I hadn't heard anything in return, but I refused to let that bode ill: John tended to take his time getting around to things.

Meanwhile we trekked north lavishly, in two cars—there were six of us, counting dogs, and I would need my own car, come August, for the drive south to Memphis. Olivia drove with me and we listened to Elvis all the way. This gave me a chance to observe how a 10-year-old, with musical roots that didn't go back much further than Ace of Base was taking to The King. And in fact, he was growing steadily on her.

Her favorite number (Colette's too) was "The Impossible Dream," the showstopper from *Man of LaMancha* that Elvis had added to his arsenal of power ballads. She had me write out the words for her. When I did, I realized it's a song of youthful idealism, hope, blind faith, optimism, commitment, struggle for the good, the pure. Of course they loved it! Elvis, the self-described comic book fantasy hero, must have loved it for the same reasons.

But Olivia was beginning to pick up on another Elvis, the quirky personality behind the Big Star. She said (always using the present tense), "Elvis is cool because he isn't two different people, on stage and off. He's the same."

"What do you mean cool?"

"You never know what he's going to do. I really used to think he was a dweeb. Then I started hearing you play his stuff over and over. And then I started playing it over and over myself. But Dad, you must admit—no offense—Elvis is weird."

"Weird?"

"Like when he sings 'shove it up your nose' right in the middle of that live version of 'Suspicious Minds.'"

"Yes, that is kind of weird."

"Like, really unpredictable. Unique. He's weird."

Olivia had tuned into Elvis in stages, just as I had. First, he was the "dweeb" or hick or hunk or whatever your initial take was. Next came respect as a performer (even if grudging). Next, more consciousness of zany or eccentric facets of his stage personality. Finally, if you heard enough of him, you ended up with (as I had) a fully developed sense of Elvis as a charismatic charmer, funny, sexy, dominant, passive, wacky, sentimental. Many listeners never got this far—certainly not those whose starting point was hostile. But I had discovered, in doing this work, something that scholars experience: the closer you get to a subject, the more faceted and esoteric your awareness of it becomes—

so much so that you have trouble speaking with ordinary people about it: *you know too much*.

Bringing my show to Rhode Island would be interesting. Carol's parents had retired there and her sister owned a summer house, where we stayed. We were part of a seasonal crowd there, going back over 15 years. The social tone, generally speaking, was what an English friend of mine had once called "county gentry." Elvis, if thought about at all, was regarded by our older-generation friends as distinctly alien and by most of our younger pals as a cornball in the same league with Liberace.

Olivia and I arrived in Wakefield before the others and opened up the house, a gray cedar-shingled old farmhouse surrounded with rock fences and meadows. Waiting on the phone table was a note, left there by Carol's father: *Call John Lincoln Wright*. I dropped everything and reached for the phone.

Contrary to my fears, John not only consented, he was *into* it.

"Anytime," he said. "Anytime. We'll have fun with it. We're not working a whole hell of a lot this summer. There's a July 4th show up in Clinton. We've got an outdoor show coming up in Medfield, on the green—that ought to be real nice, how about that?"

"That's great. When?"

"Next Friday. You ready?"

I swallowed. An outdoor show (I envisioned a hillside, or stadium, or speedway packed with thousands—a Lollopalooza, a Woodstock) . . . with John's band, The Sour Mash Boys. "*And here he is folks, our very, VERY special guest—The King of Rock 'n' Roll . . .*"

Friday . . . four days away. And there could be no reading lyrics this time.

"Sure. Absolutely. No problem."

"Come by and see me, if you can, and we'll talk about it."

I was aware John shared the standard notion about Elvis impersonators. "They're all crazy." But I had known him long enough to re-

alize he tended to headline his thinking with a broad-stroke general-
ization, then, when pressed, reveal subtler, more paradoxical perspec-
tives a layer or two below. In this case, before we hung up, he had
come around to something more dimensional:

"Actually, why shouldn't doing Elvis be just as honorable a performance choice as Hal Holbrook doing Mark Twain, or that guy that does
Truman Capote? Of course, there aren't a couple of thousand guys running around doing Twain or Capote all over the place, right? But what
do I know? I'm gonna clip an article from yesterday's *Globe* for you
where they're having some Elvis conference down at the University of
Mississippi. It's the same people who put on the Faulkner Conference
every year. And they've got multicultural Elvis impersonators lined
up—a Mexican, a black guy, an Asian, a woman. I mean, who knows
anything? Oh, by the way, I took your tape down to *Hillbilly at Harvard* and they put it on the radio. People called in. It's good. Especially
'All Shook Up'—did you know that was the first song I ever sang for
money? Twenty-five cents, age nine, won a talent show. I still do 'Love
Me.' It's one of my strongest numbers. Anyway, you really understand
what 'All Shook Up' is about, rhythmically. 'Uh-well-uh-bless-uh-mah
soul whatsa wrong with me . . .' What's not there yet is the undertone
of sexiness and meaning, that bottled up energy in every phrase."

I remembered T. J. Anderson's dictum: "More energy. Moment for
moment, he produced energy. You've got to infuse it with that same
level of energy."

"Anyway," John said, "you've had airplay in Boston. How many
Elvis impersonators can say that?"

When the van pulled in carrying the rest of my family, I greeted Colette, the dogs, and a slightly stunned Carol with powerful news: my
Elvis tape had been featured on the oldest continuous country-folk
radio program in the nation—and I had already lined up a live performance gig four days away.

Four days. Well, get the lyrics this time, stupid!

I heard that Van Morrison had just done a concert tour—and read the words to his own songs. The fact that he wrote them made no difference! You can blank out on your own creations just as quickly as you forget anything else.

My Pocket Songs prerecorded tracks were irrelevant, since I would be singing with a band. Theoretically, I could pick anything remotely familiar from the entire Elvis corpus. I listened to *As Recorded at Madison Square Garden* over and over, until I had finally made a provisional choice. I would open (as Elvis did at Madison Square Garden) with "That's All Right, Mama," follow that with Elvis's all-time biggest hit, "Heartbreak Hotel," then "All Shook Up," (which John seemed to think I had a handle on), then "Love Me," and then out with a rousing "Blue Suede Shoes."

It occurred to me John might be rehearsing the band. If so, it would be worth the hour-plus drive up I-95 to Boston to try out my miniset.

"Nah," John said when I phoned. "We're not going to rehearse between now and then. Everybody knows everything. Don't worry about it."

"Well, what about 'Love Me'? I mean, I don't want to poach on your material. Do you mind?"

"When The King is in the room, I defer."

Okay: so now it was just a matter of mnemonics and mechanics. Like Beethoven (who gave the appearance of madness), I took long, mumbling walks, mouthing lyrics until I could rattle them off in unbroken strings. To a casual observer, my behavior must have seemed over the edge. The kids followed along, mimicking me, so that we looked like some bizarre variation of the Coneheads—a family of aliens sent to earth programmed to chatter Elvis lyrics.

The second day, I made it harder by adding strategic distractions, like dribbling a basketball down the road or simultaneously reciting the Pledge of Allegiance. I shunned my family (or they shunned me, I wasn't sure which) until I finally felt comfortable with everything.

"Do you feel ready enough for us to have some people over, Elvis?" Carol asked.

"Absolutely."

It was impossible for the subject not to come up. Especially with *As Recorded at Madison Square Garden* on the stereo (full blast, thanks to the kids) as our dinner guests arrived.

"I just don't get it," said Ellen finally, after hearing me go on a bit. She parked her elbows nicely but there was trouble in her eyes. "These people go all over the place worshipping Elvis? They just pick up and go? Don't they have jobs?"

"Don't be so dense," said Natalie, who enjoyed arguing with Ellen. "Some people follow tennis, or golf, for God's sake—they subscribe to magazines, they seek out other nuts, they join clubs."

"Think of it as a hobby," said Ted, Ellen's husband, whose eternal role was that of interpreter between his wife and the world. "One of our vice presidents—remember Freddy Carlton?—he goes all over to Harley conventions."

"Or there's skydiving, or snow-boarding," said Hunter, a big tall slam-dunk of a guy who did most of these things himself. "Or Dead-heads—"

"Or Republicans," suggested Carol.

"All right, all right, but I don't care what you say—and this is nothing personal, Bill—there's just something weird about it."

The flashpoint was always there. Bring up Elvis—not to say Elvis *impersonators*—and the room suddenly filled with *attitude*. Terms like "these people" would start to enter the conversation, and there was the assumption of mindless cultists, who must also be tasteless low-class boobs.

In the previous day's mail I had received the summer newsletter from Images of Elvis, the contest folks in Memphis. In it, Doc's wife, Jackie Franklin, wrote the following: "We're still not sure that a lot of the publications about impersonators are not just an attempt at campy humor. The Elvis impersonators are shown as one-dimensional, kooky, no-life, obsessed dreamers, and this is the typical caricature that we are presented with any time an Elvis impersonator is portrayed. Well, we're mad as heck and we're not gonna take it anymore!" I thought of reading this to Ellen, but it wouldn't have changed her way of thinking; and anyway, I was trying to resist my impulse to be a St. Paul impersonator, sent to convert the gentiles of New England to some new warm-fuzzy acceptance of Elvis impersonators. I wasn't in this to change minds.

And if I were, I would start with those Elvis fans who themselves disparage impersonators. This, for example, from *Elvis International Forum*, Summer 1995: "Elvis impersonators are like dining at a real cheap restaurant; ninety-eight percent of the time it isn't worth it. The King was really unique and only the best impersonators can convey just a fraction of the charisma that he had. Yet some people ['these people'] feel at home around anything resembling The King. It was for this reason that people flocked to see *Honeymoon in Vegas*. Although the story was lame, the real Elvis was on the soundtrack and scores of false Elvises were sailing through the air." And so on.

Where was that coming from, I wondered, in a professed Elvis fan magazine?

But right now, I didn't have the luxury to care. Ellen was making noises about coming up to Medfield to "see what this was all about."

"Don't," I told her. "It may not be pretty."

"You sound like you expect the worst."

"It could happen."

Chapter
20

Medfield is a picturesque little old Massachusetts mill town, a suburb of Boston, but with a character of its own that seems imperturbably "historic." The Village Green concert was one of a season of free summer events staged in the broad expanse of lawn surrounding the original old mill and a brackish pond. We barreled up in the van, the whole family, on the edge of hysteria from having first witnessed a gruesome highway crash, then gotten hopelessly lost trying to find the town.

I had blacked out the gig to anyone beyond the immediate family circle, but I did call one friend, Bruce Lichtenstein, a videographer, who lived in Ashland, just one town over. "This is your chance to record history," I said.

"I'll come right over," said Bruce, "but I warn you: I'm on childcare duty and I can only last as long as my two-year-old."

"Don't worry. I'm bringing babysitters."

It was a stunning late afternoon, the kind of resoundingly golden atmospheric effect that you only see in New England, and rarely there. We circled the park and, noting where the flatbed stage was located, parked strategically at the rear edge of the green, about 50 yards from the stage. While Carol and the kids went off to buy a picnic supper, I joined John Lincoln Wright and the band, who were setting up their equipment.

John looked small and trim in his Acme boots, black leather pants, and summer cowboy hat.

"How're we going to do this?" I asked John, nerves building. "Is there someplace for me to change?"

"One of the Port-O-Johnnies, I guess. But that wouldn't do."

"Never mind, I can use the back of our van. When do I come on?"

"Second set. Four songs and I'll bring you up."

Bruce, who resembles a rounded David Letterman, arrived with a high-tech professional camcorder so tiny it looked like a sporty snapshot camera on a minitripod. He also had Kate, his two-year-old.

"This camera's total state-of-the-art High-8, special effects, hi-fi sound, great mike. Kate, however, is very low tech and completely unpredictable. I hope we're gonna make it through this."

Kate grinned up at me, showing a future of orthodontics and male conquests. "Where's Elvis?" she wanted to know.

"That's Elvis," said her dad.

She shook her head. "No way."

"You wait, kid," I said. "You wait."

The green was filling up with a sizable crowd: families on blankets, old folks in lawn chairs, preteens in little gangs, teens smoking in the bushes—a PG-rated crowd, spirited, but not rowdy. Olivia and Colette swept Kate away, as promised, into a pack of kids and dogs. It was showtime: John took the stage, opening his set with a coy mention of "an Elvis sighting." I listened for reaction; there was none.

"Relax," said Carol, when she saw me penning my song titles into my palm with a laundry marker (how else would I remember the order?). "This is perfect."

It was. As a performer, John had always struck me as a combination of Jim Morrison (the moves) and Merle Haggard (the sober authority). Showing his twenty-five years' experience, he handled the crowd adroitly with a mixture of funk, courtliness, and irony. A couple of dozen kids, mostly little girls, had gathered down front, and were doing impromptu dance-free stomps. But I was too jumpy to appreciate it—although I began to ease up as I got into John's set, which was the skilled work of an old master, with a superb pro band who would shortly be mine, all mine!

During the break, it hit me all over again how tough the nuts and bolts of this thing were going to be. The real Elvis had his logistics planned to the nth detail. John was busy selling his CDs to fans and couldn't be much help. I was on my own.

"John, when you get a second—"

"Hang on, I'm making money."

"Are you sure five songs isn't going to be too many?"

"I'll throw you off if I have to."

Over the expanse of dark village green I could see our white van. Everything had been said, really. I realized I was hanging onto John for security. It was time to go change. I walked through the gathering dusk alone, anonymous, and clambered into the van by the hatch door.

As a changing room our Voyager left a lot to be desired. I had thought I would have complete privacy. But knowing that I could easily lock myself into the rear of this monster, I kept the hatch cracked open. This, in turn, left the interior light on, and several curious passersby actually stopped to peek at me wriggling out of my clothes and into the jumpsuit. It was hot in there too, which made me sweat, complicating the change. And then, sweaty, bewigged and all, I realized I was trapped back there: I would have to stay hidden until time to go on, since once I appeared as The King, I couldn't just stand around.

The second set had started. After four songs I listened hard for John's intro— *Damn: he took another request*. I waited, then strained to hear again . . .

"Ladies and gentlemen, he's in the building somewhere . . . The King. The King of Rock 'n' Roll . . ."

Like an oxygen-starved diver, I burst out of the van, into the atmosphere, and strode, not too awfully fast—Elvis never moved fast—

toward the stage. Nearing it, I could hear: "Elvis . . . it's Elvis!" I climbed up onto the stage from the rear, slipping through the protective ropes like a boxer entering the ring. Feeling an unexpected wave of acceptance from the crowd, I mugged and posed, hamming it up while the band vamped expertly behind me. Encouraged, I even heard a distinct female scream (Carol, as she would tell me later). I felt good. There was just enough space for me, I was physically close to the band, and John's mike was waiting for me. Here goes nothin', I thought, grabbed the mike and jumped in: "*Well, that's all right, Mama, that's all right wit' you* . . ." And we were off.

It wasn't bad. It wasn't bad at all.

The mike was set for John's big, growly voice, so I could hear right away that I was a little underpowered (my everlasting problem) but it goaded me into singing louder, going for intensity, presence. The lyrics held in my head for the most part (the few scat jobs to cover bloopers were almost unnoticeable). The band could play this stuff in their sleep and knew exactly how to cover for me if I dropped a beat here or there.

My biggest problem was reading the song order off my hand. Wearing the official Elvis nonprescription shades, I was close to legally blind, which meant I spent a lot of time between songs staring at my palm—which must have looked to the audience like some bizarre self-hypnosis ritual. I'm not sure I ever got the order straight, but it didn't matter: the guys were as reliable as a jukebox. Whatever I called off, it was there.

Meanwhile, John Lincoln Wright had taken up a position near the front of the stage, from where he organized the girls—mostly in the seven- to nine-year-old-range—to cheer for me, which they did with ready gusto, as if somehow programmed in the womb to scream for Elvis.

During "Heartbreak Hotel" I made my one scarf move, tossing it into random space to flutter where it would. Two little girls snatched it simultaneously and wrestled over it, in the grass, just like grown-up

Vegas groupies. For the final verse I knelt at the edge of the stage, singing down to them, into the screams, and suddenly, through my myopic haze, there was my own Colette, jumping up and down and screaming with the others! They knew what to do, these little preteen versions of Elvisian maenads, and did it lightheartedly, with a touch of humor, the same way they would hug Barney or Mickey Mouse.

Time seemed to fly. John came onstage with me and made a duet out of "Love Me." Then, putting a kind of bookend on the quarter century since I had first heard his Beacon Street Union version blasting out of a radio, we traded verses on "Blue Suede Shoes," and it was over.

"The King . . . The King!" John shouted. I raised both arms, Rocky-style, and left as I had come, through the ropes at the back of the stage.

Now, however, there was a horde of kids waiting for me, mostly boys wanting autographs. This I hadn't figured on. The longer I hung out, the larger the crowd got.

"Elvis! Me next!"

"Elvis, sign my shirt!"

By now it was nearly dark. I decided to make a break for it, and sprinted toward the van, but the kids followed every step of the way and I found myself surrounded. This wasn't like a polite book signing. These kids were a pack of small coyotes, shoving their hands in my face and saying, "Sign this, King!" and "Hey, Elvis! You came back from the dead!"

"Are you, like, fake?"

"I see your underwear!"

I signed about twenty hands with one boy's indelible magic marker (sorry, moms), reverting to TCB if the hand was too tiny for a complete flourish, "Elvis Presley."

One kid hung around and was an insistent pain in the ass. This was the one who had spotted my underwear, showing through the rear of my suit, and he wouldn't let me forget it. I told him, in his mother's hearing range, to go home and pray. He said the f-word. I told him Elvis didn't talk like that. He said I had gray hair. I said he had a big mouth. At that point his mother intervened and he was suddenly gone.

To chase off the remaining urchins, I had an inspiration: suddenly and dramatically, I grinned at them and at the same time ripped off my wig.

"Arrrrrgghh! Elvis, you don't look so good."

"Well, what do you expect—I'M DEAD!"

At last I was back in my T-shirt and shorts, anonymous again. I rejoined my family, drawing not the slightest flicker of interest from anyone in the vicinity. "That's my Dad, he was Elvis," Colette said to Kate. Kate stared at me, especially at my wispy, gray pate, uncomprehending.

"Got it," said Bruce, packing up his gear. "I even threw in some MTV effects. You're gonna like it. I'll send you a dub in tomorrow's mail."

"Nice job, Elvis," said Carol.

"How'd it seem from out here? Honestly, I mean."

"Well, I overheard two old ladies in lawn chairs. One of them said, 'He's all right, I s'pose.' The other said, 'Well, it was free. What do you want for nothin'?'"

"Elvis isn't really for the senior set."

"But you were great."

"Ah! Lay it on thick!"

I was most concerned with Olivia's reaction. Being 10, she was right on the cusp of preadolescence. At any moment she was going to wake up mortified at her middle-aged father's exhibitionistic hubris.

"How was I, honey?"

"Dad," she said carefully, "you were cool. But don't bring me along anymore, okay?"

In the waning twilight, John wrapped up his final set and, in honor of July 4th, just days away, gathered the children in front of the stage. While the band broke their equipment down, he led them in patriotic songs, a cappella, passing the mike around to one clear little voice after another. Lounging on our blanket, fifty yards away, we heard "It's a Grand Old Flag" . . . "I'm a Yankee Doodle Dandy" . . . "The Star Spangled Banner" . . . "This Land Is Your Land."

Finally, in the full darkness, came "America," and I heard Colette, who now had the mike. "America, America . . . God shed his grace on me-e-e . . . and crown me good with brotherhood . . . from sea to shining sea . . ." This, I thought, was surely America, at its most iconographic: an old New England green, free country music, kids singing in the soft night—and Elvis. Later in the week, I had another life to live— a book to review, a mixed doubles tennis tournament, drinks here and there, something at Carol's parents' club. But tonight I had been Elvis, lost in America, an icon in a land where iconography had replaced topography. I had had my first real taste of what happens when you step out into the wider world as Elvis—the storm-force wind of attention, curiosity, and even love that blows your way.

I had to be careful. This could get addictive.

Chapter

21

Okay: I want you to talk about me in the third person. Like I'm not even here. We'll just refer to me as 'he.' "

I was at John Lincoln Wright's house in Cambridge and we had just finished watching the video. I had a tape recorder running now that John had finally stopped chuckling.

He lit a cigarette and popped open a beer.

JLW: Right. Go ahead.

WMH: Well? How'd he do?

JLW: Obviously "he" studied real hard at the vocal inflections, did a great job with that. The power of his voice? Not a whole lot there. Doesn't hit the high ones. Given—he was doing a lot of early Elvis material, when Elvis had more of a tenor kind of voice than the deeper heavier baritone he ended up with. The early ones need that sexual energy stirring underneath it.

WMH: Was there sexual energy in Henderson's performance?

JLW: (laughs) Well, they're gonna have to do some work on the uniform, you know? Elvis had a big athletic body. He wanted to be a football player. It was a young truck driver's body. Henderson is a little bit more . . . well, he's sort of professorial. Sexual tension . . . ? Mm. I don't know.

Although, *although* . . . in his performance, the little girls, the kids in the front, they were *getting* it, truly.

WMH: Do you think he has tyke appeal?

JLW: Tyke appeal? Well, sure, I guess. As Muddy Waters said, "The men don't know, but the little girls they understand." Leave it at that.

WMH: Well, regardless, he's finding it awfully hard to pull this off. What do you think is the challenge in trying to do this thing, trying to do Elvis?

JLW: The challenge is that you know you can't mess with it too much: the songs were *that way*. To do your own version of Elvis is walking on very dangerous water. Like when Rod Stewart did his version of "All Shook Up." I was appalled, you know? Because I said, oh no, they changed the beat! They took the tension away. The sexual tension was gone. Ain't the same tune. That was the beauty of the early Elvis music, that underlying nervousness and tension that it had. And it's apparent: the older you get the more you can hear it, too.

WMH: You did a version of "Blue Suede Shoes" on an early Beacon Street Union album. I remember in 1969, sitting in a bathtub in an apartment on Beacon Street and hearing it on the radio before I ever knew you. It practically blew me out of the water. How did that come about?

JLW: It was actually one of those little accidents of music history. We cut our first album and then we went on the road to promote it. Then we had a bunch of recording sessions set up in New York City, but we didn't have any new original songs to speak of, just a handful. So we were messing around in the studio. The producer, Wes Farrell, said, "Play anything you know, let's just hear what you do. Play some other stuff." And at a certain point he said, "Do you know any Elvis?" The one I liked, of course, was the Carl Perkins thing that Elvis did, "Blue Suede Shoes." He said, "Let's do it. Let's cut it."

And surprisingly, MGM Records, which was a strange record company in those days, decided to release "Blue Suede Shoes" as the single from that album—and it actually did well on the West Coast, got on some charts. Got some airplay here in the Boston area, but not much—enough for you to hear it, I guess.

WMH: That was your version of an Elvis impersonation. A tribute, anyway. Do you find it interesting that, in a sense, anyone can do it, anyone can put on the wig—

JLW: Well, this guy Henderson! He's got no more business being Elvis than my grandmother does. But he put the suit on and said, "I can be Elvis" for about 20 minutes in the show we did with him, and he had 'em going. Of course, there was a little audience-coaxing. I went out to the side and tried to get the kids up at the front of the stage to scream at the appropriate moments. But they did. They really did.

WMH: And his confidence zoomed.

JLW: Well, sure. I knew him when he played fiddle, quiet guy, writer for the local paper. I never saw anything until he put the Elvis suit on—and all of a sudden people were screaming at him. This is a quiet professor from North Carolina. He was transformed for 20 minutes. And people in the audience, whether they thought it was a joke or not a joke, responded in kind. They said, this is fun.

WMH: Do you think there's something magic, literally, about putting on that suit?

JLW: Putting on the suit. Maybe. But it's double-edged. After I did "Blue Suede Shoes," my producer called me, I was back in Boston here, and he called me and said, "MGM is wondering if you're interested in doing a remake of Elvis." He said they wanted to put me on the cover in the gold lamé suit—kind of like Phil Ochs did in *5 Elvis Fans Can't Be Wrong*, which made all the folkies despise him—anyway, a remake of an Elvis album—a whole album of that music. At that time I said, absolutely not. I thought it would've made me a joke, so I couldn't do it. I would've been an Elvis impersonator—Elvis, updated for the late 60s. And I said I can't do that, I don't want to do that. Not musically, just personally. Either it's a sick joke or it could even be the greatest thing that ever happened in my career—but I don't want any part of it.

WMH: You felt like you'd be losing your self?

John Lincoln Wright, circa 1967. Could this kid have been the first major-label Elvis clone? (Photo courtesy of Steven Hansen.)

JLW: Absolutely. Absolutely. I was kind of a hippie, a long-haired kid. I would've had to put on costumes and then live up to what the costume and the aura represented, and I didn't feel I could pull that off—and I think it was a smart decision.

WMH: This is fascinating: you actually had the opportunity to be one of the first—and, given the major label connection, perhaps *the* most successful Elvis impersonator—

JLW: Of all time. Right. Elvis hadn't even done the 68 comeback special at this time.

WMH: And you pulled back. So what makes some guys wholeheartedly go for being Elvis, even though they know it's impossible—and other guys say, no, that's not for me?

JLW: Well, I'm a musician.

WMH: But they're musicians, too. Some of them are top-notch.

JLW: Yeah, but most of them don't have a history of being band leaders and recording and touring like I have all along. A lot of them are guys that decide at a certain point in their life that they want to get another job, and they're going to try it at the karaoke bar to see if it works. You know—"this is a way I can get a paycheck, pick up an extra couple of hundred bucks impersonating Elvis once a week somewhere." Some of them get successful, sure, and they do cruise ships, go to Vegas, they're in packaged shows that travel around, and they're probably getting a nice paycheck. But that's not the creative part of the music business, it's the imitative part. Like the Marilyn Monroe that shows up at Filene's. My feeling, quite frankly, is: get a life, try to find something you can do that's yours.

We walked out into the warm late morning and meandered toward Harvard Square for some lunch.

"So what's next?" John asked.

"I just saw this." I pulled a copy of *Elvis International Forum* out of my bookbag and showed him a listing I had noticed: ELVIS DAY AT THE TWENTY-EIGHTH ANNUAL STRATHAM FAIR. STRATHAM'S FIRE DEPARTMENT, A NON-

PROFIT ORGANIZATION, IS HOSTING AN ELVIS PRESLEY DAY. TO ENTER CALL— (a New Hampshire phone number). "It says enter. I suppose that means it's a contest."

"That's good. That's exactly what you need. Throw yourself into a contest, blind. Don't tell 'em you're writing a book or anything. Just enter."

"And you know what?"

"What?"

"I'm going to win the damn thing, too!"

"Oh, boy . . ."

After lunch I walked across Harvard Yard and up Oxford Street to visit my friend Sebastian Lockwood, a poet. Sebastian, like John Lincoln Wright, was blessed with natural charisma—that of a charming young English gent crossed with a crazed mythological word-beast. He and his girlfriend, Simone, took a break from preparing for a performance piece Sebastian was presenting that night, at Passim (the old Club 47). We sat in his back "garden," as he called it, and drank gin and bitters in the sun. I was still full of myself from Medfield, plotting triumphs, trying to figure new ways of displaying my Elvis prowess, now that I had had a successful debut.

"Maybe Passim," Sebastian suggested idly. "They have a sound system. You could use tapes."

Simone knew someone who booked brunch acts for The House of Blues.

"The House of Blues! Yes! I could do something esoteric—a whole blues set! Maybe I could get the Sour Mash Boys to back me."

"Mmm," Sebastian hummed vaguely, not willing to stretch quite that far.

Simone, an exotically beautiful woman, was particularly interested in the notion of impersonation. We talked about how you do the impossible—merge into another's identity. In San Francisco, she had been present at an unusual feminist event—a Frida Kahlo impersonation contest.

"Frida Kahlo? Who's that?"

"She was a Mexican painter, married to Diego Rivera. She had been badly injured, so she had a strange way of walking. Apparently she was incredibly charismatic. Men and women both were mesmerized by her. A cult grew up around her. So they have this contest—"

"Frida Kahlo impersonators! Fabulous!"

"Yes, and you know, the winner didn't look like her at all. But she found a way to convincingly portray Frida Kahlo's afflicted way of moving. That's the way to do it. If you can isolate one element of the way the real Elvis expressed himself in behavior—maybe something you share with him—and portray that element, the rest will fall into place. And it won't matter if other details aren't exact."

I thought of the "50 Ways I'm Like Elvis" from *All the King's Men*. What did I share with Elvis? Not much, when you got right down to it. About the only thing I could come up with was a certain style of humor. Like Elvis, I loved dry, snappy one-liners and surreal comedy in the Monty Python mold. Elvis (according to his road manager, Joe Esposito) couldn't tell a joke. I can't either. But he had an off-beat, repartee-based jokiness, did off-the-wall things, mimicked and mocked and freaked around with wordplay, all of which I saw as my own style. So what could I do with it? Kid around on stage? It wasn't much to work with.

Sebastian's 7-year-old son, Myles, joined us. Because he had been thoroughly indoctrinated in alternative music culture by his older brothers (who were skateboarders and hung out with the wild things in Harvard Square), I decided to throw the video in Sebastian's VCR and get a reaction from him (Sebastian and Simone hadn't seen it yet either).

"Cool," Myles said, watching John Lincoln Wright introduce me. But I could see his heart wasn't in it. While Sebastian and Simone fed me back the "wow!" response I was looking for (and Bruce really HAD gone out of his way with the MTV weird-motion effects), Myles seemed to be biding his time until he could switch the program back to Ren and Stimpy. Suddenly I saw it with his eyes: a middle-aged, black-wigged dude in white spangly pajamas, cavorting in front of a band of ex-hippies. No wonder he wanted his cartoons back.

"Bill's going to enter a contest, Myles. At a fair up in New Hampshire. How would you like to go?"

"A fair? With rides?"

"I'm sure there'll be rides. Want to go?"

"Cool. Let's go."

Chapter

22

Back in Rhode Island, Carol's parents were giving a cocktail party at their beach haunt, the Dunes Club, in Narragansett. It was dressy (for me): summer blazer and tie. I had bought a tiny TCB lapel pin in Memphis and decided to confound the party guests by wearing it. These would be well-heeled folks in their sixties and seventies, an intelligent and tasteful crowd, but certainly no Elvis fans in the bunch. Most of them, as one woman of that generation told me, "took one look at him on the *Ed Sullivan Show* and never gave the man another thought." A tough crowd to please, but I was determined to talk about Elvis, my project, my wig—whatever came up—unstintingly and without shame.

"Maybe you should wear your jumpsuit," Carol suggested. She and her sister Nancy had been honing in on the video and noticing defects in the suit—the crotch was too low, the pants too wide, too short, too much flare in the bell-bottoms.

"It shows so distinctly on the video. It looks fine from the waist up, ridiculous from the waist down."

Nancy volunteered to tackle the crotch problem.

"Maybe I should get a real suit," I said to Carol. "I mean, this one's fine as far as it goes, but the real suits are custom-cut stretch gabardine, satin lined. They're replicas of actual suits Elvis wore. It makes a big difference in the way you look."

I had obtained a catalog from B&K Enterprises, outfitters to professional Elvises. They did indeed offer every suit The King ever wore (once your eye is trained, you recognize particular designs), each one with its own distinct appellation from the pantheon of Elvis show wear:

Gold Lamé
68 Comeback
Cape Fringe
Fringe
Chain
Concho
Checkerboard
Star Burst
Pinwheel
Eyelet
Owl
Comet
Black Butterfly
Conquistador
Planet
Blue Swirl
Powder Blue
Nail
Tiffany
Nail-King of Spades
Stone and Nail
Egyptian
Topaz Stone
Sunburst
Turquoise

Black Spanish Flower

Stone & Nail Flame

Thunderbird

Aloha Eagle

Pinwheel & Stone

Phoenix

White Phoenix

Rainbow

Tiger

Old Indian

Peacock

Dragon

American Eagle

Arabian Suit

Flame Suit

Alpine

Gypsy

Sundial

My own personal favorite was the Dragon, a mere $4,700 (although I would have settled for a Peacock, at $3,500). These were not the most expensive: you could pick up either the Gypsy or the Sundial for a cool $5,000. Most of the impersonators I had seen stuck to the low end—the Chain, or Fringe, or Checkerboard, or Pinwheel—in the $1,200 to $1,300 range.

I passed the catalog to Carol. She flipped through and passed it back. Nothing more was said.

I did have a minor brainstorm, however. Since we were only a short drive away from Boston, I would call Ollie and find out who had made my suit in the first place. Surely going to the source would be the way to get it right—and perhaps fancy it up a little as well, with a few more jewels and studs to bring it to a new level of pizzazz.

*   *   *

"Her name is Karon Yee," Ollie said.

"Who?"

"Kar*on*, as in Sharon. Yee as in, I don't know, Yee Olde Curiosity Shop. I'll get you her number. She's a wonderful character, sort of a performance artist of a designer, never does the same thing twice. Loves weird gigs. Once she designed Sherlock Holmes caps for a dozen cats, for a cat food commercial. It was a custom job—cats have unique head sizes and shapes just like humans. Loved it. She adored this Elvis job— especially because the jumpsuit Elvis guy was so huge. He has a double chin like a basketball. I still can't believe you're wearing it at all. Call her, she won't believe this."

He was right.

"Oh, my god," said Karon Yee, laughing at the odd twists the cosmos can throw back at you. "I never in a million years thought *that* suit would walk back into my life!"

We made an appointment for a fitting, a design upgrade, and some much-needed wig enhancement.

I didn't wear the jumpsuit to the party, of course; I wouldn't have made it past the doorman at the Dunes, no joke. It was one of those elegant club affairs in a high-ceilinged party room with French doors thrown open to a vista of manicured lawn that sloped down to sand and surf. A good many of the fifty or so guests had seen each other at five other parties that week, had known each other for half a century or more, and were most likely related by blood or marriage or school affiliation. Black-and-white-clad waiters and waitresses circulated with trays of hot and cold hors d'oeuvres and drinks. The conversational level was an animated roar loud enough to drown out the surf. I roamed here and there, provoking impersonator talk as I could.

"Elvis impersonators? Why would anybody want to impersonate that awful man?" said Mrs Whittington, a towering white-haired lady, more as a declaration than a question.

"Stop me if I'm wrong," I said. "You took one look at him, on the *Ed Sullivan Show*, and never gave the man another thought."

"Not until this instant, and why should I?"

"Well, suppose I said that more people know his name, world-wide, than know the names Mohammed, Ghandi, Buddha, Christ, Mozart—" I had no idea if this was literally true, but it was a safe bet.

Mrs. Whittington's husband, a red-cheeked old country squire, leaned in with his gin and tonic: "Watch yourself now—you're going to say he's more popular than Jesus. Isn't that what did the Beatles in?"

Mrs. Dobbs, a small, fireplug of a lady piped up: "I don't dislike him—in fact, he rather reminds me of my favorite nephew. But why? That's my question: why this man?"

There it was: *why?*

"Yes, why?" echoed Mrs. Whittington. "What's it about, all this misplaced interest? All these people who've never heard of Buddha and so on?"

"I'm not sure it's possible to explain it. First, I think you'd have to have had a better reaction to the *Ed Sullivan Show*."

"It's too late for that."

"I don't agree. It's never too late. And if you're sharing the planet with ten thousand Elvis impersonators, don't you think you owe it to yourself to be at least mildly curious about Elvis Presley, rather than just dismiss him as an article of bad taste?"

"Well, I think these impersonators are exactly that, in bad taste."

"But Bill's one!" crowed Mr. Whittington.

"*NO—!*" Mrs. Whittington's hand flew to her chest. "Tell me you're just writing about them!"

"No, I *am* one." I recalled Rick Marino and his baseline self-definition. "I—am—an—Elvis—impersonator. And proud of it."

"Lord."

Carol's father, sensing a brouhaha, stepped in. "You know, the Historical Society had an Elvis impersonator at a tea up at Brown. The president of the board was there. Kind of an odd program. The impersonator wasn't very good, but there was something about him. I talked to him, he had a friendly air, he seemed to be a good sort of person."

The fireplug lady said, "But aren't they like the people in these awful militias that are springing up all over? I mean these creatures that use threats and bombs and all the rest? These gun-type people?"

"Now there's nothing wrong with guns," said Mr. Whittington. "Let's not get into that one."

I said, "They're not the same people. The militias, the paranoid right—that's all about being against things. They're against limits on dangerous behavior, against government, they think the president is plotting with the UN to take over their private septic tanks. Elvis people are *for* things—"

"What is it they're for?"

"Fun. Good feelings. Promoting good memories associated with Elvis. Charity—"

Mrs. Whittington glanced toward the ceiling. "Oh, please, not *charity*—I'm going to cry."

"Well, it's true—whenever they do something, they cover costs and give the rest to some charity or other. Impersonators are always doing benefits for some poor kid's hospital expenses, that kind of thing. I'm not trying to put a halo on it, but it's a fact. Look: I've read fiction where dark political forces want to build power bases on these brooding Elvis cult figures with robotic followers and all that—but the premise never works, never. It just doesn't hold water. Politics, revolution, power—none of these things drive Elvis people. They didn't drive Elvis."

"Well, I know what drove Elvis," said Mr. Whittington. "The same things that drive me: sex, drugs, and rock 'n' roll."

And so it went. As expected, I didn't change any minds. No one asked me about my TCB pin (one lady did notice but told me later that she had learned the hard way, over the years, not to inquire about such things). Once again, I saw my basic premise played out: that wherever you go, Elvis is a litmus test; that there is a huge sociological stripe separating everyone of a certain age into two groups: those who are at least open to enjoying Elvis, think he's an interesting, perhaps dynamic performer—and those for whom he can never be more than an illegitimate usurper, a bumpkin, a vile truck driver, or worse.

But though this rankles the fans, or people like me who, as it were, "know too much," the truth is it's ultimately of no real significance. The world keeps on turning regardless of attitudes toward Elvis; life goes on unaffected. As Dave Marsh wrote of Elvis himself: "if he remained disreputable to the intelligentsia, it was of little consequence to him, since such people were basically foreigners in his world anyhow."

Still, the social tension produces some deliciously snappy moments, like the one in *Jailhouse Rock*, when Elvis (as the ex-jailbird Vince Everett) chews out the lah-de-dah party guests at his girlfriend's parents' house.

The girl (Judy Tyler) runs after him into the backyard, complaining that he insulted her parents.

Elvis redefines what happened: "Some old broad pushed me into the corner with some stupid question."

To upper-class Judy, he's being touchy: "They were just trying to bring you into the conversation."

To Elvis, who knows a skirmish in the class wars when he's been in one, "They can shove their conversation. I'm not even sure they were talking English."

Ultimately, however, Elvis plays his strong card, suddenly laying a preemptive kiss on Judy, with near-brute force:

JUDY: (slapping him) How dare you think such cheap tactics would work with me!

(He does it again. She melts.)

ELVIS: That ain't tactics, honey. That's just the beast in me.

So this time the beast wins out. But the eternal truth is that elite society (self-defined) and Elvis society (self-chosen) are like two desert islands, hostile and separated by a forbidding expanse of ocean. They may gossip about each other, peer across at each other, they may sometimes sneak back and forth, or even fight small, insignificant battles in disputed waters. But there they sit, geographically disarrayed, and will everlastingly, or until the day some Greater Power decides to intervene, destroying, then rearranging from scratch, every feature of this mutual but disconnected topography.

That summer I developed a fantasy that involved becoming a permanent saddle sore to the rich and cultured watchers of *Masterpiece Theater*. It was this: one day, Russell Baker has had enough of trying to fill Alastair Cooke's shoes and retires. I get the job and take it—on condition that I may do my introductions and commentaries *as Elvis*, fully wigged and jumpsuited.

"Good evening," I say. "Welcome to my world . . ."

Then I introduce the latest toney BBC literary import in a way that would make the average blue-collar guy want to sit up and watch adaptations of *Portrait of a Lady* or *Pride and Prejudice* or *A Dance to the Music of Time*.

Fat chance. But it was fun to toy with in idle moments—as a break from the real work of becoming Elvis.

Chapter

2 3

n Don DeLillo's novel *White Noise*, the main character is "chairman of the department of Hitler studies at the College-on-the-Hill" where his friend, a "visiting lecturer on living icons" is trying to establish "an Elvis Presley power base in the department of American environments."

Now, as it invariably does, life was imitating art down in Oxford, Mississippi. The week before I was due to arrive in Memphis, the University of Mississippi was indeed putting on an international conference on Elvis Presley.

The *Boston Globe* article John Lincoln Wright had clipped for me focused on a "why Elvis?" sort of controversy: the mayor of Oxford, Mississippi, had vetoed an appropriation granted to the conference by the town board. By contrast, they had welcomed the Faulkner Conference for years. According to the *Globe*, the mayor "said he was encouraged to withhold the funds by many townspeople, including 'old ladies in book clubs.'" But Dr. William Ferris, director of the sponsoring Southern Culture Center, observed that, unlike Elvis, "Faulkner came from the privileged, educated elite, and . . . there is a deep and enduring division between the powerful elite, whose literary canon is represented by Faulkner, and the working class and blacks whose values are represented by Elvis."

This sounded like a tipoff to me: The King's pop-culture onus was now being laundered for the academy by making him "the focus" of working-class and black "values."

It was a familiar process in academia by now: is the market clogged with too many Hawthorne or Faulkner or Flannery O'Connor scholars? Then simply create some new jobs by rack-stretching the canon to include a Madonna, an Elvis. It made perfect sense that now, a man named Dr. Vernon Chadwick had created an English course at Ole Miss that merged Melville and Elvis (students called the course Melvis). The same Vernon Chadwick was pictured in the *Globe* behind his teaching podium—young, lightly bearded, sporting a "cool" collarless shirt and a lock of hair that tumbled rakishly over one eye. This alternative rock star of a professor was apparently the point man of the Elvis Conference.

"You're not going?" said John Shelton Reed, who was giving the keynote address.

Reed, a widely read commentator on Southern culture, was a friend and neighbor, and I had phoned to ask him to be my eyes and ears at the event.

"It's hard to believe you won't be going. I mean, to the world's first conference on *Elvis*?"

"Can't. I'm too busy being Elvis. I've got to stay focused. What are you going to say in your speech?"

"I don't know yet. I'm certainly not an expert on Elvis. I guess I'll talk about the kind of world that produced him."

Reed knew plenty about that—the rural South of Elvis's childhood—and probably more about Elvis himself than he was letting on. My suspicion was that a good part of the reason for this conference was to grab some new professional turf for southern studies, which had been on a roll lately, not just nationally but worldwide, and John confirmed that. But he had his doubts about the legitimacy of what he would find in Oxford.

"It's probably going to be a motley crew down there—lots of press who'll come for the pseudo-event part, the Elvis impersonators the first night, and when they get their story, they'll leave. Then it'll be a mix of scholarly stuff and local color and the kind of cultural studies where somebody has one insight, if they're lucky, and instead of looking for evidence or data or facts, they just elaborate on that one insight over and over and over."

I wasn't a scholar—not even a pseudoscholar. What I was (hadn't I just announced it at the Dunes Club?) was *an Elvis impersonator*. And proud of it. Didn't it make sense that an Elvis impersonator might skip a gathering that had very little to do with the art and craft of *doing* Elvis?

Beyond showcasing a few PC multicultural Elvises on opening night (while, no doubt, the dignitaries from Graceland watched with frozen grins), wouldn't the conference's real meat be presentations of papers that introduced new theoretical Elvises? Elvis the trickster-anticolonialist; Elvis the crypto-feminist; Elvis the black whiteman, or white blackman; Elvis the overvalorized phallocentrist?

This I could do without. I had serious business to get on with.

Chapter

24

ow that I had blabbed to everyone about the contest in New
Hampshire, I had to get off my duff and do something about
it. I called the number listed in *Elvis International Forum*
several times with no luck, then finally got through to Jackie Hersey, entertainment coordinator for the Stratham (pronounced STRATH'm) Fair.

"I'm an Elvis impersonator, from North Carolina," I said, "and I saw
your listing in *Elvis Forum*. I hope it's not too late to enter."

"North Carolina!"

"Well, actually I'm in Rhode Island now."

"That's still a ways. Let's see. I've got one contestant coming from
Maine, one from Boston."

"How many do you have?"

"Five—you'll make six."

Perfect, not too big a field. We'd each do two sets, on the main
stage, up to five songs. There wasn't a band, so each contestant needed
his own back-up tape. First set was at three; then, after the nine o'clock
set, the winner would be announced. There would be prizes for nearly
everyone; for the winner—$100, a plaque, a cruise for two to some
local New Hampshire island, a tour jacket from King's Connection, an
Elvis tie and belt buckle. All *right!*

But I would have to put together a tape pronto (the contest was 10 days away). That meant figuring out what I wanted to sing—planning a set from available tracks, then dubbing the selected tracks, in sequence, to my master tape.

I needed help. I called Rick Marino.

"Okay, here's what you do: get in touch with King Tracks, they've got a lot of concert stuff. Whatever you use, the first two songs should have no pause between 'em. Then pause for about three to five seconds to sip some water, whatever. Then into a ballad. You'll probably want to say a few words, but if you're just programming a pause, remember: five seconds of *dead air* is a long time on stage. You can do this all kinds of ways. I sometimes use Elvis's own live show tapes, just sing over his voice—if you do that, tell the sound man to turn down the 'mids,' which has the effect of kind of diminishing the vocal. Sometimes, when my voice just isn't up to it, I use my *own* tapes—I mean, I lip sync myself! I like a flat sound, so I never put reverb on the mike. You might want some, though, because if you don't have super pipes, the reverb warms up your vocal sound. Not that I'm implying anything—but hey, man, this is great for you, you'll learn something, you need this. Let me know how it turns out."

King Tracks. I had seen their ad in *Elvis International Forum*: "LIVE, EXCITING AND DYNAMIC TRACKS FIT FOR THE KING. Dedicated to giving you the best sound background tracks you can sing along with. Over 60 songs not available by any other company. Obscure and concert versions from the '50s through the '70s. New Releases every month."

Since time was a factor, I phoned the King Tracks office in Tennessee and arranged to have a brochure faxed to me. They had some off-beat selections—"Rock-a-Hula Baby," "Clean Up Your Own Backyard"—but pretty much covered the waterfront on standard Elvis fare, including my pressing interest, concert versions. I decided to order two "customized" tapes (your choice, up to four selections per tape, $16.98 plus s&h), which, combined with my Pocket Songs CDs, would guarantee enough raw material to work with. I faxed them back immediately, and they agreed to FedEx my order, as follows:

2001/See See Rider (Elvis's opening, 1973 live version)
Suspicious Minds (1973 live)
Polk Salad Annie (1972 live version)
A Big Hunk o' Love (1973 live)
Blue Suede Shoes (1969 Vegas)
Hurt (1976 live)
Can't Help Falling in Love (Elvis's perennial show closer, including
    the repetitive vamp that covered his exit from the stage)

I had contacted Karon Yee in Boston and made an appointment with her for a fitting (Nancy's crotch work had helped, but not enough) and to discuss upgrading the pizzazz of my suit and wig (which was getting disheveled and certainly did reveal patches of gray peeking through from underneath). I found her in her studio at The Piano Factory in the South End, a building the size of the Pentagon that once turned out pianos but was now converted to apartments and workspaces for artists. Karon Yee was a short, husky woman, Chinese-American, with a pronounced Boston street accent and a ready laugh, but something that told me I wouldn't want to be on her bad side.

Ollie was right, no job the same. "Right now I'm doing costumes for a new rock band, Eric's Kitchen," she said. "It's the guitar player from Spin Doctors, his new group." She babbled fast, her words tumbling over each other in a torrent to get it out as quickly as she was thinking, which seemed awfully quick. "I'm working now on a female costume for one of the girls in the band." She showed me a black leather corset, with clear plastic breast cups, ribbed with black. She checked her watch—had an appointment to pick up some items at Hubba-Hubba, a shop in Cambridge that specialized in leather S&M and dominatrix wear.

"You understand, I'm not a commercial client like Ollie," I poor-mouthed. "I don't have a corporate budget."

"That's okay, that's okay, I'll cut you some slack because this is gonna be such fun, jeez, I can't believe this suit's come walkin' back in here, like a minizombie or something! Try it on."

She looked me over with an expert eye, jotted some notes on a yellow legal pad. She would take in the crotch some more, lose some of the zipper, narrow the shoulders a bit, lengthen the legs. She had an idea for a burst of ruby spangles that would supplement the brass studs and add color to the shoulder area. Sixty dollars cash and we were in business.

"I'm taking the girls to Maine for a few days," said Carol. "We're getting out of your way."

"Well, I guess I have been a little intense."

"It's no problem, I just think you need the space."

She was right. With Stratham looming—and Memphis only a couple of weeks later—I was going back into Beethoven mode, pacing, ignoring basic hygiene, mumbling to myself, humming at inappropriate moments. What I really needed was to turn the whole house into a practice studio, and I could only do that if I were on my own. Having seen me at Medfield, the girls had "been there, done that" and Carol had seen enough as well. So I would be on my own at Stratham, along with any curiosity seekers from my old life in Boston who cared to show up (word of the event and my incongruous role in it was getting around).

"Knock 'em dead, Dad."

"You're gonna win, Daddy!"

The van backed out, family waving, mugging, blowing kisses . . . and then they were gone. I was alone, with only the dogs to watch me work.

About fifteen seconds later, a FedEx truck pulled in with my King Tracks order. This was ideal: no time to mope. I could get right to work.

The tracks, however, were a rude disappointment. "2001," the whole purpose of which is to build up an elegant, august suspense, had a puny synthesizer sound for brass and strings. The synthesizer even managed to *miss* the penultimate chord (which, in Richard Strauss's version, is a magnificent held tonic, in which the full power of a concert organ thunders beneath full orchestra). Richard Strauss would have spun in his grave.

Okay: to use the Vienna Philharmonic would be a bit pretentious, but I'd have to go with the *As Recorded at Madison Square Garden* version and splice it to the King Tracks vamp. A few of the tracks were adequate: "Polk Salad Annie," "Suspicious Minds," and "Hurt." The lead guitar parts were excellent (although keyboards sucked and the drums—probably a drum machine—sounded like a child's starter kit). The guide singer, a Roger Miller clone, did clean, accurate renditions of Elvis's actual performances. With these and something from the Pocket Songs CD ("If I Can Dream," assuming I could pull off the dramatic extremes) I was covered.

Now: how to mix them all down to one tape?

If I had been at home, with my own tape deck, it would have been quick work. But at the Rhode Island house, there was nothing up to the task. I called a few friends. Nobody was really equipped. But after all, wasn't that what summer homes in the country were for—to turn the clock back to 1937? I filled the time drilling lyrics, listening to both Elvis's versions and the anonymous guide singer for inflections, diction. I sang through the tracks over and over, out of sequence—to the dogs, in the car, while jogging, while stalking through the house, stereo turned up full blast (who cared what the neighbors thought?).

But I needed a tape!

"Go to a recording studio," suggested a friend. Sure, and pay $150 for 20 minutes' work? I was too cheap—I had already spent far too much money on this project, and the week in Memphis was going to set me back plenty.

Finally, staring disaster in the face, I did something I wanted to avoid. Bruce, my videographer friend, was something of a renaissance media man. He was even a musician and could compose and record music tracks in his *basement studio*. Why hadn't I contacted him earlier? The awful truth was that, at Medfield, he had told me he was going through a kind of biblical Job period. New house, new baby, nagging flu, being audited by the IRS, wanting to turn off his phone, but having to answer calls for possible freelance work and a sailboat he was trying to sell to cover short-term cash-flow challenges. He was in no shape to do favors—in fact, it was amazing, in retrospect, that he'd even shown up to shoot the Medfield gig.

How could I call on the poor guy?

Easy. With Stratham now two days away, I was desperate. As I had told John Lincoln Wright, I wanted to win this thing. The milk of human kindness had dried up and blown away. I was demonic, driven, an Elvis without pity.

Bruce, to his everlasting credit, said he'd make some time for me the night before the contest—which was tomorrow.

I FedExed him my master tapes and discs with the following directions:

(1) CD: "Madison Square Garden": Bands 1 and 2 (to 00.18 or 00.32).

Straight cut to "piano tinkle" on King Tracks "See See Rider," stay with it till ending, where cut back to CD at (same track) 02:00 and fade out on applause (be sure to be OUT by 02:10, where he says "thank you").

(2) Butt to opening chord of "All Shook Up" (same tape)—all the way to end.
(3) Butt to opening of "Suspicious Minds" (same tape)—all the way to end.
(4) Butt to opening of "Polk Salad Annie" (other King Tracks tape)—all the way to end.
(5) Butt to opening of "If I Can Dream" (CD: "You Sing the Hits of Elvis Presley," track 19)—all the way to end.

(6) Butt to opening of "Can't Help Falling in Love" (first King Tracks tape)—go to ending, on piano glissando (at END of gliss), cut to CD "Elvis in Madison Squ. Gar" (Track 21, 01:40)—ON MATCHING CYMBAL SMASH. Stay with CD till Track 22, 00:31 where start fade (OUT by 00:37).

Who said Elvis impersonation wasn't rocket science?

Next day, I planned a long loop that would take me up through Boston to Karon Yee's, to pick up my suit, then out the Mass Pike to claim my tapes from Bruce, and finally back to Rhode Island, where I had been invited to dinner at a friend's.

At Karon's loft, I marveled at my enhanced jumpsuit, newly speckled with red teardrop rhinestones, and the rejuvenated wig, that now lapped luxuriously down my neck. Feeling great about things, I got back in my car and drove to Bruce's house.

But one more plague had leveled Bruce: his central air-conditioning had blown out, and there was a heat wave on. It was so hot in his basement that, once we got our session under way, the mountainous 8-foot rack of digital electronics—especially the audio control "smart-box" (some kind of automatic signal controller)—began to misfire. I had no idea what was happening, but I knew that equipment like this thrived on cool, dry atmospherics. So did Bruce, who, as the miscues mounted, was starting to resemble a panicked wildebeest.

"What's going on?" I asked, glancing at my watch.

"Well, that, that—thing there, that box, it's supposed to send encoded playback tracks to the computer, into its sequencer program, then out, mixed, to the recording machines."

"And it's not."

"Nothing is simple."

"I'm going to have that engraved on my skull." He tried again, his eyes bugging out, to make the splice in the two versions of "2001." We had a long way to go. I could see genuine desperation clanking into the room like Marley's ghost. The phone rang and Bruce swiped it up: a possible buyer for the sailboat. Kate toddled in, saw me, and said, "Elvis took off his hair!"

"She's been repeating that ever since the gig," said Bruce. I thought of what a piece of trauma theater that must have been for the little tykes—like Santa whipping off his beard, or Ronald McDonald lighting up a cigarette. "Where's Mommy?" asked Bruce. "Asleep with the baby. Go upstairs." "No." "If you go upstairs, you can have some cake. It's in the box next to the fridge." She was instantly gone.

I was overdue for dinner in Rhode Island. Should I call and cancel?

Bruce sighed. "No, no. I'll make you a rough practice dub now and you can pick up the master tomorrow. I'm sorry, man, it's just, it's just . . ."

"No, Bruce, *I'm* sorry. I should never have asked you to do this."

"Well, contrary to appearances, it's happening. Don't worry. I know what's going wrong, I just can't finesse it right now. The master'll be done, I promise. It's Saturday, the IRS won't be out, I'll put off the sailboat people till afternoon. The room'll cool off overnight. As soon as the baby's in gear, I'll get on it."

With my practice tape, I had at least a scratch version of the right tracks in the right order. I shoved the cassette into my car radio and howled obsessively all the way to Rhode Island. With dinner late, I even had time to toss off a beer and a few scotches to cool myself down. "Relax," my friends kept telling me. Their tone reminded me of the way the trained orderlies in mental hospitals address temporarily dangerous inmates. A couple of bottles of wine went down with dinner. It seemed like a great festive evening—I believe it was somebody's birthday. I didn't think about Stratham or Elvis or Bruce once.

Nor do I remember driving home and falling into bed.

Chapter

2 5

In the morning I awoke with a crushing headache. Fool! Idiot! All that work and you didn't even have enough self-control to stay reasonably abstemious the night before?

I rolled painfully to one side of the bed, groped for my phone, and called Sebastion.

"I've really screwed up," I said, in a forced whisper.

"Elvis has a hangover," Sebastian relayed to someone in his kitchen: I imagined a group of neighborhood Harvard intellectuals chortling over mugs of herbal tea at this hapless Elvis impersonator who couldn't pull himself out of bed.

I heard Myles in the background: "Aren't we going?"

"Well, if Bill's not up to it—"

"I'm up to it—" I snapped.

"Dad, the rides."

"Yes, the rides, but really we're going to see Bill do Elvis, aren't we?"

"But I've seen that—I saw the tape." Even though Sebastian's hand was clapped over the receiver, Myles came through loud and clear: having seen the tape, why should he be expected to sit down and watch the real thing—when there were all those rides? Perhaps Col. Parker had been right to react cool headedly to Elvis's death: after all, it was on vinyl where Elvis was _really_ alive. "Nothing'll change," he had said. "It'll be just like when the boy was in the Army."

Anyway, yes, I would damn well be there, if they had to put me on life-support. Sebastian said in that case they would certainly be there— at least for the first show.

I hung up and dumped a shovelful of Advil down my throat.

I spent about an hour drinking coffee, mumbling along with the scratch tape, trying to make my eyes focus. Slowly it dawned on me that the clock was becoming a factor: it was late morning, the day was ripening. Jackie Hersey had told me to be at the fair by two, for the three P.M. show, and that had seemed ideal. My original plan had been to bound out of bed at daybreak, breakfast on the road, pick up my concert tape from Bruce, then zip into Boston to cruise the garment district in search of scarves and proper footwear—the kind of cheap plastic ankle boots Larry and I had failed to find in Jacksonville. Now, here it was almost afternoon, and I was still home and still in pain. It was obvious that, in the shape I found myself now, I'd be lucky to end up in New Hampshire at all. White sneaks would just have to do one more time. As for scarves, I'd allow one stop along the way—_one_: I'd veer off at one of those everything-for-everybody malls, pick up a few gossamer polyester rectangles and keep on trucking.

There must have been something a little scary about me to the saleswoman whose help I tried to enlist. Here was this grimacing middle-aged crazy with a lopsided pair of eyes (the headache agony had taken up residence in the right hemisphere only), and all this spooky intensity about buying _cheap, plain_ scarves. She tried, but once I saw the kind of junk she pulled out for me, I got the idea: these places were there to sell splashy imitations of fashion items, not simple, honest scarves for Elvis impersonators.

Suddenly, the situation turned around. A humble Dollar Store was nestled in a corner of the mall. There, astoundingly, I found exactly what I wanted: a dozen all-silk scarves, some white, some saffron, some blue—a buck apiece! No waiting at the checkout counter—I was in and out in three minutes!

Back on I-495, speeding toward Bruce's, I could feel my headache begin to wane, another distinct miracle since headaches often stay with me for three days. Bruce was waiting on his front stoop, dangling the back-up cassette, mixed, mastered, sliced, diced, pureed—a thoroughly professional production. He had a sweaty, haunted look. His air-conditioning was still dead, he said; the heat wave had sat for days, like a sodden pachyderm, on all New England, and his family was slowly going bonkers.

"At least the IRS hasn't sent a repo man for my sailboat yet. But I tell you what—I need a break from my life. What do you say *I* do Elvis for you today?"

"Bruce, I realize things are rough, but trust me, you don't know what you're saying—you can't believe what you'd be in for."

"Oh, that's what all you rock stars say. You can't tell me being Elvis wouldn't be a breeze compared to *my* life. But don't listen to me, I'm babbling, babbling. Right now I'd try anything for some relief, it's just a mad impulse, a baroque fantasy, like throwing myself in front of a moving blue suede shoe."

"Bruce: if I win today, I'll buy the sailboat."

"If you win today, you can *have* the sailboat."

On the road again, I sang along with the tape. Bruce had unaccountably added extra silence between numbers. No matter: I'd chat my way through, do a "relaxed" set. Singing through a second time, I caught myself pushing the Subaru to 90 mph. I was losing my voice. Come on, control, control. I made a stark reassessment of the time factor. There was now no way I could be at the fair by two: I wouldn't even make it to the Stratham area by show time. The miracle of the disappearing hangover was now blighted by the sheer bald stupidity of my tardiness. A grown man—a researcher, for goodness sake, on a mission—and here I was blowing it like some dysfunctional rug rat.

I crossed into New Hampshire, still excoriating myself, and noticed heavy clouds darkening the sky. A few fat drops of rain splatted against the windshield, then became a sudden raging torrent, so fierce that cars and trucks were pulling off the interstate. I pressed on, realizing the downpour would at least delay the start of the contest (which would have just been getting under way).

As suddenly as it had begun, the torrent ceased. I accosted pedestrians all through Stratham until I got directions I could comprehend. The sun was blazing again, through great gaps in the disintegrating cloud bank, by the time I found the fairgrounds and was waved by a cop into a soggy grass field among hundreds of parked cars and pickup trucks. I grabbed my suit bag and wig box and hiked the several hundred yards to the entrance.

The fair was more elaborate than the little country expo I had expected. There were carnival rides, music, noise, food smells, animal shows, crowds flowing in two or three directions, and a confluence of dissecting paths and trails. Around a bend was an amphitheater, ancient Greek style, with seats descending a hill and a permanent stage at the bottom of a natural bowl. A blue-clad male figure, some sort of ancient Greek singer/actor/priest was enacting a popular orphic rite for a crowd of about two hundred communicants—that's the fanciful twist my mind produced anyway. Text and setting were as familiar to me as The Doxology: he was chanting ". . . Caught in a trap . . . can't walk out . . .": an Elvis impersonator (one of my competitors, I reminded myself) in the midst of his set.

I slogged down the edge of the hill and around to the rear of the stage, where hidden from the audience, there was a large house trailer. At the side of the stage, a woman with a clipboard turned out to be Jackie Hersey.

"Ah—Bill Henderson. You're here, great." She contemplated her clipboard. "I'll pencil you in last. Got your tape?"

I handed it over, just thankful not to be tongue-lashed.

"Now, how do you want to be introduced?"

Bilvis? El-Bill-Vis? Elvis Henderson? "Just Bill Henderson."

"From Rhode Island? Or I could say from North Carolina, sounds more impressive, like you came all that way."

"Fine, fine."

"You can change in the trailer—it's so broiling hot out here, the guys are staying inside with the AC."

I looked toward the trailer. This would be a first: I was about to go among other Elvises not as a journalist, but purely and simply as one of them. I ambled toward the trailer, trying to look like I had done this a hundred times, reached for the doorknob, and turned it.

"Shut the door behind you," somebody said.

It was almost as hot inside as out. I saw several shirtless young men, teenagers really, lounging on the floor, directly in front of the air conditioners, hogging the air flow. These, I found out later, were members of a trick cyclist act that would follow the contest. The Elvi, three or four of them, were standing, in various stages of transformation. One of them looked ready to go on, a tall, lean, white-suited Vegas Elvis. "Looking for the limo?" he joked, on the assumption I had walked through the wrong door.

"Who's going next?" I asked.

"Me." He straightened up a bit, probably thinking now that I was a contest official. "I'm number two."

"Then I've got some time, I'm going on last," I said.

"You?" He refocused. "You're kidding."

Once, in a shop window, I had seen a T-shirt that I dearly wished I had bought and was wearing now: NO ONE BELIEVES I'M ELVIS.

Another Elvis, short, in a black jumpsuit, offered his hand. "I'm Elvis Bishop," he said, thrusting out his hand. "Where you from?"

"Bill Henderson," I said, "Rhode Island."

"Isn't that the home of the Rhode Island Red?"

"Yeah, nice place, kind of small."

"RHODIE" bellowed one of the trick cyclists, raising his fist. "The nation's smallest sewer! I can say that, I'm from Pawtucket."

The door opened and in came the blue-suited Orpheus from the stage, sweating profusely.

"God almighty, it's hot out there."

"Chuck DeNault, you're up," Jackie yelled in. Number Two took a deep breath, fastened his cape, and descended into the heat.

"I'm too old for this," said Orpheus, unzipping his suit.

"Not as old as me," I muttered.

"Man, I'm older than God," he said. "How old do you think you are?"

"I'm fifty-two."

Orpheus made sure he got that right, then broke into a grin. "Well, I'll shake your hand, man. I thought forty-three was old. You've got real scrotum, I mean it. If you can make it through this heat you deserve your own solid gold walker."

I found the closet area and began to unpack, figuring the jumpsuit would be my protective coloration in this crowd. Elvis Bishop continued a conversation about Chuck's suit that had apparently been in progress when I entered. "He keeps dropping his studs on the floor. It's bad glue, man. I stitch 'em on. That way you're sure. I'm making my own American Eagle right now . . ."

Aside from the sweat-drenched Orpheus and myself, everyone was indeed young. Counting me, we had three Vegas Elvises in white, Elvis Bishop in black, Orpheus (who told me he was Fred Hazard, a disk jockey from somewhere nearby) in blue.

A dark, vaguely Polynesian-looking guy squatted against one of the walls, wearing something that resembled a mid-60s Hollywood Elvis getup—blue shirt, thin red tie, sport jacket with skinny lapels. There was a distinctly familiar look to this Elvis, as though I had seen him on TV. He seemed set apart from the others, with a shyness or reserve that took the form of prideful silence. I realized he wasn't Polynesian; he was African-American. That led to a double revelation: this had to be Robert Washington, the "black Elvis" from Maine that Doc Franklin had mentioned. I had read his name in the Images of Elvis newsletter—and

I *had* seen him on TV: he was one of the EPIIA Convention Elvises, the one who had struck a pose in front of the Stardust Casino and said, "And now, back to Blue Hawaii . . . on TBS."

I introduced myself. "You're going to be in Memphis, aren't you? Doc said you're an automatic finalist."

"That's right. I placed in from the January contest."

"Well, I'll see you down there. I'm going too."

He gave me a mild version of that look I was getting used to by now: the "did-I-hear-that-right?" eyebrow lift.

The others had cracked open the door and were straining to hear Chuck, who, according to Elvis Bishop, wanted to win this one bad. "He's doing the Trilogy—he promised he wouldn't do that to me. He's hungry, he's hungry. But I don't care. I'm set: I got something from each era, plus a spiritual. You don't have to go for the bleachers. Let him do the Trilogy, I'm set . . ."

I was taking off my pants just as two young women, one with a camera, entered from the other half of the trailer.

"Hi, I'm Cindy from *Salt Magazine* in Portland," one of them said to me, then came close and whispered, "Sebastian told me about you."

"Sebastian!"

"He's out there, with his little boy."

"Okay, but did he also tell you—?"

She put a finger across her lips. "Shh, don't worry, *Professor* Elvis. Jenny and I are doing a piece on Elvis Bishop. We'll just be hanging around, okay?"

Right: wink-wink, nod-nod, I thought. *But these girls better not blow my cover, that's all.*

I got into my jumpsuit but left the wig off—it was too hot; I would wait until the utter last minute to seal off the top of my head.

"I'm going to that academic thing in Mississippi, too," said Robert.

"The Elvis Conference?"

"Yeah, the first night. They're having me, El Vez, a couple of others."

Appropriately multicultural. I looked at him: he was multicultural all by himself. A light-skinned black man, maybe some part American Indian (as Elvis himself had been), impersonating the most famous poor southern white boy in the history of the world. Ironically, my own fictional Elvis, Byron Bluford, had also come from Maine—South Portland, to be exact. Something, like a premonition, or an approach of déjà vu, prompted me to ask:

"Where are you from in Maine?"

"South Portland."

This was almost too much to bear without breaking out into some incomprehensible act, like a war whoop, or a dissolve, in giggles, to the floor. *South Portland!* Oh, ye gods! But come on, hang onto yourself, Bill: if you freak out, he won't know why and it'll just look weird. I changed the subject back to Memphis. Robert had a history there going back several contests. "Last year I was on track to win. There was this other contest being run at the Americana, which is the old Eagle's Nest, so I entered. I was in the finals for both contests. Doc came backstage after I did my set there and said, 'You in that other contest?' I said, 'Yep.' He said, 'You going back there tomorrow night?' I said, 'Guess so.' He just turned around and walked out. I lost. Doc's okay, but you don't cross him. He's . . ."

"Territorial?"

"Yeah, big-time."

Everyone had taken to pacing or listening at the door to whoever was on stage. Intermittently, we chatted. The talk was of nuts and bolts: equipment and sources—how to use a Thompson Eliminator to strip the vocal out of an Elvis track, where to buy studs. There was a kind of locker-room camaraderie, as if we all played the same esoteric sport. We were just a bunch of guys engaged in a serious hobby—mountain climbers or fly fishermen. I recalled the dinner conversation: "Don't they have jobs?" Sure they did: Elvis Bishop was a truck driver; Chuck DeNault was a cop in Kittery; Robert Washington was a factory worker (another eerie correspondence to my Byron). Not that they were all best buddies, by any means: when Robert went on, Chuck remarked, "There goes Mr. Ego." Listening to Jackie introduce him as "a national finalist" in the Memphis contest, Chuck complained bitterly: "Now that isn't fair, to introduce him with his national track record and all. It'll influence the judges."

Elvis Bishop didn't agree. "She didn't say *the* national finalist, she said *one* of the national finalists, okay? That's just saying what's true. And anyway, he was damn good. I know because I was there."

"He brought his fan club down from Maine—he's got forty or fifty fans out there."

"Well, I feel for you there. I don't have anybody here but my girlfriend."

They listened carefully to Robert's patter. "He shouldn't refer to Elvis in the third person," said Chuck.

Robert Washington at Stratham, giving a clinic in extreme Elvis movement.
(Photo courtesy of Jenny Walters, *Salt Magazine,* Salt Documentary Center.)

Elvis Bishop agreed: "When you're out there, you're representing Elvis, you *are* Elvis, you don't talk *about* him."

Knowing Robert was on stage, I suddenly wanted to be out front watching. The trailer was like a holding pen. I wished I could see each of the other guys, but once having changed, I really couldn't go out-side—none of us could. As in Medfield, the reality was that, once you were Elvis, you couldn't just go hang out any old place.

But we could all hear, and it was a tough audience back in the trailer. When Mike Strater, from Chelsea, MA, was out there, his version of "Are You Lonesome Tonight?" was minutely critiqued:

"That's too fast. He's talking too fast."

"He's about to lose it."

"Don't tell me he's gonna do 'standin' there, in my underwear . . .'"

"Did he?"

"No, he didn't."

I realized I was two away from my turn. I would be getting the same going-over. It was time to wig up. "Are you nervous?" asked Cindy. I tried to fend off the question: "Elvis was always nervous."

"That's right," said Elvis Bishop. "Thousands of concerts, years and years on the road, and he never shook it off: he was scared stiff before every show."

In front of a tiny hanging mirror, I asked Robert to find any gray hairs he could at the back of my neck and stuff them under the wig.

"So *that's* what it's all about," mocked Jenny the photographer, sensing something campy and moving in on it with her camera.

"Bill Henderson, you're up!"

I stepped out into the oven of an afternoon as Mike Strater finished his set.

"Tell me quick about your tape," said Jackie.

"It starts with '2001'—"

"Want us to put any pauses in?"

"No, hold off until the vamp part, do the intro there, then let it run."

"Gotcha."

I was uneasy. Mike Strater came off to desultory applause. "Jeez, it's hot out there!" Was the crowd wilting too? Before I could follow that thought too far, I heard Jackie Hersey introducing me. But where was my music?

". . . all the way from North Carolina. BILL HENDERSON!" Smattering of applause. I should enter. But I hadn't heard "2001" yet. Maybe they decided to skip right to the vamp? No such luck. The endlessly long, pompous chords of the opening began. The crowd and I would have to wait, twiddling our thumbs, while "Thus Spake Zarathustra" thundered for the fifth time this day (only Robert Washington had been clever enough to skip it altogether). Richard Strauss overkill, and in 90-plus degrees! Would they even remember my name by the time it was over?

Oh well. Eventually, after what seemed like the entire Precambian era, came the famous drum licks leading into the vamp. I strode manfully up the cement stairs—and out onto what felt like the biggest, emptiest stage in the universe. It even included a Vegas-style runway, leading out into . . . into what, I couldn't see, because of my myopia problem. Were there people out there? I had to assume so—I could see the mike stand, like me, all by itself in this vast desert of a stage. It seemed like a 50-yard walk to it. My cue was coming up. I arrived at the spot, struck a pose, and reached for the mike stand to tilt it toward me, Elvis-style (Elvis, of course, would have had a ceremonial guitar slung around him; too much paraphernalia for me). As I did, the mike fell loose in its clip and drooped like a flaccid penis—an omen? There is a similar moment, in *That's the Way It Is*, where the same thing happens to Elvis in a recording studio. He breaks up. I hoped the crowd would pick up the allusion. They didn't.

Here came my cue.

And there it went. Just like karaoke, except no words on a monitor.

I jumped in where I could, whipping the mike out of its stand and hand-holding the stupid thing, contrary to tradition (lucky the guys in the trailer couldn't *see* this minor breech in custom; otherwise they'd be buzzing about it).

It panicked me to know that I was spooked by the situation. There was no band here to give me moral support. I was absolutely alone on this huge expanse of stage. My tape was running mindlessly, inexorably: were I to flub an entry, there would be no mercy for me. I felt my body freeze in position. I couldn't move. My mouth went dry. I realized, too late, that I should have practiced some kind of movement sequence, some steps, some "body language," SOMETHING! The Medfield gig now seemed so safe, so comfy, with its tiny piece of stage, the band guys right around me, and John Lincoln Wright orchestrating screams for me from the girls.

Suddenly I was dropping lyrics, slurring, scatting, mumbling, as the tape moved forward through time. It was an acute case of Murphy's Law: since there was absolutely no margin for error, I seemed to be committing as many mistakes as humanly possible. *Come on!* I screamed inside my mind. *Get hold of yourself!* I tried to move, but it took the form of walking from spot to spot and striking inert poses. The extra pause between songs, inserted by Bruce, seemed like an eternity each time I finished a song, heard a few claps, and waited to go onto the next. I tried a little patter. "Hot enough for you?" At one point I reached down and retrieved a fat rhinestone ring, dropped by one of the guys from the stage floor. "It's mine now," I quipped, although the audience couldn't possibly know what I was making reference to.

Something seemed wrong with my voice: I couldn't sing low with any power. Was the tape deck running slow? I was no J. D. Sumner, but the bass end of my voice wasn't *this* bad.

Sweat was now running into my eyes, down my neck. I couldn't see faces in the broad daylight: were they smiling? Frowning? Who knew? Would this set ever end?

With rote pointlessness I passed the mike from hand to hand and meandered around the upstage area in slow circles, afraid to stride out on the runway into the crowd, afraid even to acknowledge them and their pitter-pattery applause, which at this point I felt was completely unearned. Plugging on through "If I Can Dream" without a total break-down (a pyrrhic victory itself) I heard at last the welcome lead-in bars to "Can't Help Falling in Love" and knew the ordeal was almost over. Win this thing? I was lucky not to have been stoned to death out here.

Coming off, I walked into the whole gang of Elvises, who had been directed to appear backstage to sign autographs.

"Nice set," somebody said in a monotone.

"You've got some friends over here," said Jackie Hersey.

In the small, waiting throng of autograph seekers were Sebastian and some old friends, Dorothy, Caroline, and Buck. Caroline had a video camera stuck to her eye and tape was rolling. I went out to meet them.

"Good show, Elvis," said Sebastian, with hearty English cheer.

Dorothy seemed stunned, or in a state of heatstroke-inspired hilarity. She had just read *Stark Raving Elvis*, she said—and now stood before a broken-down author/icon of the main character himself.

"I wondered when I'd see you again," she said, "but I never in a million years would have thought it would be . . . like this."

"It must take real courage to stand up and do that," said Buck man-fully. Courage, I thought. Insanity. Not even a book contract was worth what I had just been through. And Memphis coming up in a week? Could I really stand it? Could I put myself through something like this again, only in the relentless glare of Elvis Presley's own holy city and the event of all events for Elvis initiates?

Someone was tugging on my scarf, which I had hoped to bestow upon some lady or other but hadn't—nor did any lady even lean forward for it (or if she did, of course, I couldn't see). I looked down and there was Myles.

"Can I have it?" he asked. "Will you sign it?"

I took the pen and signed "Bilvis, Stratham '95 . . . R.I.P." Then a TCB flash. "There you go, son." He ran off to have the others sign. As I spoke to the grown-ups, trying to strike an ironical, wisecracking

William McCranor Henderson

tone to mask my trauma, I realized Caroline was still rolling, getting it all. Jenny's automatic camera advance was firing away. I decided to do something visual, something that would express in some comic way the outlandishness of my failure.

"Here's something for you," I said to Jenny. "I'm going to give you a before and an after. Here's before . . ." I smiled nicely. "Now here's after . . ." I reached for the wig and whipped it off, as I had done in Medfield, but for all to see now, in broad daylight, not just to scare away a few pesky kids in the twilight of Medfield green, but to clown my way to a sneaky vestige of dignity.

I played it for laughs, pretended to be startled by the wig, as if it were a tarantula. Then I spoke to it: "Alas, poor Yorick . . ." I said, balancing it on my fingers at arm's length. I raised it to my head for a me-and-my-wig buddies shot. I pretended it was burning my fingers and blew on it, to cool it down.

Clowning, just like Elvis used to clown (you wish). Laugh, clown, laugh . . .

Back in the trailer, while the others were still out signing, I changed in silence. Jackie Hersey stuck her head in: "See you at nine, okay?"

"I won't be able to make it."

"You won't?" There was slight irritation in her voice. We were her entertainment, after all. "Well, that's when we're announcing the results. You won't know whether or not you won."

"I didn't win."

"How do you know? We haven't even picked up the judges' cards yet."

"I know and you know. And I've got kind of a long drive home, anyway. My family's just getting back from a trip and I really ought to be home. Thanks for everything; it's been great. I'd love to stay, but I really have to pass."

"You were okay, you know."

"Yeah, yeah. Thanks."

* * *

I emerged. It was good to be an anonymous baldy again. No one recognized me. I found Sebastian and Myles up the hillside, checking out the rides. Sebastian and I stood and talked quietly while Myles rode the Scrambler. He told me Myles had been lukewarm about the whole Elvis thing until he saw Robert Washington, who made his little eyes pop with his athleticism (he had done a standing back flip!) and his "cool."

"Caroline's going to send you a copy of the tape," Sebastian said. "Let's find some time to watch it together. I've got some thoughts for you."

"Sure. Down the line." Thinking about the Mack truck that had just run me down was the last thing I wanted to do now. I was hungry. I missed my family. I just wanted to get out of here.

"Look," Sebastian pointed. There, on the Scrambler, squealing like five-year-olds as they swooped through the air, were Cindy and Jenny. Fun, that was the right idea. It shouldn't be fraught like this; it should be a simple pleasure. After all, hadn't Elvis said to Norman Taurog or some such Hollywood director, when discipline on the set got too tight for the Memphis Mafia, "Sir, if it isn't fun, we just don't want to do it"?

I said so long to Sebastian after signing Myles's hand, my last official act of the day. The Stratham fire department was serving up pepper steak heroes at an excellent price. I sat at a table full of families—tired adults, squirmy, sticky kids—stuffing my face anonymously. After a while I picked up my suit and wig, found my way to the car, and drove on home.

Chapter

26

Back in Rhode Island, they had arrived home before me, thank goodness, and the house was lit up warmly in the darkness and full of life when I drove up.

"Did you win, Dad?"

"Look at my poison ivy, Dad."

"How'd you do, Elvis?"

I didn't make much of it. No, hadn't won, but it sure was a kick, fascinating experience, all that. And then I moved them on to their stories about the Maine woods, and that was that, until Carol got the real stuff, in explicit detail, after the kids had gone to bed.

I let a day go by before I called Jackie Hersey—a day of staring into space, reading Proust, listening to Mahler . . . a day of trying to cocoon myself into forms of oblivion that were as far away from Elvis World as I could get.

Here's how it all turned out: 1st Place . . . Robert Washington. 2nd . . . Chuck DeNault. 3rd . . . Mike Strater. 4th . . . Elvis Bishop. 5th . . . Fred Hazard. And 6th . . . ?

Well.

Jackie said that by nine o'clock, it had turned nice and cool; the crowd was four times as big; people were asking for me (I wonder).

The judges had been winners of an on-the-spot Elvis trivia contest and ranged in age from 13 to middle-aged. They rated each contestant on Vocals, Body Language, Audience Response, and Costume.

"Everybody won something. Even you."

"No."

"You won an Elvis clock, a tie, a penknife, if you had only been around to collect."

The next day, a videotape arrived from Caroline. I didn't want to watch it. In the same mail was my summons to Memphis, a letter from Images of Elvis, Inc., telling me that my sound check was scheduled for 4:00 P.M. on August 16 (the very date of Elvis's death, I noted). "You may use the band that we provide, or you may use your own accompaniment tapes." At this point, I felt, what would it matter?

"Snap out of it," Carol said. As a dancer, she had performed in every possible situation, good and bad. "One tough experience shouldn't devastate you. Come on, pick yourself up and get back into it. You can work on this stuff. I'll help you."

She was right.

After a stiff cup of coffee I was thinking I should do something immediate and practical.

I reached for a phone and called up my karaoke buddy, Dave Williamson, down in North Carolina. "Listen," I said, "this stuff is harder than I ever thought. It makes Shooters II look like Ding Dong School."

"Uh-oh."

"That's right, uh-oh. But I've been thinking—a little company would help. This Memphis thing is just over the hill and I'm going to need a bodyguard."

"Really?"

"Well, not *really* really. But someone to play the role, wear the red tour jacket, hand me my water and scarves. Do you think you could be up for that?"

"Sure, absolutely. My mother-in-law lives in Memphis, you know. Only thing is, I'm about to take off on a river trip down the Mississippi with Shannon and Will. In fact, you practically caught me heading out the door."

"Oh, well—"

"But I'll be there."

"Are you sure?"

"Bill, let me tell you something. You have no way of knowing this, but if God Almighty told me I could do only one more thing on earth before I had to die, it would be exactly what you describe. I'll be there."

Well. That was heartening. I felt better. But I still wasn't ready to look at the videotape. What else could I find to do?

Look for shoes!

Karon Yee had told me about some "flash" rock 'n' roll clothing stores on Newbury Street where I might pick up a pair of cheap plastic versions of the basic white Elvis ankle boot. Then I would bite the bullet and stop off in Cambridge to watch the Stratham tape with Sebastian on his large-screen TV.

Okay: I was functional again. I would observe, take notes. Carol would give me some movement tips. "Some days you get the fox, some days the fox gets you," goes the saying. Another day would come. With a little work I could beat this thing! With a little luck, I might even get the fox!

The Newbury Street shoe expedition was a bust. Several very pleasant young salespeople with tattoos, pink or blue splatty hair, and rings and spikes in their lips, ears, cheeks, tried to help me. I thought I had scored when I did see a white plastic ankle boot—but it had a thick, three-inch high heel, not the right look. I decided to put off the search until Memphis, where surely I could find what I wanted on Beale Street, where Elvis himself had shopped in the early days.

At Sebastian's, I popped the tape into his VCR. Caroline had captured a minute or so of Robert's set. There he was—snaking along the runway with the elegance of a tiger. A moving icon, confident, muscular, graceful, cool. Then came a smattering of Mike Strater, then Elvis Bishop . . .

"I'm next, I believe."

It wasn't quite as awful as I had expected—I actually looked halfway decent in the upgraded wig and suit, topped off by the glasses. But it was clearer than ever that (1) I had almost no body moves—and some of those I did have were all wrong; and (2) there was (as I had felt) a lack of intensity, a detached coolness. This was a solipsistic, introverted performance. Elvis's connection to his audience had been electric; I was aloof, wooden, with a chronic lack of intensity that kept my presentation on a low burner.

Sebastian saw something in particular. He had watched the other performers, and being raised a Catholic, had noted their ritualistic relationship with the audience. "To me, the others were doing something that seemed like altar work. Get down on one knee, take the silk, bestow it. These guys would use the runway so they could kneel and sing right to individual women in the audience. The Elvis clothing was like a priest's vestments—they were *invested* in the robe. They weren't so much imitating Elvis as becoming avatars through Elvis.

"And they were sexual, too, in a chaste sort of way, just as priests are sexy. These women wouldn't go to a male stripper club, but Elvis erotica is acceptable because it has the sexual charge of religion. You should go to high mass and see the real thing—the silk and spangles, the worshippers lining up for communion."

Bread and wine become body and blood . . .

"When you came on," Sebastian continued, "I was watching hard for some transformation in your persona. Jenny the photographer was in a whole different place: 'Aren't you just laughing hysterically watching your friend do Elvis?' She wasn't getting it. I was beyond camp. I wanted to tell her to shut up and let me watch. But there was a gulf between you and the audience. Something distanced you from them. What you were doing was more a performance than a ritual. Something demanding but isolated, like a thousand push-ups. You kept them out. You didn't let them participate."

Yes, he was right. I had felt it. Now I saw it.

Cocktail party wisdom was that Elvis impersonation was somehow so weird as to be anti-social. But no! The exact opposite was true. It was profoundly *social*. And I hadn't been social enough to place any better than last!

All right: I had a week. Get busy.

I opened an old file and found my early notes on Elvis's style of movement:

the lasso
the squat
the blind man's rock
glass on palm
arm-fling cutoff
bowling cutoff
open-handed punch cutoff
air guitar
fist pump
shakey leg
body palsey
backhanded throwaway

I screened *That's the Way It Is* again, the Vegas performance section. It's 1969: Elvis at his mature best. His basic stance was feet spread, heel pumping, a rhythmic shifting of weight from leg to leg on the strong beats. He sometimes "conducted" the band with his head, sometimes his hand. The left leg was constantly going up and down. He used the stirring motion and the "lasso" a lot. He'd punctuate a strong beat by drawing his fist back suddenly and pumping the elbow. His cut-offs were broad: arm fully extended to the side, he'd make a sidearm wind-up-and-throw motion—sometimes the throw itself was the cut-off, sometimes it was a hold (a *fermata*) until he swept the whole arm back again.

I needed a place to work out. Our friend Liza invited me to use her new exercise room: it had wall-to-wall mirrors and a VCR for workout tapes. It was perfect: I could monitor my movements directly in the mirror while, over my shoulder, keep an eye on the TV Elvis. With the VCR remote in my hand I could make him repeat a movement over and over, as I tried it out on my own body.

Carol came with me the first day and we looked at the Stratham tape. Her analysis: I had to *move*—start with the basic back and forth weight shift; I had to *support* with my pelvis and straighten my chron-ically hunched shoulders; I had to make articulate hand and body moves, gestures that "read." Carol watched a few numbers from *That's the Way It Is* and jotted notes on Elvis:

TAPS HEELS NOT TOES

EXCELLENT POSTURE—SHOULDERS BACK, PELVIS CENTERED

FREEZES IN POSITION (ARTICULATION) . . .

We watched my tape again.

Carol said, "You should be constantly in motion: for you, that's part of gaining the intensity you need. That goes for your face, too. You look distant, private, your face lacks animation. Elvis's expression is always dynamic, changing, he uses his head to make broad gestures, he uses the details of physical presence to create drama."

Slowly, I began to get it.

Liza and her husband John looked in, noticed something happen-ing, and urged me on. I began to feel an ease come into my movement, as though parts of my body were waking up.

"Shoulders!" said Carol.

"Pretend you're in a body-building contest!" said John.

It was hot, tiring work.

At home, I put my back-up tape on the deck, top volume, and sang along with it full voice. I was able to remember most of the lyrics I had blown in Stratham, since they had been simmering in the back of my brain ever since. "If I Can Dream" went particularly well. I whooped it up when the tape finished and yelled upstairs: "How about that? What do you think of THAT?"

"Great, Dad!" Olivia's voice replied. And she meant it.

With one day to go, I called Fetzer in Memphis. I had reserved a room at the downtown Comfort Inn, which was connected to Fetzer's apartment building.

"Great," he said. "It's a little complicated, but you can get to my place without even leaving the building. There's just one thing."

"What's that?"

"I've quit Graceland."

"Oh?"

"Yeah, they wouldn't give me a raise. I mean, I've enhanced my status, I just got licensed to carry a gun, I can get better work. So I went to 'em: I said, look what you've got here, a security specialist, licensed to carry, ability to write, rapport with every employee at Graceland—now wouldn't that indicate some kind of advancement, even just a minimal raise, even just some more hours in my schedule?"

"And?"

"Nothing, not a flicker. So I quit. I'm starting work for an outfit called Protek now. Much better pay."

"Good hours?"

"Yeah, lots of 'em. Twelve hours a day. But there's one problem . . . I'll be working nights, seven days a week. I'm gonna have to miss your show."

That was a blow. I was counting on Fetzer's presence to lend me some credibility and moral support. That left Dave, my bodyguard—

who was now somewhere on the Mississippi with his daughter Shannon and photographer Will Owens piloting a 26-foot houseboat in the name of literacy (with READ TO KIDS emblazoned on its sides). According to his wife, when last heard from he was still hoping to be in Memphis, but at this point it wasn't a sure thing. The river was a living thing and unpredictable. He had already been delayed by weather problems and mechanical failure.

What was going on here? Was this some kind of cosmic pattern? Was I to be "tested?"

But suddenly there was no time to think about it. The pure logic of events had taken over: I only had time to pack my suit and wig, throw some things in the car, pick up some maps from AAA, and hit the road for Memphis.

Chapter

27

Once you get beyond Nashville on I-40, and nothing stands between you and the mighty Mississippi but Memphis itself, a momentous thing happens that makes you know that you are entering Elvis Presley country: Elvis himself informs you. An immense cardigan-clad billboard Elvis Presley looms up to remind the traveler that this is a major frontier crossing.

"WELCOME TO MY WORLD . . ." says the colossal billboard Elvis, and he means it, literally.

At that point, I knew it would be a straight shot to Memphis—WELCOME TO MY WORLD meant that nothing of consequence now stood in the way, and in a matter of hours I would be, like never before, *among the Elvises*—as well as face to face with their impressario, Doc Franklin.

Doc, whom I only knew from the phone, was an interesting anomaly in that he had grown up comfortably and was thoroughly urbane, professional, and middle class in a way Elvis Presley could never have hoped to be. In high school, Doc ran with the well-groomed kids and had gone on to Vanderbilt and the University of Tennessee and now had a grown son who was a Memphis M.D. ("the real doctor in the family").

For no particular reason, Fortune chose Doc, as it did others, for a random walk in the Elvis god-light.

"I got out of school in June of 1961 and set up practice in Southaven, down the road from Graceland," he told me. "And probably within a month's time, Elvis's Aunt Delta brought the first dog to me."

Only three years younger than Elvis, Doc was soon taking care of every animal that passed through Graceland.

"The dogs, horses, everything. Scatter, the monkey. I took care of the ranch he had for a while, all the horses out there, the cattle. For years I guess I was doing something or other at Graceland just about every day.

"Then in 70, I wanted to branch out so I opened a great big country music nightclub called Bad Bob's about three blocks or so from Graceland. I was a big country fan. And I mean we had real performers in there—you know, Mickey Gilley, Jerry Lee Lewis, the Mandrell Sisters, Charley Pride, all of 'em. It was *the* big country nightclub in Memphis. Elvis told me several times, 'I sure wish I could come to Bad Bob's.' But he couldn't, of course. He couldn't do everyday type things like that.

"And of course, even before Elvis died, there were people around singing like him. We had a couple of guys in town that sang like Elvis all the time—even though the truth is, Memphis is an impossible Elvis impersonator market. I mean, Memphians just don't go for it.

"But these impersonators would come to town, and they would all sing at Bad Bob's. Some weeks we would more or less turn it over to Elvis impersonators. Then when Elvis died, it really took off, and my wife Jackie finally said, 'Well, let's organize it.'

"We used to have buffet lunches with Elvis impersonators, special dedications to Elvis and this and that, so it was always very, very heavy Elvis.

"And now—lord, we've got the judges, the past winners from all over the world, the newsletter, contestants from everywhere, international media attention and all that. And it's going into its tenth year. All due to Elvis."

Doc Franklin's unlikely connection with Elvis, a fluke of personal history, had rippled through the lives of everyone around him, creating a virtual "major league" for Elvis impersonators. The connection had evolved elegantly, kaleidoscopically across the years, to a point where its power could devolve even unto the likes of me.

It was late afternoon when I hit the Memphis area.

On my way into the city I would pass close enough to the Best Western to swing by and check in with the contest. Doc was certain to be there now, setting up the ballroom for opening night and the week ahead. I pulled off the interstate, into Democrat Road, and found a space in the hotel parking lot—which seemed to be remarkably full of 18-wheeler truck rigs. (I later found out that the Best Western gave a cheap rate to truckers, many of them Elvis fans, who found it convenient to stay near the airport while waiting for a load.)

The Best Western ballroom was the size of a small Wal-Mart. You passed through the lobby, down a wide spiral staircase (beside a "Blue Hawaii" pool-and-palm-tree area), and through the entrance doors, where Doc had set up an entry station. Here, you would pay, pick up brochures, buy your Images of Elvis souvenirs, and have your wrist banded with a plastic color-coded bracelet (a different color for each night). Inside was a sea of round dinner tables, each seating ten, and at the far end, a high stage, even bigger than the stage at Stratham, with a runway that jutted forward like the prow of an aircraft carrier.

On stage, a four-piece band was in place, setting levels for a sound check. I looked around the room for someone resembling Doc—having talked to him several times on the phone, I expected a small, ferretlike man. "Are you Doc?" I asked a likely candidate. He laughed and replied in an Australian accent, "Not me. Doc's over there." The man he pointed out seemed unaccountably huge, a tall galumph of a guy with big arms and a towering balancing act of a body. This was a man you would trust your horse to.

"Doc?"

"That's me." The voice was indeed Doc's.

"I'm Bill Henderson."

"Ah! Doctor Henderson from North Carolina. Well, I have to say, you *look* like an English professor."

"We're going to work on that."

Doc introduced me to his youngish wife, Jackie, an attractive, pleasant lady, and she checked me in and made sure I had my Images of Elvis free paraphernalia. As activity swirled around him, Doc kept a lofty eye on things and still managed to chat with me. "This thing'll make you feel like you woke up on a planet where the basic life form is Elvis impersonators. You'll see the best ones, too, past winners and all—they're back. But I'd say this thing's almost getting too big. We've got over 60 legitimate entries this summer, not including ringers like yourself. Of course, we have the January contest that provides some of our finalists here, but I'm trying to help develop some feeder contests around the country—Decatur, Fort Worth, Orlando—that'll take the load off our preliminaries here in August."

A tall, husky, boyish kid with horn-rimmed glasses ventured forward to speak to Doc. He had a power forward's body, but the virginal air of an Eagle Scout, and was still carrying his suitcase.

"I'm scared to death," he confided to Doc, after pumping his hand.

"Well, that's natural. We got a boy here, won all of Australia and New Zealand, and he's scared, too. The only people who don't get scared are too stupid or else too old, like Dr. Henderson here."

The joke flew right over the kid's head. "Tell me, sir, how's the judging going to work?" he asked anxiously.

"Well, it's complicated, it's almost like space science to me. You got the different categories, point scales, scores getting carried to the third decimal, photo finishes and all, but don't ask me to explain it now."

"You got something for degree of difficulty?"

"Yeah, but I leave that to my judges. That's a musical judgment. I don't know anything about music, I'm a veterinarian."

The boy looked down, then turned his gaze back up to Doc, his face strangely intensified. "But you met Elvis."

Doc shrugged. "Many times."

The talk turned to tapes versus the band. Doc favored using the band, "for showmanship."

"Let's say you want to wander into the audience and give out some scarves. Or say you want to have a little fun with somebody—kiss a few extra ladies—the band can cut you some slack while you're working. But with tapes, you better not miss a beat or you'll get run over by your own tracks."

The Eagle Scout nodded stiffly. Somehow I just couldn't imagine this guy toying with the crowd. (Nor could I really see myself in such a relaxed, commanding role.)

"How many days are you staying around?" Doc asked me, after the Eagle Scout had withdrawn.

"Right through."

He sized me up ironically. "You want to get in the finals, don't you?"

"Doc, I want to take this sucker!"

Chapter

28

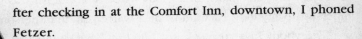fter checking in at the Comfort Inn, downtown, I phoned Fetzer.

"Well, I'm here."

"Come on down to my floor. Becky's cooking some eggplant casserole. Then we can head out there and catch the show. I don't start at Protek until tomorrow night."

I had to change elevators and negotiate my way through a combination-locked security door, but eventually, I followed the smell of eggplant casserole and the sound of rockabilly music until I was at Fetzer's apartment door.

"Come in and listen to the master!" Fetzer roared over his stereo, letting me in. He introduced me to Becky, his ex-wife, a tall, vivacious blonde, from Ripley, 50 miles north. Becky had been up since 4:00 A.M. (she was a hard-working small-town lawyer) but you couldn't tell. Nor was there the slightest sign that she and Fetzer were "exes." The two of them made a spirited couple—both smart, charming, endlessly curious, and, like racehorses, possessed of an almost overabundant store of high energy.

"Recognize the voice?"

It was an early rockabilly recording, but beyond that I drew a blank. "Is it Carl Perkins?" I guessed, not really believing it.

"Warren Smith."

"Warren Smith? 'The Red Cadillac and Black Mustache' guy?"

"Yep." Fetzer showed me a picture of Smith, an unattractive guy with a plain face, crew cut hair, a pinched nose. He was fronting a trio exactly like Elvis's fifties combo. "Warren Smith, the early Sun artist. Look at that band. Elvis didn't invent the *Ed Sullivan Show* thing, it was already out there. He might even have stole it from old Warren, who I firmly believe was better than Elvis, but he had one big problem: a rotten awful personality. Everybody hated him. But if I was going to impersonate anybody, I'd want to be a Warren Smith impersonator."

"Everybody says you look just like him," Becky mocked, echoing an impersonator in-joke Fetzer had picked up while working at Graceland.

I couldn't fathom his extreme enthusiasm for Warren Smith: the more I listened, the more he sounded like a run-of-the-mill Hank Williams imitator. We listened to "The Fool," and Fetzer started to sing along in his powerful (if unsteady) Ernest Tubb baritone. This got Becky up and moving.

"Can you dance, Bill?" she demanded. Before I had a chance to hem or haw, she was putting me through my basic (very basic) beach-boogie swing dance repertoire. Fetzer's voice boomed. Becky and I did the bop.

"Come on, Elvis, show us your moves!"

Moves—hey, I actually had a few now! I went into a lecture-demonstration, based on my study of the past week—focusing on what I had now come to believe was the root of all Elvis's moves, the heel-tap (the secret, I could show, of E's celebrated "shaky leg!"). But then, what good were the moves if they had no effect?

"There's one thing I'm worried about," I said. "And that's that when I'm up there, with my bodyguard and all those scarves, that not one woman'll come forward for a scarf."

"Well, then you go out and hook one," said Fetzer. "Chase one down."

"I'll be there!" said Becky. "I'll bring my sister, too, and my mama! We'll all come up, how's that?"

"That's what I need. I've had bad dreams about it. I'm standing there on the edge of the stage, looking out into the dark, holding out a scarf—please, please, take this scarf!—and NOTHING. Nobody there. Just darkness."

"Don't worry, Bill. We'll be out there."

"All right," Fetzer drawled, wiping his mouth. "Let's get over to the Best Western and show those Elvis dudes a thing or two."

It was Fetzer's last night as a free man and he wanted to kick back and enjoy it. Strutting into the Best Western ballroom, he escorted Becky to a front table, close enough to touch the performers. The stage runway jutted to within a few feet of their chairs and put them precisely where they wanted to be: where the action was at its white-hot center.

Fetzer right away picked out a favorite Elvis, Jim DeShaw, a plump, dynamic "young Elvis" from Dallas. Another fave was an insolent hillbilly cat type, Rick E. Aron.

Doc had noted that there were a ton of young Elvises these days. "You hardly ever saw them until a few years back. Then Kevin Mills won the contest, doing young Elvis, and every year since, there've been more."

An idea struck me: watching Rick E. and Jim DeShaw, I saw in both of them a defiant, in-your-face stance that struck me as distinctly "alternative" in character. Was there a Generation X factor working here? These Elvises didn't go out into the audience and fondle the ladies; they stood there and glared, daring you to like them—or *not* like them. "Who cares?" they seemed to be saying. "As far as I'm concerned, it's all the same whether you like me or not."

"That's pure Elvis. Defiance. Roots!" Fetzer crowed, and he

whooped it up big for the "roots" Elvises. I was familiar with the early Elvis stance; I had watched the clips from *Elvis '56: In the Beginning* over and over. They weren't directly relevant to what I was trying to do, but I thought I had picked up something Fetzer wasn't seeing: that in the midst of defiance, the youthful Elvis was coaxing, teasing, playing his audience—the women especially—for every ounce of emotional response he could get out of them. Unlike Warren Smith (the guy nobody liked) Elvis wanted *desperately* to be liked, even loved.

Becky, within five minutes, had had heart-to-heart talks with five or six of the women at the front tables. One pretty middle-aged lady had come for the entire week, with three generations of her family, and attended every year. She had been an Elvis fan as a girl, but so poor that she had never been able to buy a ticket to an Elvis concert. Now that she had money, she was letting her money buy as much live Elvis performance as it could.

A German, Ralf Wolter, came out in an idiosyncratic white suit with a red satin shirt. He was young and tall, with matinee idol looks—a large sensitive mouth and a wistful, almost melancholy presence. He sang with no accent, but his thickly accented spoken English was hard to understand. At one point, he seemed to have a problem with the band. Or perhaps it was the band's problem: with anything more complex than "Blue Suede Shoes" or "Hound Dog," they seemed unsure of the basic chord changes.

I had been handed a song list by the guitar player:

All Shook Up
An American Trilogy
Are You Lonesome Tonight?
Blue Suede Shoes
Burning Love
Can't Help Falling in Love
Don't Be Cruel
Good Rockin' Tonight

Heartbreak Hotel

Hound Dog

It's Now or Never

Jailhouse Rock

Johnny B. Goode

Lawdy Miss Clawdy

Little Sister

Love Me Tender

Loving You

Memphis, Tennessee

Mystery Train

My Way

Polk Salad Annie

Return to Sender

Rip It Up

See See Rider/2001

Shake, Rattle, and Roll

Steamroller Blues

Suspicion

Suspicious Minds

Teddy Bear

That's All Right, Mama

Too Much

Treat Me Nice

Unchained Melody

Whole Lotta Shakin'

You Gave Me a Mountain

A decent basic repertoire. But could they deliver? They had been together for only three weeks. Could a pickup group, no matter how talented each member, meld so quickly into an "Elvis band"? They had a strong drummer, in the Ronnie Tutt tradition, a must in any Elvis band. But the guitar player's solos were generic rock, and he showed no knowledge of (or interest in) the Scottie Moore/James Burton solos so familiar to fans. Worse than that, I could hear the band actually missing crucial chord progressions that were central to the harmonic patterns of some of the Elvis staples. So: tape or band? I still didn't know what I was going to do. But the more problems I saw on stage, the more I was leaning toward using tapes.

Following Ralf Wolter (and using tapes) came John Tally, the Eagle Scout, transformed by an elaborate jumpsuit and cape, and calling on "the King up above" to help him out.

"A mutant," Fetzer hissed into my ear. "If he's so young, why's he doing the mutant Elvis?"

Tally's suit was genuinely splendid—I couldn't quite place it in the Elvis suit hall of fame, but Fetzer said he recognized it as an exact replica of one of the suits on display at Graceland. Big, stolid, and full-voiced, he had everything but maturity. He shunned the rockers and went straight for the heights, the Olympian material, those monumental power ballads. His every move was an accurate replica of some move Elvis had once made, perfect in a sense, but too carefully sculpted—like a student's slavish copy of his master's drawing. And, as I suspected when I observed him with Doc earlier, he lacked looseness, spontaneity. When he came out into the audience to bestow scarves, he was a bit stiff, which in turn made everyone else tighten up sympathetically.

He made one strategic error: giving a scarf and a kiss in the midst of "How Great Thou Art," a *sacred* number. This was a genre-crossing taboo—simply not done. He closed with "An American Trilogy," the most dramatic of the Elvis production numbers—typically done with an American flag backdrop (as in Pete Willcox's show at Pigeon Forge). Tally closed big, turning his back to the audience and raising his arms so that the cape unfurled like a wet butterfly flaring into life fresh from its cocoon. *Showing the cape,* I realized, had a powerful effect on an Elvis audience, and resonated on the animal level, as when a male peacock fans its plumed tail. This was powerful iconography, and the crowd responded.

Fetzer wagged his head back and forth, unmoved.

It was after midnight before the first slate of preliminaries was finished. Now the fun began. Doc had lined up exhibitions by three "pros." Kevin Mills, Young Elvis extraordinaire, was here from Tunica, a gambling haven just across the Mississippi state line, where he was now working a steady gig at the Sheraton Casino. Steve Chappell, last year's winner, was also on hand, as was Michael Hoover, from Virginia Beach, the contest's first-ever winner and one of the most durable, popular Elvises on the national circuit. I was looking forward to these guys, not just as the cream of the crop, but also because they represented such a wide spread of Elvis types.

Kevin Mills came first: small, quick, agile, he exuded the supreme confidence you need to dominate a crowd (not surprisingly, I noticed this was true of all the pros). He was from New Jersey, son of a pizza shop owner, an unreconstructed northerner who made not the slightest attempt to sound southern. Even when rapping the classic talk-intro to "Polk Salad Annie" ("Some y'all nev' been down south too much" and so on), he sounded more like Danny Devito than Elvis. Kinetically, Mills was about as perfect an early Elvis as you could imagine, again and again pulling off body moves that thrilled the crowd. He started with the gold lamé jacket, then stripped down to basic black for some of the more sexually suggestive numbers, like "Trouble," "One Night," and "Little Sister." He never got frank or suggestive, however, and was a favorite of the little girls (there were at least half a dozen) sitting on the floor beside the stage making faces and snapping pictures. At one point he hopped off the stage and ran a minigauntlet, receiving awkward little prepubescent pecks from all of them.

Steve Chappell, the reigning champ, who followed, was a different story. Glaring down at the same little girls with a look that said Where did these bugs come from? he screwed up his brow.

"Boo!" he said.

His face was round, his lips rubbery. He had short, kinky, brown-ish hair. His body was big. He roamed. Pretty quickly he established the all-important sense of *authority*. "I might not look right or act right," his manner said, "but I'm the boss. I'm in charge." Like Kevin Mills, he didn't project an abject reverence for Elvis. The identification with Elvis seemed to be just a starting point, almost a superficiality. His version of the sorrowful "Hurt" was anti-bathetic, emotionally discon-nected. He went out and jumped up on a tabletop to start it. He finished on stage, toppling backward into a cross-legged parody of Elvis "relaxing" on the boards—then bounced up, Buster Keaton–like, with-out a trace of expression on his face.

He played flirty games with three or four women who hovered near the stage. His "Concho" jumpsuit had a beaded macramé belt that hung down to his knees in the form of a sash. At one point he backed up to the edge of the stage and invited one of the women below to "pull my sash"—she was only too glad to reach between his legs, grab it, and yank on it like a bell rope.

"You like that?" he said. "Come on down tomorrow night and watch Irv Cass strip down to his swimming trunks. Is Irv out there? Come on up here, Irv! Huh? He's not?"

"I've never seen an Elvis impersonator like this guy," I said to Fet-zer.

"He's an original, all right," Fetzer said, and added, "Which has got to be a paradox, I suppose; if you're an impersonator."

"Look at him!" Doc was needling me, in his stretch slacks and XL LaCoste golf shirt: "Overripe, overeducated, definitely overage. You ought to be home grading papers, Professor."

He was lurking around the entrance table, arms folded, one of the stations along the roughly circular peregrination that led him, endlessly roaming, through the ballroom as night boogied along toward morning and the show went on and on and on.

"What time is it, somebody? Man, I tell you, these late nights are hard on a working veterinarian. I've got amputations coming up, two dogs tomorrow, two later in the week. I don't know if I'm going to be able to keep my eyes open." Arms folded, he drifted on to his next station.

Up on stage, Michael Hoover was closing out the night. He was a husky, sweet-faced guy in a lime-green jumpsuit. With short hair, Hoover might almost have been a candidate for Superman. He had a bright, high baritone and a straightforward professionalism that brought Rick Marino's style to mind.

Elvis performance, I thought, is a kind of semiotic language: Michael Hoover didn't have to strain at being Elvis; he simply "spoke" the language so effortlessly it was as if he were in his living room—not really *working at* anything so much as simply going about his normal life. For him, personal style wasn't the issue (as it was for Steve Chappell): Michael Hoover was simply a fluent speaker of "Elvis."

All right, I was here, it was three in the morning. In one night, I had seen more Elvis impersonators than in my entire life. Enough was enough: I was in training. It was time to go.

I said good night to Fetzer and Becky—we agreed to meet for a late breakfast in the morning.

Back in my hotel room, I was amazed to hear yammering voices in the suite next door. I knew there was some kind of high school basketball tournament in town, but this wasn't the noise of carousing high schoolers, this was something else: it sounded like an entire family of people who had shouted for so many years that they had no idea how to speak quietly. There seemed to be two booming male voices, one high and one low, and an indeterminant number of women and children, making trips to the ice machine, the Coke machine. And this was 4:00 A.M.!

Not that I let it bother me. The other hotel guests could complain—I was deep in sleep almost before I had finished arranging the rubbery hotel pillows beneath my head.

Chapter

29

Morning—very late morning.

Fetzer and I got on the Main Street Trolley, a lovingly re-stored old trolley line meant to lure tourists downtown, but also a practical way to travel Main Street. At the Beale Street stop, everybody got off—everybody but us. We were headed even deeper into hardcore urban Memphis, where Elvis's favorite hamburger joint, The Gridiron, still operates much as it did in the 50s, when Elvis and his boys had their own special booth near the back.

We sat in Elvis's booth.

My digestive system wasn't ready for hamburgers yet, but (much to Fetzer's consternation) the management had just that week canceled a Gridiron tradition, the 24-hour-breakfast. We were too late: it was lunchtime. I settled for a bowl of chili.

"Well," I said, "what do you think about last night?"

"Amazing," Fetzer said. "I wish I could be there tonight. But I got the theme for your book."

"Oh?"

"It's the generation war between the young Elvises and the mutants."

"That sounds like your book, not mine. And by the way, whether you know it or not, you're sitting here talking to one of the 'mutants.'"

"Well, I understand that—so go ahead and tell me what you see in the 70s Elvis."

"Okay: maturity, command, range, a kind of splendor—"

"What I see is decadence. He started off with something pure and exciting and by the 70s, it was all glitter and pomp and bad covers of stuff like 'Steamroller Blues' and 'My Way.' By the way, when Sid Vicious sings 'Moy Woy' he gets the real meaning out of it, which is: I might've messed up my own life, and a bunch of other people's, too— but, by God, I did it my way! I mean, no wonder it's the all-time number one on the barflies' hit parade—!"

"Can we stay on the subject? I mean, I don't particularly like 'My Way,' but that doesn't mean Elvis didn't do any good stuff at all during the 70s."

"Name some."

"'Hurt' . . . 'Moody Blue' . . . 'Kentucky Rain' . . ."

Fetzer shrugged and maintained his puckish, slightly tilted grin. Obviously a few exceptions only proved the rule. For Fetzer, Elvis was born in 1935 and, for all practical purposes, died in 1958, period.

"You know what I'd like to see?" said Fetzer, his face brightening with a new idea. "This would be a natural extension of the contest—a Christ-impersonator event!"

"Like on-stage healing?"

"That's right: Miracles—feeding the multitudes! Costume—how good is your halo? Crucifixions! Resurrections!"

"Oh, come on, Fetzer—"

"Well, it wouldn't be so awful different from what they go through in 'American Trilogy,' would it? I mean, nobody's actually getting nailed to the cross, but there's some kind of straining toward being Christ going on there. I mean, Elvis is a religion, don't tell me it's not."

"That's easy to say, and there are similarities. I don't think they go deep enough, though. Most Elvis fans are devout, go to church on Sunday, and so on."

"But who do they actually *worship*? Elvis. They believe he was a piece of Godhead, come down here in an earth suit. Christ and Elvis, Elvis and Christ. I know, I've talked to plenty of these people at Graceland."

The Elvis-as-Religion argument again—a dog chasing its tail, as far as I was concerned. And anyway, I needed shoes.

"Let's go to Beale Street—"

"And get you some mutant boots? I don't think Beale Street's the place anymore. There's about five stores along Main Street that's bound to sell them. Along with some extra rings for your fingers."

We walked back up Main in the heat. As usual, Fetzer knew everybody. A cruising panhandler . . . two dwarf street musicians . . . a woman selling Afrocentric art on the sidewalk.

At the corner of Beale, we ran into Jim DeShaw and his dad. The young DeShaw was dressed perfectly for the fabled Beale Street of old: his hair carefully slicked, his clothes all "cool" urban zoot creations in loud mismatching pastels. His dad, who looked about my age, had a bushy head of graying hair, cut short, and looked pretty cool himself, all in black.

"I'm looking for Lansky Brothers," said Jim.

"That's it, there," said Fetzer, pointing. "Or was it. It's just a junk discount store now, a flea market almost. You can buy all the Elvis souvenirs you want for at least half what they'd cost at Graceland."

"They got jewelry there? I need some jewelry. I got a show in Dallas coming up. '12 Elvises,' it's called. I only get five minutes, but the money's great. I want to look good, man."

"You aren't doing anything past 58, I hope."

"Not me. My own band down there, Speedster, we don't do anything past 57. That's it, man. The music stopped right there."

Fetzer beamed and nodded broadly.

*   *   *

The search for shoes got under way in earnest. We worked through a half dozen forlorn shops where hungry-eyed black or Asian entrepreneurs, their businesses hanging on downtown by a garish thread, tried their best to come up with something that would do. "It's not the season," one of them said. As if, I thought in my growing identity as an impersonator, as if there could *be* a season on Elvis Presley footwear. We tried several suburban malls. Even less luck there. We were foundering. In a final Hail-Mary gambit, Fetzer led me to a bleak strip mall where there was a business that catered to security and hospital employees. "You just might find something designed for an orderly or a guard that has to wear white." It was an interesting store: I could have left with a billy club, cans of mace and pepper spray, handcuffs, a badge. Their only footwear turned out to be black, brown, or white clodhoppers so heavy that I would have looked like I was doing Elvis as a space walker.

The heat was getting worse. As we dragged ourselves back to the car, every step seemed impeded by invisible shackles. I began to feel like I was running a fever. I was losing time, time that I could be spending in my air-conditioned hotel room practicing, running my moves, creating my rap.

"Fetzer, I'm giving up. The white sneaks will have to do."

"They might take off points."

"Can't be helped."

At the hotel, I lay on my bed with a yellow pad in front of me. It had occurred to me that I should be ready to say something when I went out on stage Wednesday night. Something that would relax the crowd, maybe draw a laugh, a chuckle. "Ladies and gentlemen, I'm out to prove that college professors have soul—and I don't mean the kind of scholarly soul they were serving down at Ole Miss last week. I'd call that 'filet of soul' . . ."

Too cute, too arch.

"Folks, I know you get asked this question every five minutes, but—is everybody having fun?"

Too much of a cliché, even with the disclaimer.

"I tell you what, I'm havin' the time of my life!"

So what?

I was sagging. If I could only gather the energy to dig out my boom box, I could work out with my tracks. But the shoe search (bootless!) in the 103 degree furnace of early afternoon had undone me. An illusion of paralysis came over me; the yellow pad drooped to my lap. In a last-ditch attempt to stay conscious I reached for the TV remote and punched the on button. There was something about the Grateful Dead. And Death . . .

Jerry Garcia dead? When had *that* happened? Where had I been? An announcer was speculating about a Jerry Garcia death cult rivaling Elvis's. But the effect was like news signals arriving in faint bursts from the other side of the galaxy.

I tried to ponder the light-years of separation between planet Elvis and planet Jerry. I tried and simply couldn't. My mind buckled under the task—except for one clear thought that blazed up like a nova: the separation itself was not what mattered. Even though a Deadhead was as dissimilar to an Elvis fan as a passion fruit to a banana, the mechanism was identical. On the human level, we were looking at the same phenomenon: performer becomes laden with mana; his tribe builds a world, a way of being, a past, a present, and a future, all based on the power of that mana, the spiritual sustenance that comes from living and endlessly reliving the miracle of that performer's mighty presence.

Did I think that thought?

No, not then, not in those words. A flash blazed and subsided, the words came later. I was too tired then for words. Too tired even to mourn Jerry's passing (a shock, but not entirely unexpected).

I punched off the TV and fell into deep, blank, sleep . . .

And somewhere in that sleep, I was young again, with long, flowing hair, as it had once been, years ago. I had just bought an ancient hippie van and my girlfriend and I were on our way to a greater California, where everything was green and bronze-red in the endless sun, where the water flowed like sparkling burgundy wine, where everyone was beautiful and loved everyone else and no one ever got any older than twenty . . .

Good-bye, Jerry. Good-bye, old man.

You were cool, too.

Chapter

30

Rolling into the Best Western, nearly show time, I saw Elvises here, Elvises there, Elvises everywhere. Outside, an army-clad GI Elvis was posing for some fans; at the front door, a pampered-looking dude with the air of a golf pro (and a rack of Elvis suits) was descending from his van/limo, with an entourage.

I spotted the "Israeli Elvis," Yaniv Rozen, in casual civvies, shooting pool with his voluptuous blond fiancée Machal. Some of my Jewish friends held Elvis Presley in awe and horror as a kind of crypto-Nazi figure, because of his Nordic looks and the fact that he was an unrepentant southerner. I knew they would be incredulous (even indignant, perhaps) at the notion of an Israeli Elvis—I was mildly surprised myself—so I wanted to find out as much as I could while I was here.

"Yaniv! Got a minute to talk?"

Rozen whispered something to Machal. Because the two of them spent much of their time entwined, as if joined together at the hip, seeing them together produced an erotic effect, as though they were highly sexualized Siamese kissin' cousins. But this time (alas for me) Machal shrugged and went off in the other direction.

Rozen had an awful photo business card: in it he wore a white "Nail" jumpsuit with American Eagle belt. Oversized drugstore shades dwarfed him, bad lighting fattened his lips, and the total image was that of a diminutive, goggle-eyed action figure. This was too bad: although slim, he was tall, about six feet, and much better looking than his picture. I could see Rozen had a knack for friendship. He and Machal were almost always surrounded by others. He was popular with fans and the other impersonators alike. "These are my friends," he told me, settling into a chair near the pool table. "They understand what I'm doing, we are all doing the same thing, we all love Elvis, we go out, we have fun together."

He had some of the princely hauteur that you see in native-born Israeli men, but it was leavened by a playful, almost goofy gregariousness. Back in Israel, he was in direct marketing, pioneering a telemarketing system which, he said, wouldn't be anything new in the U.S. but was revolutionary in Israel. Israel wasn't anywhere near up to speed on Elvis impersonators, either.

"There's no place to work, really," he complained. "The club scene is tawdry—a singer and a stripper. You have to break into the hotels, where there is tourist business. I'm not there yet."

"Are there Elvis fans in Israel?"

"Yes, but they're scattered. Not organized. What we need is fan clubs. Then you get events, concerts—and I would have better success if I were taken up by a fan club."

I asked if he knew about The Jewish Ancestor (Elvis's maternal great-grandmother, Martha Tackett Mansell). He grinned with satisfaction; he knew all about her.

"Elvis liked Jews. I know several of his guys were Jewish. Larry Geller, the 'guru' guy. The Memphis Mafia boys, George Klein, Alan Fortas, Marty Lacker. And I know about the Star of David he had put on his mother's tombstone, for the great-grandmother, and the Hebrew charm on his necklace . . ."

"How'd you get into doing Elvis?"

"My father is a great Elvis fan; he played Elvis music constantly. I heard it from when I was a baby. But in Israel this is unusual. You are a freak."

Rozen had turned up at last January's contest as a tourist, no jump-suits, nothing. Doc told him to get up and sing anyway. Now he was back, and the feeling was one of coming home, reminiscent of the old Jewish cliché, "like a Jew in Jerusalem."

"Being here in Memphis gives me a spirit I crave for back home, but you can't find it. To breathe the air of this place, to go to Elvis's home—can you believe, the other Israeli Elvis impersonators have never been to Graceland! But they are not serious—they come out around January 8th or August 16th and do lip-sync stuff, lookalike con-tests. There might be 10 of us in Israel, but Israelis think any kind of impersonation is weird. They think I'm crazy. Wearing sideburns—no one does that in Israel. They can't understand I'm doing this because I want to show my love for Elvis, not just for fun or money . . . to wear the suit, to get up and sing the songs . . . it's love."

Recently he thought he had a chance to get the point across to all Israel. A reporter from a prominent Tel Aviv daily wanted to do an in-depth story on him. He gave her four hours of his time, explained why he did it, what it meant to his life; he put on his suits, one by one, for pictures.

His father had just faxed him the article from the paper and he was furious. The reporter had burned him. She made him look stupid, buf-foonish—which, he felt, was most likely her plan all along.

"This is what we face with the media. Not just in Israel, but in U.S. too. She asked me, 'Would you do this for a living?' I said, 'No, I have my job, my profession. It's best for doing Elvis to be a serious hobby.' 'But if someone offered you 10 million dollars?' I laughed. It was a silly idea. 'For 10 million? Sure.' This she turned into 'he wants to go pro because he thinks if he does, he'll make 10 million dollars.' Now what is my employer, who gave me a vacation to come here, what is he going to think when he reads this? This is in a paper that everybody reads. I am very angry."

Impersonators as clowns: déjà vu all over again. But at least the Israelis had an excuse: only a half century away from genocide, surrounded by countries that wanted to push them into the sea, it was no wonder that they might view Elvis impersonation as comically irrelevant to their national preoccupations.

Things were picking up as darkness fell. Elvises began to appear, in full costume, in the foyer of the ballroom. Some would be performing tonight, but others had already gone on, like John Tally, the "Eagle Scout" from the night before. And some weren't scheduled until later in the week. So they gathered like peacocks, to schmooze and strut, hanging around the ballroom foyer as though it were an anteroom in Louis XIV's Versailles. Fans with snapshot cameras, looking for an Elvis or two to have their picture taken with, kept them busy posing. There was action of some kind wherever I looked: Doc held forth, a visible beacon, at least a full head taller than everyone around him. A crew of tuxedoed professional waiters, most of them elderly blacks, swirled and circled, waiting for drink and food orders from the tables (I wondered what they made of this unusual group of crazy white folks). There was a good bit of casual contact between the younger Elvi and their fans: I saw one "hillbilly cat" disappearing into the elevator with two girls; one had her hand under his shirt.

Jim DeShaw and his dad were perched at a table off by themselves. They had decided to pack it in tomorrow. "We're going back to Dallas, man. It's fixed," Jim said. "I might make the finals, but I know I won't win. He's already got his finalists, and already got his winner. Rick E. knows who they are. You never win the first time. I could stay, but I won't win, so why hang around?"

There was a stir back at the entry table. Rick Marino had arrived, with a small entourage from Jacksonville. Aside from his hair, there was nothing about him that said "Elvis." True to his word, he was there as a tourist, in shorts and T-shirt.

"We're just here to watch, catch some of the action, see some old friends," he said. "Check with me later about who you think's got the inside track."

"Rick, *I've* got the inside track," I said, with my best poker face. "Come back Wednesday night and see for yourself. You won't believe how far I've come."

"Wish I could. We're leaving Wednesday morning. But you're right, I wouldn't believe it. And I don't have to see it to not believe it, either—but good luck, son. If you win, I'll buy you a Cadillac."

He and his bunch settled in at a table along with Mike Albert, another pro, an auctioneer from Ohio ("I'm getting booked everywhere. I don't know at this point if I'm a part-time Elvis, or a part-time auctioneer!"). That day, Albert had done two shows at Libertyland, the amusement park Elvis used to rent for his friends, and Doc had scheduled him to do a showcase here later in the week.

"Contests are too weird," said Rick. "I don't have anything to do with 'em anymore. I once entered one in Orlando as a favor to the organizer. He asked me and Michael Hoover to enter, to give it some class. But there was this rule that your place was determined on a first-come, first-served basis, and by the time we entered, we had to settle for the last two places. I asked Michael if he was going to use tapes. 'No,' he says, 'I think I'll go with the band—even though they suck—because by that time the judges will've heard the same back-up tracks twenty times.' So this dumb contest was full of wanna-be's, guys with spray-painted suits, lip-syncers. By the time me and Mike went on, the judges were burned out. We didn't even place, man! I didn't care about the prizes, but I had to suffer the humiliation of gettin' skunked! But . . . here's the funny part: they forgot to hand out the prizes. I was in the room later, after it was all over, and saw the trophies just sittin' there. I told my bodyguard to grab 'em. Michael and I went home to my house and I awarded 'em myself—first prize to me, second prize to Michael—and anyway, I got my picture in the *Sentinel* and the Orlando Magic ended up paying me three grand to do a half-time show, so what the heck? What goes around comes around."

Rick E. Aron, the Young Elvis from Santa Rosa, California, was table-hopping, hanging out with groups of younger impersonators, chatting with girls—and perhaps at the center of the "young Elvis conspiracy," if (as Fetzer was convinced) there was one. He was 21, and his face had the degenerate innocence of a boy vampire. He told me he had done his first Elvis impersonation for his family at age four. He was Italian-American (real name Lenzi), and music flowed in his blood—he said he identified with his grandfather, who sang grand opera, but had never been able to make a living at it. While he got a temple rub from a fan (he, like a lot of us, was suffering from intermittent headaches from the smoky, recycled air inside the Best Western), he laid out his theory of the contest. It was fixed: Doc exerted control over who would win. This year's winner was already decided. It would be Irv Cass (whom Steve Chappell had taunted in his absence). And yes, there was a prejudice in favor of the Vegas era.

But what about Kevin Mills, who won as a 50s Elvis?

"Yeah, he blew in and took it in his first shot. But that was a kind of quirk. I think Doc realized he needed something new, some new energy, and here it came in Kevin. I think there's definitely a bias in the other direction. The contest really ought to have divisions: Young Elvis/Old Elvis . . . New Performer/Experienced Performer."

I tried out my Generation-X theory on him—that the early Elvis style echoed today's alternative stance. He agreed, but then he threw me a complete curveball:

"Actually, I love the 70s Elvis. I can't wait to put on the jumpsuit and do that material. I just can't pull it off yet—my face hasn't grown into it. I'll tell you this, though: when you see me in the finals, you're going to see me go to black leather. This is a first: I've never done it before."

Black leather: the midcareer Elvis of the 68 Comeback . . . Elvis at 33, reentering the lists as a mature live performer. Black leather was a gateway to the later jumpsuit Elvis. And, Rick E. told me, he was going to end his set with the quintessential song from that transitional moment, "If I Can Dream," which is about as far removed from early rock-abilly, in style and spirit, as you could hope to get.

I wished Fetzer were here for this, the coming out of this neo-phyte-mutant.

The band took the stage now, and opened the evening with a per-functory "Great Balls of Fire," sung by their bass player. I found a seat at a front table, ordered a beer, and settled in for what turned out to be a full evening's demonstration of how broad and accommodating was the platform on which Elvis performance was built. One by one, a gallery of Elvises passed before me, each unique, yet each an offshoot of some genuine performance facet of Elvis himself. A few examples:

Irv Cass was indeed the same Irv Cass that Steve Chappell had re-viled suggestively from the stage the night before. Now I saw why. Like the Chippendale's male strippers, Cass front-loaded his act with raw sexual exhibitionism. His male anatomy was visible as an articulate bulge down one of his pant legs. His "shakey leg" shook wildly. He humped and ground his pelvis like a hoochy-koochy dancer until the move took on a monotonous, worn-out numbness.

At the other end of the taste spectrum, Ken Cox based his act en-tirely on the religious Elvis: middle-aged, dressed in a simple black shirt that shimmered with a Milky Way of tiny rhinestones, he began with a little speech: "Every day of his life, Elvis warmed up with it, went to bed with it, and said he should have stuck with it. With that in mind I'm going to do an all-gospel tribute."

An atypical Elvis offshoot was Chris Cave, an Ole Miss student who had performed at the Elvis Conference, where he billed himself "The World's 7th ranked Elvis." Cave built his persona on Elvis's madcap sense of humor; this led to a sort of Elvis-based college comedy act. Cave was a frat-mixer Elvis, the sly, jokey sophomore sent in to warm up a crowd of freshmen pledges. He was genuinely capable of "doing Elvis," as he proved on "Polk Salad Annie," but seemed to prefer to work for moments of high bad taste and physical slapstick. He was small and nerdy, with a wiseguy style that lent itself best to insult comedy. A woman brought him a cup of water; as soon as she turned to walk away, he pretended to toss the water down her back. Another woman came forward for a scarf: he mimed blowing his nose into it (she walked away in disgust).

Chris T. Young, a seeded finalist from the January contest, made an impressive impromptu appearance, announcing that he was going to do a set of seldom-heard Elvis songs. "This is a real treat," I heard a woman say, "I mean—after hearing 'See See Rider' twenty times!" Young moved through his set with assurance, an attractive figure, dark-haired, about 25, perfectly fitted in a stunning Peacock, the design embroidered in multicolored silk on white—very tasteful, no Liberace spangles. I particularly noticed his fluent scarf technique—he seemed to have about a dozen different moves for delivering the rectangular satin to the women who came forward, each move calculated to be sexy, affectionate, yet casual.

As Young bowed out to applause, Doc slipped in beside me.

"That was unusual," I said. "A real connoisseur's choice."

"Yep. That kind of thing doesn't go unnoticed either," Doc said. He motioned toward the entrance with his head. "By the way, there's somebody at the front looking for you."

Lo and behold—there stood my bodyguard!

Dave Williamson was fresh off the Mississippi. The river trip itself had given no problem, but on land, Dave insisted on driving (and maintaining, hopelessly) an ancient pickup truck that broke down wherever he went. "Let's see, we lost the taillights, the brakelights, some lug nuts from one of the wheels. The windshield wipers broke. We lost the headlights. Going home we lost a shock absorber and the boat started bouncing 'cause the truck was bouncing, which almost sheered off the transom and we nearly had a 60 hp Evinrude fall off in the interstate. I sent Shannon and the Evinrude on home in Will's car and I parked the boat with some brother cops in Knoxville—and here I am. How's it going here?"

"All I can say is, thank goodness I wasn't scheduled for evening number one," I said to Dave. "I just wouldn't have been ready."

"What will it take you at this point?"

"Well, I don't think I'll have any memory problems. I have to figure out how to incorporate some of these things I've been seeing them do. Tomorrow's a night off. I just need some time alone in the hotel room. I'll be ready."

The evening's pro showcase featured Mori Yasumasa, from Japan, with his own band. Mori had won the contest in 93 and was back this year, playing gigs around town, recording at Sun Studio, and touring Elvis country with a group of nine Japanese Elvis fans in tow.

"I want to tell you boys two stories Mori told me," Doc said, as Dave and I stood at the entrance, among a full flourish of peacock Elvises. "And they're not funny, either of them, although I guess they do have a certain grim irony. First story: Four years ago, Japan's leading Elvis impersonator, Kyoshi Ito, died. He was Mori's mentor. He wanted his ashes scattered at Graceland, maybe with a little ceremony. Graceland refused. So one day, in the spring, a Japanese tour group came through the mansion. They got around to the Meditation Garden and, on a signal, they all pulled out little plastic Baggies, opened them up, and scattered Kyoshi all over the grounds.

"Second story: Today, this very morning, Mori and his own tour group went down to Tupelo in two rented cars. Now, you understand, for them this was like a trip to Bethlehem. Well, some dumb Tupelo cop stopped them—'cause their eyes pointed the wrong way, y'know—and asked for their driver's licenses. They had international licenses, but this lug had never seen one. So he impounded their cars and they had to come back to Memphis on a bus. Now, isn't this a sad irony: Japan's leading Elvis impersonator (now that Kyoshi's gone), visiting Elvis Presley's birthplace, and they treat him like that?"

Wagging his head mournfully, Doc folded his arms and moved along to the next station on his route.

Japanese Elvis virtuoso Mori Yasumasa.
(Photo courtesy of Patty Carroll.)

The second story took on an even deeper irony once Mori went into action. He was quite simply stunning—an explosive, acrobatic, charismatic performer. It was no wonder he had won here. Despite his small, boyish stature and his dark Japanese looks, he was a virtual catalog of Elvis's full performance repertoire. Watching him, I realized he was the best example yet of Rick Marino's dictum that the top impersonators use Elvis as a platform for their own personality. He made no attempt to look like Elvis. Mori was always Mori. Elvis was the medium for his work, the language he was speaking—a starting point and constant reference, sometimes a distant reference. It was a little odd in "Polk Salad Annie" to hear him saying, in a Japanese-Southern accent, "Some o' y'all nev' been down south too much." Yet, when "American Trilogy" came along, and he sang "in Dixieland, where I was born in," you almost believed it. Mori probably would never have an audience anywhere like this one, and he knew it. In halting English, he improvised a little speech: "In Japan, I am very lonely for Memphis. In Japan, they love Eh-vis, but sometimes . . . they don't like . . . *impah-sonator!*" (Same old story, I thought.) Emerging from a final wave of applause, he led a spontaneous cheer: "WE WANT EH-VIS, WE WANT EH-VIS . . . !" Flaming cigarette lighters went up all through the ballroom. Mori leaped to the edge of the runway and lunged toward the universe of twinkling flames, launching himself into the air, and disappeared into the vast house, glad-handing, giving kisses, finally making his exit through the peacock Elvises and out the front door.

"Whoa," breathed Dave.

"Yes!" I assented.

Chapter

31

n the morning I picked Dave up at his mother-in-law's house north of the city and we headed down the highway, into Mississippi, to Holly Springs and Graceland Too.

"The whole round world has been through since you were here," Paul Macleod said. "Last week with that conference over at Ole Miss and this week, with it being Tribute Week and all, this place is spinning like a top."

Paul looked a little weary today. But we were paying customers and, since Dave, a first-timer, was along, he led us through a slightly muted version of his usual no-pause-for-breath tour. "I tell you, it's one thing after another. We had a guy from the *New York Times* come by here doing a feature on us. *A Current Affair*'s on the phone, they want to bring the cameras in and do something. It just don't stop. Hey, this'll interest you, Henderson: a fellow was through here just yesterday from Disney World." He flashed a Disney World business card at me. "They want to hire a thousand Elvises for Elvis's birthday. This here's the business card that he left. I'll copy it down for you . . ."

The back door opened and Elvis Aron Presley Macleod, all six feet eight of him, appeared with a friend. They had gone out for a case of Coke and were back now. The friend, a muscular youngish man with a bushy flattop haircut, was, as it turned out, an Elvis impersonator himself, from Cherry Hill, New Jersey. He had sought out Graceland Too last year, befriended the Macleods, and now was back, as a houseguest, to take in the Vigil.

"You ought to bring him by the contest," I said to Elvis. "I'm on the bill tomorrow night, you know."

"We'll be there."

I asked Elvis's friend, whose name was Mark de Francisco, why, with his obviously full head of hair, he wore it so short:

" 'Cause I'm a police officer. I could grow it like Elvis, but I'd never hear the end of it from the other cops—cops are like that, you know. I already hear plenty from 'em. It doesn't bother me, though, because doing Elvis is just too important in my life. To be relating to people in a positive way, for a change, like they're actually *glad* to see you, instead of they just got burglarized or assaulted or whatever—it's good for my head. When I arrive someplace as Elvis, it's all fun and good feeling. I don't get enough of that at work."

As he talked, worry lines came out in Mark's face. I could see he wasn't as young as I had thought.

"I've put a lot of money into my wig—about a thousand dollars, custom wig, human hair. If you're going to be up close to people you have to. I've upgraded my suits, too. That costs big money, but you have to if you're serious. It's funny: when I do a party, I show up as me. And I can just see the disappointment in their faces when they open the door—oh jeez, he doesn't look like Elvis, what is this? I set up my sound system and go change. When I come out, it's like I've arrived for the first time. 'Elvis!' Transformation. When I start to sing, with my karaoke tapes, they think I'm lip syncing (which to me is the best compliment I could get). They sometimes don't understand it's really my voice. Like I'll work a girl's name into a song for a birthday party— Susan, let's say—and some guy'll say afterward, 'How'd you ever find a tape of that song with Susan in it?' I've performed for as many as 65,000 and as little as 2. The two was a guy and his girlfriend, in a honeymoon suite. He was going to propose and wanted me there, singing 'Love Me Tender,' can you believe it? I did a wedding, they just wanted an impersonator at the wedding. People want you around, they want Elvis there."

This visit I was able to see Macleod's record room, since his 86-year-old mother was awake. Mrs. Macleod was perched on the side of her big brass bed, an afghan thrown over her nightgown, watching a daytime drama on TV. She was a surprisingly pretty woman for her age—I had spotted a much younger picture of her, on the wall of another room, that confirmed her attractiveness. She welcomed us with genteel courtesy while keeping an alert eye on her soap opera. Rare recordings covered the wall, framed, many of them oddly colored, red, blue, or marbled, indicating that they were special promotional pressings, thus extremely valuable. The thought crossed my mind, as it had before, how easy it might be for thugs to drive up in the middle of the night in a Ryder truck and rob the Macleods blind. I mentioned this to Paul Macleod.

"Let 'em try," said Macleod. "We got enough guns here to make a revolution in Mexico, peace in Bosnia, and still have some firepower left, so anybody that comes in here like that better have a small army or they're gonna go out in a box—my trigger finger's just jerking to hear me talking about it. That's not what we're here for, we're here for peace in the world, out of respect and love for Elvis Presley, but if anybody thinks they can clean us out, they better get their affairs in order first."

"That was an amazing scene," Dave said, on the drive back. Dave was something of a connoisseur of amazing scenes. The previous autumn he had taken a solo vacation in Haiti—arriving just two days after the U.S. invasion force. Right now, he was trying to interest his editor in an "inside a nudist colony" article to follow his "I-was-a-bodyguard-inside-Elvis-World" piece.

"Well, it may seem bizarre to you," I said, "but during the Dark

Ages, the little monasteries that preserved Western Culture must have seemed bizarre to the average visitor."

"Hm. So you're equating Elvis memorabilia with Western Culture?"

"Not equating. I'm drawing a parallel. Here's my hypothesis: if you agree that preserving the spiritual essence and material relics of Elvis has any intrinsic value—and I know lots of people don't, I grant you that—but *if you do*, then what is the most dynamic means? We have Graceland, the Vatican, sitting there in Memphis raking in money from pilgrims, essentially running a theme park. On the other hand you've got independent monastic shrines, like Graceland Too, and smaller ones all over the place, along with the Elvis impersonators who are the sole means of preserving live Elvis performance—and by the way, Graceland would love to burn all these guys at the stake, so to speak, if they could get away with it from a public relations point of view, which they can't."

"Okay. I'm still with you. I think."

"Well, don't you see the parallel? Look at history. A tradition stays alive as long as individuals hold onto pieces of it and do things with those pieces, enliven them and pass them along. When some varnished entity at the center takes hold, you get slow death. Christianity is alive today not because some pope in the Vatican was able to grab and hold all the marbles, burn all the heretics, crush all the heresies, but precisely because he *couldn't*. So every time the spirit enters some self-anointed country preacher and he jumps around like he's dancing on a hot tin roof, that's a defeat for Vaticanism and monolithic central control."

"And a victory for individualism and—"

"Renewal! Renewal-ism, to coin a new word."

I kept my eyes on the road, but I could tell Dave was gawking at me. "And you are on the side of renewal-ism?"

"Of course! Who wouldn't be? Except the lords of corporate control, who want all the marbles. General Motors. Graceland. The banks, the insurance companies. They are the enemy of spontaneity, the enemy of diversity, the enemy of the small, the special, the various. The enemy of the soul. Why? Because all these things splinter the market and throw little monkey wrenches in their money machine. Do you know where Jack Soden came from?"

"Jack who?"

"Jack Soden, the CEO of Elvis Presley Enterprises, Inc.—the pope of Graceland. He came from the banking industry. Now his job is to extend centralized control over what is essentially a patchwork of grassroots enterprises all over the world. And he's off to a good start. My guess is that if Paul Macleod ever got organized enough to become some kind of real attraction, Graceland would strike with a vengeance."

"Because it represents what they're afraid of: heresy, creative anarchy, individualism—"

"Renewal-ism!"

"The enemy of centralized control!"

"You've got it!"

By 3:00 P.M. Fetzer was awake and stirring. He had a small window of free time before having to report to work at six. We met him for "breakfast" at a diner near the hotel.

"I still think you ought to do Young Elvis," he said, slurping coffee. "That's the only worthwhile Elvis manifestation."

"Now how am I, at age 52, supposed to do Young Elvis?"

"You could get away with it. Look at Mick Jagger. He's older than you and he still does Young Mick Jagger."

"Listen, Fetzer. You're a damned rockabilly purist. That's fine, there's nothing wrong with that. But don't think you can impose one narrow vein of sensibility on the rest of the world. That's—"

"Centralized control—" Dave chimed in.

"Yes. Just because Fetzer is stuck in one taste rut doesn't mean the rest of the whole Elvis spectrum sucks."

"Whoa, wait a minute, all I said was that early Elvis is better, that's all. It's not because I'm in a rut. It just is. I mean, Vegas—he came back as a gas bag, he stopped being an innovator."

"Fetzer, how long is *anybody* an innovator? What are you saying— do you have to be a transitional figure for twenty-five years? The 70s Elvis isn't about innovation, it's about consolidation. He was pulling from everywhere, consolidating everything he touched into a mainstream performance interface, a sort of front end that *everybody* could relate to, not just rebels and hillbilly rockers."

"Don't get hot over this, Bill."

"I'm not hot, I'm just an eclectic, that's all. I'm for eclecticism, I realize it now, I've isolated the gene. I'm a sixties person. I mean, why does everyone have to run around stomping things out, closing doors?"

Fetzer chewed on his sausage for a minute. "Well. You can do what you want. Next year I'm gonna enter this damn thing as a Young Elvis, and I'm gonna sing 'Red Cadillac and a Black Mustache,' and when I win, I'm going to make a speech declaring I'm not an Elvis impersonator at all, I'm a Warren Smith impersonator and all those Vegas Elvis slobs can just go jump into hell, and if the judges take off points for that, I'll remind them that I'm just being historically accurate because Warren Smith had a horrible personality and Elvis stole his early stuff from Warren Smith—and if that throws the contest into chaos, so BE IT."

On that note we declared a truce and strolled out into the heat to find some dye for my chest chair.

My adrenaline was still surging when Dave and I pulled into Graceland just after nightfall. The four lanes of Elvis Presley Boulevard had been roped off for the death night candlelight vigil. Parking was free in the Graceland lots. All night, thousands of candle-bearing fans would process through the mansion grounds. We watched the candles snaking up the hill through the darkness, in an endless twinkling single file.

I spotted a tall, red-suited, rhinestoned Elvisoid, standing outside the darkened car museum. I had seen him before at Graceland, exactly as he was now. Apparently this was his peculiarity—to dress like Elvis and stand around Graceland, a wanna-be. He was a fake—a nonperforming impersonator impersonating a genuine impersonator. It was this kind of psycho, I thought, and those like him, who gave Elvis impersonators a bad name.

"Hey!" I said, walking up to him. "Excuse me, but who told you you had a right to wear that suit? Are you an Elvis performer?" My mouth was dry, my hands were fluttering. "Have you ever done anything to earn this—?"

The guy backed up. Through his amber shades I could see mute confusion in his eyes. He was used to having people ogle him, ooh him and ahh him. No one crossed the line to jump in his face this way.

Dave's hand was on my shoulder. "Come on, Bill," he said. "Let's go."

We wandered into the boulevard, which was mallish and teeming in the dark. There was a festive chaos everywhere. Votive candles in paper cups were being passed out by Graceland volunteers. We got into a conversation with Faye, a middle-aged biker mama–type from Minnesota, who had driven all night in her big clunky car. She was friendly but tough, an artist, several tattoos on her, had airbrushed her black leather jacket with views of Elvis, had airbrushed her car, her window at the Days Inn. Standard story: BLAM, fell in love with Elvis on the *Ed Sullivan Show*. Gave her whole life up to it, a votary. Quintessential hardcore fan. I decided to prove a point to Dave:

"Have you seen the impersonators' contest over at the Best Western?" I asked.

A slight frown pinched her face, as though I had used a word she didn't know. "Impersonators? Why should I?"

"It's the best show in town."

"They're all crazy, aren't they?"

"As a matter of fact, no."

"I've seen 'em at the karaoke tent. That's enough for me."

"I'm not talking about those guys. These are professionals, real performers."

"They're not Elvis."

"Well, they're doing more to keep Elvis alive than—" I swung around and pointed a finger toward the corporate suite of Elvis Presley Enterprises, "—than the gray suits that sit in these offices all day long dreaming up lawsuits."

Looking beyond me, Faye half-shrugged and, without a word, walked off with her candle.

"See that?" I said to Dave. "And that was a *fan*."

I was gripped by a desire to sit down in the road. "Okay, Frog, we're here, want to get in line?" I said. "Free candles, it's Vigil Night, it's Graceland . . . this is about as classic as it gets."

"I don't think so. I've heard tell it's a three-hour wait unless you come at three or four in the morning. I need a good night's sleep tonight. You'd better get some, too."

I took a deep breath. "I guess so."

Yammering news helicopters circled above, gathering aerial footage for their 11 o'clock report.

"Oh, what the heck, I'll watch it on TV, back at the hotel."

"TV is more real anyway."

I dropped Dave off and drove myself back downtown to the hotel, feeling jumpy, unresolved. I wanted to sleep, but I knew I wouldn't. I needed to practice for tomorrow, but I was too scattered, unfocused. Next door the Loud People were shouting to each other between the rooms of their suite. Their doors opened and I heard them spill out into the hall, laughing, banging on the Coke machine, dumping ice into coolers.

I heard a scattered mention of Graceland. "Got your candle?" said a little kid's voice.

Of course: pilgrims! No wonder they were headed out at eleven o'clock—these were Elvis people, on their way to the vigil.

Elevators sucked them away and I was alone with myself, not a pleasant prospect at the moment. I took stock. Yesterday my camera bag had been stolen, with my back-up tapes in it. So, as for tapes vs. band, I had no choice now.

Actually, the band was ripening a bit with experience—they could now handle the intricacies of "Polk Salad Annie"—but they still committed mortal sins. For instance, they still blew the chord changes at a crucial point in "Hurt"—even after I had pointed it out to them.

On the other hand, in New Hampshire I had experienced the mindless inflexibility of tapes. If you jumped in on the wrong beat, it was like trying to boogie with The Terminator. At least the band would be pliable, forgiving accompaniment, as well as live bodies on stage with me. I looked at their song list again, made a choice of six, ran over the lyrics in my head (rock solid), then started working on movement.

"Caught in a trap . . . can't walk out . . ."

Not too much, now . . . I didn't want to pull a groin muscle, tear a hamstring. Karate kicks, heel stomps, dance steps, lasso motion (careful . . . careful). I was working up a sweat. Good. I could feel the tight spring inside me start to loosen a bit. Nerves were one thing, but I had to watch out for something else here: losing my stance, my edge, my objectivity.

Of course, what did it ultimately matter whether I was any good or not tomorrow? What was there to be so damned worked up about? I was writing a book, not living a true-life adventure. I would be leaving Memphis in a few days, perhaps never to step into an Elvis suit again. So let tomorrow come. I had made an ass of myself before, I could do it again. It would be funny, engaging. I could create a protective umbrella of urbane self-mockery by writing about my cute little failure—

But no.

Not this time.

I went back to work.

Two hours later, trembling from exhaustion, I mixed the dye for my chest hair. Just For Men Brush-In Color Gel. Mustache, Beard, and

Sideburns (why didn't it say chest hair?). "Blends away gray in 5 minutes . . . lasts up to a month." It said the color was "Natural Real Black"—as opposed to what? Some other kind of Real Black? Concentrate, now—these are dangerous chemicals! (They warned you not to leave the stuff on for more than eight minutes.) I blended the two components of the power-goo and raked the result into my white thatch, setting my wristwatch. Slowly, stupidly, I nodded off—sprang back into consciousness with my chest burning. How long had I been asleep! I threw myself under the shower and soaped off thoroughly, relieving the raw reddish tissue underneath my now jet black tangle of manliness.

What time was it? *Headline News*, repeating itself every half-hour, showed its own aerial shots of the long chain of candlelight below. I threw back the heavy window drape between me and the Mississippi River. A wash of gray and cool pink reached toward the Western sky. It was Wednesday, all day. My big day.

I heard the Loud People coming home amid shouts, clatterings, bangings. They didn't bother me. My inner springs were finally sagging. I felt ready now to deliver myself up to whatever was coming.

Chapter

32

It was late afternoon before I got back to the Best Western. Clutching my suitbag, I made for the inconspicuous side entrance that doubled as a stage door for the impersonators. A heavyset man with impish eyes was leaning against the wall inside.

"Got your Elvis suit, sir?" he said, with chuckle (goofing on the old baldy).

When I nodded and turned in to the dressing room, his grin faded. He followed. "Hey, man, I was just kidding with you, no offense. You really *are* in it, aren't you? This is your night, too, isn't it?"

"It sure is."

He looked at me again, at my sparse, hoary old pate, as if I were a talking horse, and shook his head. "You're blowin' my mind."

It was my turn to grin. "Hey, no offense, but . . . don't tell me you're Elvis too."

He was younger than I was, and more eligible on that score. But there was something unpromising about him, a haplessness that told me his story in a split second: he would be remembered fondly by everyone here yet would always lose. Even though he was tall and husky, and had an aura of personal charm, the fact that you instantly

saw no chance for this guy made him an even more unlikely Elvis than
I, if such a thing were possible.

He held out his hand. "I'm Jack Howard, man. This is my third year
in this thing. Something always screws me up. Like today I had to
spend all morning wrestling an overload of asphalt onto my truck in
124-degree sunstroke heat, all by myself, because the damn hired
helpers wouldn't work in the sun—'too hot.' They were sitting in the
shade laughing at me, man. I thought I was going to have to scratch out
of this tonight, but I feel better now."

"Well, you look okay."

"I'm fine, I'm fine. I'm going to look superb. I just picked up a
great buy on a jumpsuit over at Graceland Crossing. A red Pinwheel,
wool and polyester gabardine, like they don't make anymore. I was at
the karaoke tent, a guy over there in the crowd, a dealer, just happened
to have one that fit and he laid it on me. Said, 'I want you to have this,
man!' First time I've ever had a good suit."

He held it up.

"The fabric seems awfully heavy."

"That's the wool in it. Elvis wore wool gabardine. To get wool
nowadays—from B&K, for instance—you have to pay hundreds extra."

"It looks hot."

"After this morning, I could go on stage in an arctic snorkle suit
and it wouldn't bother me."

Jack and I left our gear in the dressing room and headed toward the
ballroom for the five o'clock sound check. It was going to be a
crowded night: 13 contestants were scheduled.

A special, noncompetitive "Children's Showcase" had been going
on all afternoon. I had seen some of the little Elvises hanging around
during the week, dressed in their junior-sized jumpsuits, striking cute
Elvis poses whenever asked (or prodded by their parents). I was startled, however, to walk in on one of the hottest performances of "Polk
Salad Annie" I had seen all week. The kid was 12, small and wiry, but
intense, well-costumed in black leather, and he had terrific moves.

Once his voice changed and he grew a bit, he was going to be a killer. This, I knew by now, was not an uncommon path: one of the adult finalists here, Jamie "Aron" Kelley, had been a "youth performer" for several years. This year, at fifteen, he had earned his finalist's spot by taking first place at the feeder contest in Decatur, Illinois.

Passing the entrance tables, I stopped to let Doc's daughter band my wrist.

"Cross his name off," Doc yelled from the bar. "This is probably his last night as an Elvis impersonator."

"What's he talking about?" asked Jack.

"It's kind of a joke. He's just playing with my head."

We joined the others down near the stage, where Jackie Franklin was about to conduct a nightly ritual: each of us drew a number. The number determined the order in which we would choose our spot on the program. I drew 10. By the time we got to my turn, spot number 5 was still open and I took it. To me, that was perfect: I wouldn't have to go first, but neither would I have to sit around sweating in a pool of nerves all evening.

I looked around at our group. No one was in costume yet. This could be a group of men going through a new hire orientation meeting at a security service, a government agency, a corporate engineering outfit. All seemed to be in their 20s or 30s. The only guy anywhere close to my age looked like an ex–Green Bay Packer inside lineman gone to seed. Clearly he had been a big guy to begin with, but now he carried a layer of girth that gave him the distinction of being the only truly "fat" Elvis I saw all week. There were a couple of Young Elvises I recognized from "sing-ins" earlier in the week, but in mufti, the young-old distinction seemed to blur. One barrel-chested young guy, who could have been either, was wearing the T-shirt that I had seen once and coveted: NOBODY BELIEVES I'M ELVIS.

"Where'd you get that shirt?" I asked.

"Buffalo, Noo Yawk," he replied in a booming city-boy voice that had a familiar ring to it. Where had I heard that voice . . . ?

One by one, in order, each contestant stepped on stage and sang through a few bars with the band or with their tape, allowing the sound man to set vocal levels to match each individual voice. The house lights remained low from the children's showcase, so stage conditions were pretty much as they'd be tonight—blinding, from the spotlights, and vast—bigger even than the stage at Stratham. The sound system was excellent. Powerful monitor speakers aimed up from floor level, so you would hear yourself loud and clear—in my case, with full reverb, which I hoped would lend extra presence to my "Elvis lite" voice.

Out on stage, knowing how silly I must look to the other assembled Elvises, I made a solemn pact with myself: I would not go down in ignominy, not tonight. I would blow this crowd away. To Doc I was a joke, but I would surprise him and his judges. They weren't going to see an old professor out there making a fool of himself in thrall to a book contract—they were going to see a legitimate Image of Elvis, full, dimensional, dynamic. It was as simple as that. It had to be. And once you knew that simple fact—not intellectually, but in your body—once you grasped it, the physical knowledge of it, as surely Elvis had, you could fly.

I had to get out of this place for a while. Compose myself. Over the past week, I had fallen into a journalist's pose—onlooker, listener, notetaker—always receptive, passive, slack, asking questions, focusing on others. To hell with that. My task now was to prepare myself to be— for ten minutes, anyway—the center of the earth, the white-hot core of the galaxy, the hottest erupting spring of energy in the universe.

I needed to get away from the Best Western, this dormitory for Elvis impersonators, away from the cool, stale, smoke-ruined air, recycled all week to battle the 100-degree heat wave. Hunger struck. I had a sudden craving for fried food—a plate of breaded fish, a huge hamburger. I hit the street and began walking.

The Memphis Airport area isn't really walking territory. There are no sidewalks. Strange people cruise the boulevards in flashy vehicles. There is a sense that crime is an ever-present possibility . . . if you're driving, you could be "bumped" by carjackers; if you're walking, you could be victimized at any second by a drive-by mugging. I didn't care. I was pulsating. No one would bother me.

I walked past a couple of seedy clubs, their action heating up in the dark. Men in parking lots, some black, some white, gave me a scrutinizing eye as I passed. Motorcycles and cars with loud mufflers seemed to circle me. I had no fear. I had a protective screen of energy surrounding me. No one was going to touch me.

I saw a Denny's down the road and made for it.

I ordered a big sloppy hamburger (with fries and slaw) at the counter. In silence, I rattled through my lyrics three, four, five times, chewing to the beat inside my head.

Gradually, I became aware of another voice, a real voice, right there in Denny's. The voice was reciting a long, monotonous food order: "and some chips with that—ranch flavored, if possible—and I want the barbecue sauce on the side, with dressing on one salad, but on the other, put half the dressing on the salad and the other half right on the french fries . . ." and so on.

Another middle-aged white guy, from the sound of it.

I looked around and there, in a baseball cap, was the ex-football giant, whose name was Don Ingram. He saw me at the same time I saw him. We nodded and ended up at the cash register together.

"Want a ride back?" he asked.

"Thankyouvurreh much," I said.

Don had flown to Memphis from Santa Rosa (where he was a private detective) along with Rick E. Aron. Making their arrangements together made sense when they were buying plane tickets—they often traveled to local contests together—but in the wake of Rick E.'s popularity here, Don was struggling a bit over being a 40-ish nobody, lost in a wash of youth. The particular torture of having to room with Rick E. had his teeth on edge. "He treats me like wallpaper. Girls are slipping notes under his door here. He'll bring kids into his room and won't introduce me. I don't want to be their best friend or anything, it's a generation thing, partly, so I end up totally ignored. I have to say: excuse me, hi, I'm Don Ingram, and then he acts like I suddenly appeared out of a pink cloud or something. I was a football coach, you know. I've dealt with all kinds of kids. Rick used to act respectfully, yes sir, no sir. But now—he's a rude little bugger."

Don's rental car was small. He had to squeeze to get himself behind the wheel. As he drove, he went on talking, his accent vaguely Californian, his diction precise, like a TV anchorman's.

"I don't know about you, but this contest is a reality check for me: you get here and discover you're not as special as you are back home—you're just another Elvis; not only that, but there are *lots* of Elvises here, any one of them is as good as you, maybe better. It's humbling . . . that is, if you know the meaning of that word. Rick doesn't fully grasp what he's up against here. He doesn't have a work ethic. Sometimes back home he tells me he's just not going to put out fully for this show or that show because the fans aren't *discriminating* enough. Well, here he's going to stumble one of these times, and when he does, he's going to free-fall, because he doesn't have the equipment to stop himself."

We pulled into the Best Western and parked. Don sat immobile in the car and stared meditatively ahead, bags of fast food on his huge lap. I had an image of him, with his John Madden body, on the sidelines of a high school football game, pacing heavily—exhorting, exulting, excoriating. But now, out of his element, he sat heavily, as if leaving the car was the last thing he wanted to do. He turned to me. "Want to come eat some of this food with me?"

"Thanks, Don, I'm full. We have to get back to the ballroom—you, too."

"Yeah, yeah. I'll be over there in a while." He eyed the bags of food. "It won't take me long to polish this stuff off."

*   *   *

Things were getting lively back at the ballroom. Robert Washington had arrived from Maine, looking like he had just emerged from three hours in the gym. He remembered me from Stratham, as did his fan club president, a nice lady from South Portland, whose candid response, upon meeting me again, was, "Oh, yes—you're the one who left."

As far as Stratham was concerned, if I would always be known as "the one who left"—as opposed to, say, the one who phoned in his performance—I'd be satisfied. "Let's face it, I was a bust," I said to Robert. "I never really showed up for Stratham. But things are going to be different here. You're going to see a whole different show. I've made a quantum leap here. You're not looking at the same guy."

Robert didn't seem to know quite what to make of this declaration. He nodded abstractly, then broke into an awful cough. "I've got a rotten cold," he said in a gravelly voice. "I caught it on the plane. It's in my throat. I'll be lucky if I can sing at all."

This was going to be trouble for Robert. A poor vocal performance would cost him in the most crucial judging category. Elvis Presley himself knew that no matter how sexy he was, no matter how well coiffed, ornately dressed and bejeweled, his voice was his ticket. In the oral history *Elvis Up Close*, his personal physician, "Dr. Nick," described what that meant in terms of nightly preparation: "Usually the routine, whether in Vegas or on the road, was . . . a decongestant . . . what he called a voice shot, which was a combination of three or four different herbs that had no medical justification that you could find, but he was convinced that it helped his voice . . . There were times we would even have to put some drops on his vocal cords. Then after he was dressed and ready, he would get a vitamin B-12 shot. If he still had some congestion, we would decide whether to placebo him—you had to give him something at that time 'cause he thought he couldn't perform without it—or give him a decongestant." Elvis's great beast of a fear—indeed the gnawing anxiety around which all his drug abuse circled—was that he would be unable to perform, which, for him, was almost entirely a fear that he would lose his voice. Without it, he was just another pretty face.

Robert Washington was certainly more than just a pretty face, and I hoped he'd be able to show it, but sympathetic though I was to his problem, I had Number One to look out for—and right now Number One had a rendezvous with his suit and wig. I made my way through clusters of fans and impersonators toward the backstage area, hoping no one had decided to take advantage of lax security and run off with my suit.

Don Ingram, whose problems were less exalted than Robert's, must have breathed his food and changed in his room, because he was back now, fully costumed, and hanging out in the hall with Jack Howard and a couple of other Elvises. I peeked out the dressing room door and saw that he was wearing a weird costume: pink satin shirt, black vest, black pants with a single silver stripe and flare.

"If you're my size, you just can't do the things Elvis did on 'Suspicious Minds,' he was saying. "Not unless you're in super shape—I mean, the kneeling, the shoulder shimmies, all that—the physical demands are just too great."

Another voice: "Elvis didn't do that stuff either, not toward the end."

"That's right," said Jack. "If you want to see what he did do, you can buy the last concert for sixty bucks down at Graceland Crossing. He just stands there and shakes a little from side to side."

"Sad. You can almost see death in his face."

"Well, he just didn't have it anymore," said Don. "But he was realistic. He didn't have it, so he didn't try it. He would've fallen down."

"I know all about that," Jack said. "I wrote the book on falling down."

I slipped out of my pants and shirt. What about the underwear question? Elvis didn't wear it. (Neither did Hemingway.) That punky kid in Medfield had said he could see it through my suit. Should I go au naturel? But if you could see the underwear line, what else might you see? Did Irv Cass go au naturel? Did I want to have to worry about this? Jack Howard, always asking for advice, had queried Robert about this matter (although with his thick new red suit, it seemed to me, having his underwear "sighted" wouldn't be an issue). "I wear a ballet dancer's jock," Robert said. "Except it's uncomfortable as hell up your butt. If you want, just wear Fruit of the Loom and pull everything up like a loin-cloth—so you won't have an 'American bulge.'" Jack liked that idea, but I didn't want to be worrying about "wedgies" in the midst of my penultimate Elvis performance. I'd go as I had, for better or for worse.

I stepped into the jumpsuit and zipped it up to the sternum, no higher. My black chest hair looked great.

The wig went on, stretching like a watch cap to fit my big, oblong head; I pulled it snug by tugging down on the sideburns, then smoothed them to my face and secured them with the ear pieces of my "official" Elvis glasses.

I pulled on my tennis shoes, still the Achilles heel of my "look" but comfortable, light, and sure-footed. I walked out into the hallway.

Tony Ciaglia, a 17-year-old Young Elvis, was telling the story of how he became an impersonator. "I was never an Elvis fan or anything. Then I was involved in a terrible accident, a car crash. I was like in the hospital for months, in a coma. When I woke up from the coma, I knew all the moves, I had the lyrics down. It was weird, uncanny. I never had to teach myself, it was just, like, there."

As I joined the other Elvises, the ever-polite Don Ingram thrust his hand toward me. "Hi. Don Ingram. Nice to meet you."

"Hi, Don," I said, "it's me. Bill Henderson? I was riding in your car twenty minutes ago? Remember Denny's? How was your meal?"

"Ohmigod, it's the wig."

Doc meandered by. "Too many intellectuals back here," he murmured, scowling at me.

"How'd your seven o'clock amputation go, Doc?" said Jack Howard.

"Fine. Had barbecued rotweiler tails for lunch."

Don said, "Did they wake up yelling 'where's the rest of me?' "

"Yep. Had to keep telling 'em, come on, get a grip! Be a man, be a man!"

Doc drifted on through and was followed by Jackie, a clipboard in her hand. Contestant number three was not going to be here, she announced, something about a family emergency. To fill his spot, she had asked William Toulson, one of the seeded finalists, to "sing in."

"Great," Don grumbled. "Now I have to follow a finalist. That's not going to help my cause."

But I still follow you, Don, I thought, cold-bloodedly. That's not so awful.

Dave appeared in the hallway looking every inch a bodyguard in his new red tour jacket.

"Who else is here?" I asked.

"Becky Mills just arrived from Ripley, with her mother. My mother-in-law, Hazel, is here. Not exactly a fan club out there, but you'll be okay."

A band member stuck his head around the corner. "Where's Bill Henderson?"

"Here."

"You'll be our first victim. Everyone up until you is using tapes. Do you want to start with '2001'?"

"Absolutely."

"I'll need a set list from you."

"First contestant!" Jackie called. "First contestant, get ready!"

The evening was under way.

Dave busied himself getting a full cup of water for me and arranging my 10 scarves on his arm for quick delivery (in my entire career as an Elvis impersonator, I had given out two!). We had already practiced the scarf routine, with mixed results: he would hover too close after the replacing motion, then get whacked by my head as I rebounded from the kiss—hey, nothing worthwhile is easy! Now I paced like a tiger. *Yes,* I thought, *tiger, tiger,* TIGER . . . I could hear the first guy—all lugubrious ballads—then Toulson—more ballads. They must be going to sleep out there! That's fine. I knew Don wasn't going to rock the house. With "See See Rider" (would I have first crack at "See See Rider?" What luck!) and with my abbreviated but gutsy "Polk Salad Annie," I was going to be the evening's first rocker!

Dave was in his own world now, rehearsing his part of the show: extending the water cup, withdrawing it, extending it . . . flaring a scarf, placing it low, placing it high, hopping back to avoid a scull to the chin . . . I made one last monumental effort to focus on what I knew I must do. I'm a verbal person: I had to talk it.

"Dave."

"Huh?"

"Listen to me: I'm going to cut loose, okay? My body's going to love being out there. It's going to dance for joy. I'm going to take possession of the stage, every inch of it. I'm not scared of that ramp either, okay?"

"Bill, just do it."

"Yes, do it. Just do it." Writers appear to do it, my mind jabbered on. But they're off in their rooms, patching time together, faking it. One spontaneous lyric emotion—ten musty old years in the fabrication of an illusion, an elaborate scam. This is what I've got to beat—

"Do you need some water?"

I did. My mouth was dry. And then I remembered that, handicapped by the nonprescription Elvis sunglasses, I was awfully close to blind. Remember Stratham? *Nobody out there!* No wonder I had fallen so easily into a state of solipsism. Okay, my prescription glasses were lightly tinted and close enough to aviator style to pass. I ran back into the dressing room and dug them out of my pants pocket.

"Dave, take these. After the first number I'm going to ask you to trade them. We'll just make a thing out of it."

Now he was pacing. "Okay: water, glasses, scarves . . . water, glasses, scarves."

I paced with him. "Energy, motion, love . . . energy, motion, love . . ."

Don Ingram came off-stage, soaked with sweat. I hadn't even heard a note of his performance. "Whew, I'm glad that's over!" he gasped, slumping back into the hallway.

Quickly, the band settled in. Jackie peeked back into the hall: "Ready?"

The dread tonic-dominant-octave sequence of Strauss's Nie-tzschean solemnity (had Elvis sensed the mystery of it—*What The Hell Are We Here For Anyway?*) sounded its challenge. Okay, said the por-tentous fanfare, go out there and have your fifteen minutes of gravity and cosmic personal consequence. Go solve the World Riddle, if you can, but don't forget to boogie!

We left the hallway and stood poised at a set of stairs leading to the stage. "Ready . . . set . . . GO!"

I bounded on, almost running, radiating extroversion for all I was worth. As at Stratham, the lone microphone stand waited for me, like the skinny broom handle of the sorcerer's apprentice, ready to assist. This time the clip didn't collapse; I tilted the stand, pulling the mike to-ward my mouth, opened my mouth, and *just did it*.

What do I remember?

Becky yahooing. Flashbulbs flashing. Stage blindness (temporary, I hoped, but mostly, as it turned out, caused by staring into darkness while facing spotlights). I remember launching a spontaneous karate kick sequence (although the videotape, viewed weeks later, shows no trace of it). Problems with the band were minimal, some of them my fault; you have to conduct them, as Elvis did; I tried, with uneven re-sults. "Polk Salad Annie," my karaoke nemesis, the long, narrative swamp rocker, had become my rock 'n' roll showpiece, and I even hammed a bit in spots, like "a mean . . . vicious . . . STRAIGHT-RAZOR-totin' woman!" When it came time for the featured bass solo, I pulled out an old John Lincoln Wright trick: scamper back to the bass player and pretend to pick up the solo with the hand mike. Only this bass player didn't realize *a solo* came here, and simply kept plunking out bottom notes. Oh, well, back to the front, finish the song—lasso, lasso, lasso—it was working, it actually felt good—and give the band a big,

Memphis: Taking it to the floor . . . nobody mobbing me.
(Photo courtesy of Charles Gauthier.)

I pull off some flashy scarf work at last, with the help of bodyguard Dave Williamson. (Photo courtesy of Charles Gauthier.)

Elvis-style cutoff. Yeah! Whew. All right. Sweat. Dry mouth. Almost too dry to talk.

Okay: I remember saying a few words about exchanging glasses so I could see everybody. Dave came out: I might have just barely passed as an Elvis, but I must say that Dave was the most authentic-looking bodyguard-cum-scarf man in Memphis the entire week. He had my prescription shades and suddenly I could see a few faces. From now on I would pick specific faces to aim at. Ah, water, forgot water—but do it right: ask, like Elvis did, for "wah-wah." Mmm, that's good. Now came "Hurt," the acrobatic power ballad that I had the hutzpah to attempt. I started off missing the first note by a country mile. No matter. The band hadn't bothered to correct their notable sour chord change. No matter. I settled down and actually managed to get through it while descending into the house and giving out a scarf and a kiss (Becky). Back on stage for a few words of thanks to Doc and Jackie (sincere, but it came out like a cheap ploy for applause—which it got). And into "Can't Help Falling in Love." Oh, god, the band was starting it slowww, the studio-version tempo. Any real Elvis band would know that "Can't Help Falling in Love," as a live show closer, is always done at a brisk clip. I turned, on my way back into the crowd, and goosed them as eloquently as I could.

There is a school of thought among impersonators (Keith Henderson, for example) that when it comes to giving out scarves, you don't go into the audience and distribute them—you go to the edge of the stage and tease the women forward. I had seen it done both ways but didn't have the guts to take my chances on stage. For me, just to plunge into a sea of strangers, to circulate spontaneously among the dark tables of fans, that alone was gamble enough. I motioned to Dave and headed for the floor, determined to rid myself of every last Dollar Store scarf before I was through. First came two of the women regulars, there every night, every year—that was de rigueur. Slight coordination problems—once, I kissed the mike instead of the woman. But miraculously—they were coming forward! A blonde . . . a brunette. Suddenly, there was Cheryl, of Mike and Cheryl, the friends I had stayed with my first trip here. Hook with scarf . . . kiss cheek . . . keep moving. Dave kept a discreet five feet behind me, deftly darting forward to place a new scarf around my neck each time I whipped one off. Did I miss someone?—okay, she followed me, not to be denied. It was working! Why had I ever worried about it in the first place? Before I knew it I was down to my last scarf: taking my cue from a move I had seen countless times here in Memphis (Elvis-based, of course), I rubbed in sweat from my brow and chest and tossed it to a sweet-looking elderly lady who went for it like a cat attacking a June bug.

Now it was back on stage for the bravura finish: "falling in love . . . wi-i-i-i-i-i-i-th . . . yoooou . . . Oh, you . . . Oh, you . . . Ohh-ohh-OHHHH-HHHH!" Drum flourish and into the exit vamp. Thankyou, thankyouvurreh much. "Bill Henderson . . . Bill Henderson!" Down the stairs. Back into the womb of the hallway. "How'd it go, man . . . ?" I whipped off my hot, sweaty wig, turning me back into a satyr: half-Elvis, half-Mr. Chips. I stepped out of the suit and into shorts, a polo shirt, and boating shoes. Done . . .

Someone else was on stage already. Pacing the hall, 16-year-old Rob Hunter, a guitar slung around his neck, asked me to sing some harmony with him on "Suspicious Minds" to help keep his energy up and flowing. With the Martin acoustic and two bare voices, it came out sounding like a folk song, an urban hootenanny number from 1962. This was fun. Had I just been on as Elvis? It didn't feel like it. I could hardly remember what had happened out there.

"How'd we do?" I asked Dave.

"Dynamite."

"Was I charismatic?"

"You broke every Geiger counter in the joint."

"Let's go get a beer," I said. "Elvis has left the building."

In the lobby, Doc swilled on a cup of club soda, while chatting with a party of upscale tourists, one of which turned out to be his son, the real doctor.

"Well?" I said.

"Well, what?"

"How'd I do?"

"I haven't seen your judging sheet yet." He chewed on some ice. "But I wouldn't call Ed McMahon yet, let him call you."

I caught sight of Elvis Aron Presley Macleod and his buddy Mark, just arriving.

"Too late. You missed me," I told them. Elvis, who seemed to take

Finishing big.
(Photo courtesy of Charles Gauthier.)

most things with casual nonchalance, dangled his head in mock mourning.

On stage, here came the guy in the NOBODY BELIEVES I'M ELVIS T-shirt. He was still wearing it. Devotion to Elvis, he announced, had kept him from crossing the line into wearing a jumpsuit, which was, he felt, too close to sacrilege. I thought there was something aggressive in his purity, as if he were daring you to produce as pure a love for Elvis as his. He had the voice and accent of the classic New York City workingman. With his muscular strut, he looked like a college football player and walked with the rolling, chesty stride of a center or guard. Rather than make "moves" he simply strolled the stage, letting his short, bulging arms swing free.

"I think we're forgettin' the most impawtant person for tonight. And I'd like to take a moment out here for a silence for Elvis Prezly. How do you feel about that? You think so? All right." He knelt, on one knee, the way athletes do during brief sports prayers. "Thank you, Elvis. I love you with all my heart. I'll give it my best shot."

Vocally, it was a pretty good shot.

But without a costume, without a "show," he didn't have a chance here.

Jack Howard, all in red, seemed to be lurking in disarray out around the front entrance table.

"What are you doing out here?" I asked, sipping a beer while watching the current performer, Rob Hunter. "Aren't you about due to go on stage?"

"I'm next."

"Shouldn't you get backstage?"

"I'm going to make my entrance from here," he said. "I've talked to the spotlight operator. He'll pick me up here and follow me down to the stage." Jack looked old, potbellied, confused, like it was all somehow too overwhelming for him. "Would you do me a favor, man? I forget whether I set out my scarves or not. They're in a plastic bag. Will you go check and see if you can see a plastic bag stashed behind the speaker column?"

"A plastic bag? Isn't somebody doing your scarves?"

"Me."

"You're going to carry a plastic bag around?"

"I don't know, but can you see if they're there?"

"Wait a minute, Jack. You can't do your own scarves. I'll do scarves for you, okay? I'm through. I've got nothing to do but hang around."

His face seemed to lose ten years. "You will? Aw, man, I love you like a brother. That's great, what a relief, that's great!"

Quickly, I headed back to the stage area and found his scarves, a dozen or so, in different colors, fabrics, thicknesses, rolled up and stuffed inside a supermarket sack. I refolded them, hung a few of them over my arm, and waited. This would be interesting, I thought: master and servant in the same night.

Jackie's voice boomed: ". . . Jack Howard!"

Jack picked his way through the audience like a bemused air traveler searching for his gate, paused to flash two fingers at the crowd, and ascended the stage in a single, abortive scramble that, but for a well-placed knee, would have been the end of his show right there. After a karate-style cutoff, he walked upstage and downstage in an odd silence, the mike to his mouth. No sound. Turn the mike on, Jack! Ah, now he was ready. "Okay, I guess you could call this, 'Theme from Graceland,'" said Jack, and plunged into "Welcome to My World," a love song in the form of a real estate pitch.

As addled as he was, Jack knew how to work an audience. He sang surprisingly well, and went right to the edge of the stage, where he used tiny paper roses to coax a few women forward. Next, taking his time, he slipped off a scarf and held it out until another woman came to him, grabbing it. From that point on they were coming from everywhere, forming lines.

I went into action, standing behind him Charlie Hodge–style, draping his neck as quickly as he undraped it. Jack Howard was a very popular man with the ladies, I realized: something of the sensitive truck driver crossed with an Elvis manqué, and a sly, sweet sense of humor.

Song over, he retreated. "You've got a few roses left in the bag," I stage-whispered to him. He nodded and took a bunch.

On "Separate Ways" he ventured into the audience and was mobbed.

On "Memories," it was back to the stage, and still they were lining up. I fed him what was left of the scarves. Gently, flirtatiously, he made sure each woman got at least three seconds of the best of Jack Howard.

Now it was time to rock. He chugged water from a stray ice pitcher and got rid of his shades. Off came his big black belt: the way Jack was built—with a classic oval belly that raised his center of gravity to the danger point—he needed unfettering. Working with the band, he literally hurled himself into "Burning Love," complete with brash karate leaps and thrusts, pinwheel arms, lassos, skips, axels, punch-kick combinations, and a climactic coda (he laid the mike down on the floor for this) that recapped his entire movement repertoire, throwing in two spinning back kicks for good measure. You had to love it—here was the world's plumpest dervish, a human beer truck careening at the farthest edge of control. This made my physical performance look like a baby's first steps. No wonder the guy had hit the floor three years in a row!

"I didn't fall!" he crowed, backstage. "I didn't fall!"

Chapter

3 3

There remained the question of who would win.

The prequalified finalists were already halfway home. The night before the finals, Jackie Franklin announced the additional finalists, those whose performances here had rated high enough with the judges to boost them into the finals.

No real surprises: Jack Howard wouldn't be one of them, nor would Don Ingram, Jim DeShaw (gone home anyway), Mike Roberts (of the T-shirt), or a host of other also rans.

Some were distinctly displeased by not making it. John Tally, the Eagle Scout, was not on the list; Don Ingram told me he took it badly and flew home in a rage.

I wouldn't be one of them either. Doc had been right: it *had* been my last night as an Elvis impersonator, competition variety. Easy come, easy go.

I awoke the next morning from an obsessive dream in which I was struggling to learn how to flick my scarves in such a way that they soared through the darkness under their own power. Over and over again, they kept falling under their own limp weight. Someone was instructing me, some drill sergeant, just out of my view. He was urging me on with a voice that sounded like he had swallowed a bullhorn.

In the place where my dreams lived, anyway, I wasn't through with this thing: something in me wanted to improve, practice, absorb more, learn more, come back here next year and really show them something. The world of Elvis impersonation had become the real world for me. I was in it, of it. Its imperatives were driving me, at least for the moment. Like the fictional character I had created more than a decade ago, I woke up wanting to be the world's best Elvis impersonator. Yet, unlike Byron, I was 52 years old; at 52 you know a few more things, and in another part of me I recognized that it would never be.

Even though George Eliot said, "It's never too late to be what you might have been," I knew that, like it or not, I had already become all the things I might have been, and now, for better or for worse, I was a writer, and for the duration. With all my surging ardor to take what I had learned here and build it into a world-class Elvis performance, the reality was that I would end up back in my writing mode, return to my version of the lit'ry life, the classroom, the reading circuit, the blinking cursor waiting, waiting, waiting for the next word, the next phrase, the blessed burst of verbiage that puts you over your word limit for the day. I would write the book and go on to other things. It would fade.

I would never get there.

I also realized that the drill sergeant from my dream was actually shouting *right now* in the hall outside my room—the very real-world Mr. Loud from next door. But now I knew who he was.

"Mike Roberts!" I said, sticking my head out the door. "Nobody Believes I'm Elvis!"

"Huh?"

"It's me. Bill Henderson. From last night?"

"Excuse me?" He was over by the elevators, waiting with several packed bags.

"Picture me in a black wig."

"Oh! Oh, my god! How ya doing? You been living there all this time?"

Children and adults crowded out into the hall. They had had quite a morning, it turned out. Having scored Mike his first jumpsuit the night before (from a suitmaker who went after him almost before he had left the stage), they rolled out early, on a tip for shoes, and had the rear window gunned out of their van by an unknown (probably random) assailant.

"The bullet almost hit me," said one of the kids. "I could hear it whiz by my ear."

"We're getting out of here," said Mike's dad, a wiry old dude whose piercing tenor voice was familiar to me from through the wall—and even more penetrating than Mike's high-decibel baritone. "We'll be back, though. Mike's got his suit now. He's got his shoes. He was reluctant. He didn't want 'em till we got down here and he saw you've got to have 'em."

"I'm not an impersonator," Mike announced. "I do a tribute."

"Yeah, yeah," said his dad. "But whatever you are, you gotta have flash, that's what the women go for, a little of this—" He shook his hips.

"He's got a gig back in New York this weekend," said Mike's wife. "Now he looks right, anyway."

"Not staying to watch the finals?"

Mike shrugged. He hadn't made the finals either, although with the suit, he might have had a chance. "I'm a Yankee. They go with the homeboy down here. They're still fightin' the Civil War."

I thought about that. Of the finalists, the majority were from outside the South, even outside the U.S. I mentioned that to Mike. It didn't matter. "They go for the homeboy down here," he said again. "They're still fightin' the Civil War."

Two elevators arrived simultaneously; the extended Roberts clan filled them both to capacity. Mike's mom laid a few of his business cards on me and they were gone, leaving a ghostly calm throughout the tenth floor.

My room phone was ringing. It was Dave Williamson, leaving early for home and family. But he had caught the fever. What about the Elvis suits I wasn't using? Did they fit me? Would they fit him? And what about that Disney World monkey business in January? Would I be going, if it happened? He wanted to go too—as an Elvis, if possible. Or if not, did I need a bodyguard? If it really was to be a night of 1,000 Elvises, surely there might be a way to fit him in.

"Anytime you do this again," he told me, "remember: I'm your bodyguard."

Earlier, Dave had conceded that, for the price ($6) this really was the best show in town. Six bucks for a parade of Elvises—including showcases by some of the best-established pros in the business. Now, however, the finals were at hand: Doc was asking $20 and he would get it. For fans of Elvis performance, the finals would be the best of the best—a kaleidoscope of Elvis in the various physiques, personalities, preoccupations, temperaments, and predilections of each performer.

But as evening approached I was finding it hard to get up for mere spectatorhood. I parked in the Best Western lot and sat in my car for a while, doing nothing.

Look on the bright side, I thought: I was out of it, *hors de combat* at last. I could now sit back, truly detached, free of performance anxiety, and watch how the apparently bottomless archetype of Elvis performance yielded, contained, suggested, and supported a full panoply of pop/ritual entertainers. I ought to be in hog heaven. I wasn't.

Oh, hell, I thought, go on in.

The room was packed. I found a place to perch next to the spotlight platform.

Let the show begin.

As he had promised, Rick E. Aron unveiled a new act and it turned out to be a mistake. I watched from beside the spotlight platform as he cast off his trademark Young Elvis sport jacket and baggy pants and appeared in slick black leather. Don Ingram was standing beside me, profoundly conflicted: still seething at Rick E.'s inconsiderate brattiness, he couldn't help but coach him from the sidelines anyway.

"It's hot in this black leather," Rick announced to the crowd. "Jesus!"

"Don't say *Jesus*!" Don hissed (into my ear), trying to keep his voice down.

The band screwed up on the introduction to "That's All Right, Mama."

"Stupid shits," Don imploded.

"Well, I'm just learning tonight . . ." said Rick when something went wrong.

"Don't apologize!" spat Don. "Don't turn your back!"

It became obvious that Rick, a confident performer as the young Elvis, was shaken. His natural mode—youth, sassiness, defiance—didn't help him here, didn't carry over. As an older Elvis, you had to establish contact with the crowd directly, go out into the audience. Rick E. hadn't figured this out and had no experience with it.

The songs he had chosen were definitely "mutant" material: "Suspicious Minds," "It's Now or Never" (take *that*, Fetzer!), "If I Can Dream." But though he earned my admiration for his eclecticism, this was clearly not the occasion to be crash testing the next level of Elvis maturity. He was hamstrung. He didn't "take the stage," didn't go into the house, didn't even walk to the end of the runway (as Don observed bitterly). He had miscalculated, and—too late—he knew it. Afterward, Don told me later, he was so upset he wanted to bolt for the airport and grab the first plane out of Memphis.

Irv Cass, following Rick E., was almost his opposite. The Chippendale's Elvis was just coming off a year as a cruise ship King, doing shows every day, and it showed in the assurance with which he worked the crowd. Missing from his moves tonight were some of the overt humping, striptease pelvic thrusts on which he seemed to anchor his style. I thought this was shrewd of him—until I realized both his parents were in the audience and their presence was most likely reducing his sex rating from R to PG.

He introduced his father: "Stand up and show 'em your bald head,

Dad. Hey, Mom's back in the rear with someone else—you're in the wrong place, man!" He turned in a smooth, controlled show that even included an up-tempo gospel stomp.

There were others:

Rob Hunter, the cheery 16-year-old from my night, stuck to his strong stuff and turned in a near-flawless Young Elvis performance.

Yet another juvenile, the 15-year-old Jamie "Aron" Kelley, came out in a black early 60s outfit, a tight red jacket with two vertical white racing stripes. Very movie-era. He held a rubber guitar, which he tossed into the audience after his first number.

Doc perched beside me, proud of his handiwork. "Some of these guys are so improved I can't believe it. They come here the first year with sloppy acts. Then they go home and do something about it, get their lives together. Chris Young—now, did you know Chris Young lost 50 pounds since last year?"

It was hard not to notice Chris Young. He combined everything I felt you needed to transcend the prejudice against Elvis impersonators. He was youthful, good-looking in a bright and chipper fashion, tall, well proportioned, and moved with grace and confidence. He had proved he was an aficionado with the unusual showcase set he had put together earlier in the week. Now he came out in yet another knockout suit, The Dragon, a rainbow of colors on white, that fit him like a glove. His set was unusual without being offbeat. His moves were flawless. His scarf technique was virtuosic: once, in less than three seconds, I saw him wipe his eyes, his brow, his lips, then hook the woman gently and kiss her smack on the lips. Strong stuff.

He was followed by Canadian Darren Lee's hyperkinetic Young Elvis/Black Leather Elvis show.

Finally only Robert Washington was left.

For Robert it had been a day of medication, tea, honey, rest, waiting, and hoping for a change of internal weather. By evening, he had a thin layer of vocal possibility and was trying to keep it alive. He would go on last—good for his voice, perhaps, but never the best slot to occupy in a competition. Judges, in spite of themselves, burn out as the night moves on; as a result, the final performances are apt to be undervalued. He had to do something unusual to get their attention.

To start with, he walked in from the rear of the house, not so unusual in itself—Jack Howard had done it—but to "The Theme from Peter Gunn"? This was so unorthodox that you either had to cringe or laugh at the inspired lunacy of it. Looking terrific in a simple white jumpsuit, he leaped onto the stage and stood with his back to the crowd until the music reached its climax (50s TV watchers will recall one particularly raucous chord, repeated seven times, then breaking into a prolonged orchestral scream). He whirled around and plunged headlong into a blistering "Burning Love."

Right away I noticed the roughness and strain in his voice. Physically he looked more impressive than anybody: an athlete's body, his moves all muscular refinement, tremendous physical charisma. When he ventured into the audience it was with a huge leap into the air that took everyone's breath away as he seemed to fly across tables into the darkness. Swiftly he headed for the rear tables: "Some of you people back here haven't been getting a close look, so . . ." He circled, then jumped up on a tabletop. When the song ended, he was close to the sound booth. "Stop the tape, I gotta get some breath, man." Then it was back on stage for a ballad (one of the 60s movie ballads). He did great scarf work (his scarf lady, from the Maine fan club contingent, handed them up from the floor). He ad-libbed nicely, radiating energy and a naive charm. His voice barely holding, he made it through "Polk Salad Annie," "Johnny B. Goode," and finished strong, if ragged, with "Hurt." The crowd was on its feet for him; and considering his placement, at a point in the night when everyone was in a mood to close it out and move on, I thought he had really pulled one off.

But the voice . . .

At last, Jackie Franklin came to the microphone for the announcement. Here were the winners:

Second runner-up: Darren Lee, from Canada.

First runner-up: Rob Hunter, the teenager from Indiana.

And the winner . . . Chris T. Young, from Michigan.

(So much for Southern Culture! For anyone who cleaved to the Elvis-for-rednecks theory, these results—not a southerner in the crowd—shot it all to hell. Take note, Mike Roberts: not a single home-boy!)

Kind of a surprising list in other ways too, I thought, with Irv Cass not even placing, nor Robert Washington (I wondered if the Peter Gunn opening had counted him out). Rob Hunter's second place was a pleasant surprise and a blow for youth (Doc: "That's a shocker. I would've given him three more years first.").

Despite suggestions to the contrary, the contest results did *not* seem rigged. I was standing near Doc while the winners were announced and watched him carefully: nothing about his behavior suggested he had prior knowledge of the outcome. Certainly Chris Young deserved top spot if anyone did. He was strong in every area. As the sportscasters say, "He came to play."

Of course, I had come to play, too—and with my dilettante's ego inflated to the size of a serious competitor's, had briefly entertained the absurd thought that I too could play in this league. If sheer desire were the crucial factor, that—plus another year's performing experience—might have kept me alive a while longer, maybe even got me into the finals. But standing here beside Doc, who was more my contemporary than any of the guys on stage, I knew in my bones I never could have come close to the kind of performances turned in by a Chris Young or a Robert Washington—even a sick Robert Washington. That was the final reality for a middle-aged duffer like me. As I took a seat to watch each winner perform his victory set, the answer to the charisma question now seemed simple: either you had the pure potential for it, or you didn't. I didn't have enough. Never did. Never would. And the older I got, the less potential (if any) existed for me to go on a stage and rivet audiences with my bewigged approximation of one of the most charismatic humans in history—so why try?

The contest winner, Chris T. Young.
(Photo courtesy of Karen Mullard.)

Got that right, Bill?

Yet back at the hotel it struck me how much I didn't want this to end. I had hung my jumpsuit on a hanger. It was dingy now, with a case of ring around the collar, but in the dim light of the closet, it seemed to stand, rather than hang, on its crumpled bell-bottoms, with a ghostly readiness to jump back into action, someday, some way.

It was late, so late it was early. I put away my wig in its brown paper supermarket bag (camouflage against casual theft). I removed my flashy fake diamond ring—I would have to buy more of those. You had to have more rings than I did, rings on every finger. And the shoes. Yes, I would continue the search for shoes.

In the dark, I lay on the bed, staring out the broad hotel window across some rooftops into the pink of dawn. The August heat wave was still holding out there. I could sense the Mississippi flowing through the dark, only a few blocks away. Rivers were mythic, for good reason, because they promised that change was always possible. If you lived on the River, you would always be going somewhere. Time, age, decline— on the River, they no longer counted for much because, as the old saying put it, you never had to step in the same river twice.

Yes, shoes . . . there would be other ways to find those shoes. Rick Marino would know. Keith Henderson would know. I could even try to go wherever it was Mike Roberts had gone in search of his—although I didn't particularly want to get shot at, and anyway, tomorrow would be Sunday, and I was due home Monday, due at the university for start of classes Tuesday. Start of classes? How could that possibly be? I had moves to learn, vocal tricks to master, real work to do. And shoes . . . Doc had said I ought to ask Michael Hoover's wife, Bobbie. She knew all the sources . . .

Dancing theta waves gradually overwhelmed what was left of my wakefulness and I drifted toward sleep, fully clothed, surrounded by the chill boom of stale air-conditioning. I could actually live in this world, I was thinking, as I faded toward the darker end of the gray scale. I could do this. Really I could. I could work—I *would* work—to be better, to make a comeback next year, a triumphal return, transformed, to come back to Memphis and knock their blue suede socks off.

If this was a cult, I would be a devotee.

If this was a brotherhood, I was a brother.

Or did I simply dream that thought . . . ?

Epilogue

Dreams, of course, have no boundaries. In the future I would dream many times of "doing Elvis" with a level of ability I could never hope to muster in waking reality.

The Elvis equivalent of flying dreams, I guess.

"Is the performance part of the book done?" Carol asked me, when I returned home. "Can you stop being Elvis now?"

"I suppose so."

But that, I am discovering, was a premature judgment.

Waking reality, it turns out, offers a steady stream of opportunities to hack away at the dream of being one's own "best Elvis." And I can live with the fact that the opportunities derive not from my prowess so much as from a curiosity factor that has more to do with my being an author.

Let's face it: I am a talking dog.

But if that's what it takes to keep me in the game, I'll gladly bark, roll over, sit-stay, whatever.

Like many impersonators, I've learned that being Elvis promises to take me places I'd never go otherwise. I now have my own back-up group, "The I Can't Believe It Band." We've already gotten through one show: my thirty-fifth high school reunion dinner-dance. How many guys from "the Elvis generation" get to come back 35 years later and entertain their high school classmates *as Elvis*? Pinch me, somebody!

As I write this, publication date is still a full year away; I have *lots* of time to work on my skills before the best excuse of all kicks in (to make a fool of oneself, that is): BOOK PUBLICITY!

Meanwhile back on Planet Elvis, the beat goes on:

After a tough year, the EPIIA scrapped its summer 1996 convention plans for Chicago but is looking forward to a big return to Las Vegas in 97, the twentieth anniversary of Elvis's death.

Rick and Susie Marino had a baby boy. Rick is losing weight and gearing up for "one more big shot"—a national tour in 97.

I continue to get news tidbits via membership in my on-line Elvis fan club, ElvisNet:

Pete Willcox (who I was astounded to learn was older than me) decided to "quit at the top of his game" and left Pigeon Forge to go into the ministry, somewhere in Las Vegas.

Robert Washington (healthy this time) took top honors at the Elvis Fantasy Festival competition, in Portage, Indiana. Second place went to Chris Young. Third place was shared by the precocious teenagers, Rob Hunter and Jamie Kelly.

As for me, I'm already looking ahead to Memphis in 97, if not as a contestant, at least to "sing in."

So no, I don't think "the performance part" of the book is done. I don't think it may ever be done.

I'm sorry, Carol.

And stay tuned, folks. The "I Can't Believe I'm Elvis" extravaganza might even come to your town.

About the Author

William McCranor Henderson's last novel, *I Killed Hemingway*, was named a *New York Times* 1993 Notable Book of the Year. Before becoming a fiction writer, Henderson lived and worked in New York, Boston, and Los Angeles as a filmmaker, musician, radio producer, journalist, and screenwriter. He is a graduate of Oberlin College, and now lives with his wife and daughters in his home state of North Carolina, where he teaches at North Carolina State University.